THE DOG'S LAST WALK

HOWARD JACOBSON

BLOOMSBURY PUBLISHING

LONDON · OXFORD · NEW YORK · NEW DELHI · SYDNEY

BLOOMSBURY PUBLISHING
Bloomsbury Publishing Plc
50 Bedford Square, London, WC1B 3DP, UK

BLOOMSBURY, BLOOMSBURY PUBLISHING and the Diana logo
are trademarks of Bloomsbury Publishing Plc

First published in Great Britain 2017
This edition first published 2018

These columns were first published in the *Independent*, to which Author and Publisher
are grateful for permission to reproduce them.

A catalogue record for this book is available from the British Library.

ISBN: HB: 978-1-4088-4528-8
TPB: 978-1-4088-4529-5
PB: 978-1-4088-4512-7
EBOOK: 978-1-4088-4530-1

2 4 6 8 10 9 7 5 3 1

Typeset by Newgen Knowledge Works (P) Ltd., Chennai, India
Printed and bound in Great Britain by CPI Group (UK) Ltd, Croydon CR0 4YY

For Aimée

CONTENTS

Introduction

THIS IS MY SECOND selection of columns from the *Independent* and, given that the paper closed in March 2016, it is likely to be my last. The first selection, *Whatever It Is, I Don't Like It*, was confined to pieces printed prior to 2010; most of those in this volume are more recent.

The shutting down of any serious newspaper is a small catastrophe; the closure of the *Independent*, which excited so many hopes for a different spirit in journalism when it first appeared in 1986, is particularly calamitous, not just because I wrote for it for eighteen years, but because its ambitions to be impartial and non-assertive made it peculiarly suited to the sort of writing continental Europeans designate as feuilletonistic – that is to say at once popular and literary, serious without solemnity, perhaps intimate in tone, sometimes taking the form of fiction, eschewing dogma, at all times assuming a shared disinterestedness in matters intellectual and stylistic, and therefore a patient leisureliness – an absence of any hunger to have their own views confirmed – on the part of readers. The end of the *Independent* is thus one more proof that we no longer read in the expansive, altruistically curious manner we once did.

So how do we describe the way we read now? This introduction is not the place to go into that. Several of the pieces that follow address the question, sometimes fatalistically, sometimes with resigned good humour, depending on how bad the picture looked to me at the time. My education predisposes me to see the worst. And, for reasons that we don't need to go into here, jeremiads come naturally to me. Though for a feuilletonist of the sort I became in the course of writing for the *Independent* – I have to say I hadn't thought of myself in those terms previously – any prophetic tale of woe must contain an awareness of the prophet's absurdity. I had many an argument with the several editors who came and went between 1998 and 2016, but none ever questioned my right to hold contradictory positions simultaneously, or to make fun of myself in the very course of making fun of others.

Here is one way in which we no longer read the way we did. Asseveration is today the rage: a passion to pronounce with certainty, to aver or declare if you're the writer; an impatience with discourse of any other sort if you're the reader. Irony, whose methodology is often slow and covert, finds little favour in those channels of conversation which the social media have made possible. The writer, literal-mindedly meaning what he says, stands and delivers, whereupon the respondent, literal-mindedly believing him, gives the thumbs up or the thumbs down. If you happen to believe that most judgements worth making occupy a hazy, indeterminate space somewhere between 'like' or 'dislike', and are in a perpetual state of being formed and reconsidered, you will find there are few symbols on the Internet you can make use of. We still await the creation of an emoji that can suggest reluctant demurral laced with intermittent enthusiasm floating precariously on a sometimes calm, sometimes tumultuous sea of doubt.

We've had it, is what I'm inclined to say. Soon, all that literature understands by drama, subtlety and equivocation will be gone, and bald statement will be all we have left. But I also know that mankind has a genius for getting itself out of the worst of scrapes. So take as a valediction and a promise these effusions from a defunct paper which for a short while got the joke even when I wasn't joking.

Howard Jacobson, 2017

The dog's last walk

THE OTHER DAY – AND have no fear, this isn't another Crufts story – I watched a dog go for a last walk with his owner. Don't ask me how I knew it was his last walk. I could tell, that's all. Finalities are unmistakable. Perhaps I should have looked away, but neither dog nor owner was aware of me. So my silent requiem was not, I thought, obtrusive.

I'd been shopping with my wife in Marylebone, buying what you buy in Marylebone on a Sunday – farmers' market breads and cheeses, rare-breed potatoes, oak-smoked garlic cloves. The good life. We'd paused on a bench in St Marylebone Gardens, right opposite the Fitzpatrick Mausoleum, an elegantly domed stone memorial to Susanna Fitzpatrick, who'd given up the ghost in 1759, aged only thirty. That teaches you something when you're sitting there laden with indulgences, though I'm not sure what.

A small child was struck by the mausoleum too. She kept running up to it and knocking on its bolted wooden doors. 'No one in,' her mother told her. But the child wasn't convinced. 'Knock, knock.' A quick listen, a quick retreat, and then back again. It was just as she had finally decided that there really was no one at home, or at least no one she fancied meeting, that the dog appeared. A black Labrador as old as Methuselah. 'Done in' is the best description I can give of him. A Macbeth dog who had grown aweary of the sun and for whom each day was now too like the day before.

He walked with agonising difficulty, his hind legs arthritic, his back a terrible burden to him. It was as though will alone kept him upright. He was barely able to round the mausoleum, and kept

3

stopping. With each tired step he took, his owner stooped to say something to him and patted his head. Laid her hand upon him would be a better way of putting it. A long, infinitely gentle touch, as though to lend him some of her vital spirit.

Whether she was urging him to get up and walk a little further, or telling him he could just sit down now in the gravel if that was what he wanted, take his final rest there and then, I couldn't hear. But by some agreement they reached a bench where they could pause: she on the seat, he, folded under himself, at her feet.

She was an elegant woman in her middle years. Soberly coiffed and dressed in a smart grey wide-skirted coat and black boots. Had I been a dog I'd have been proud to have such a woman take me for a walk. 'This is my mistress, where's yours?' But the Labrador was past all erotic vaingloriousness now. He didn't look at her or make any acknowledgement of her presence. For a moment I even wondered if he were blind.

Children scooted past him, cruelly young, carelessly wheeling close to his paws, but he didn't flinch. It seemed not to be sightlessness that afflicted him, though. He didn't have that air of relying on other, sharpened senses. It was more indifference. The presence of children didn't arouse his curiosity, nor did the wildness of their spirits agitate him. What harm could they do? Lay on, Macduff.

I can't fully explain why he reminded me of Macbeth. It had to do with his blackness – 'come, thick night' – the sense of something once strong ebbing from him, the dignity of his defeatedness. He'd reached that point of knowing himself to be beyond amity with another being.

His owner seemed to understand that perfectly. She didn't ask for anything from him. She didn't badger him. She held his lead with an exquisite gentleness, careful to do nothing abrupt, as though the lead were the last thread that bound them. She leaned forward, stroked him, laid her hand upon his head, and whispered to him. What did she say? God knows. But he gave no sense that he was required to respond in any way. I doubt she lied to him. I doubt she told him it was going to be all right. She had a gravity that was the mirror image of his. Between the two of them existed all that was serious in life.

The most sombre beings I have ever known are dogs. I never had one of my own, but I sometimes accompanied my father when he walked his Labrador. That dog, too, lived a long time, and in the end decided he would take his final walk on his own. Somehow he escaped the house, made straight for the lake around which my father had walked him for years, and strode calmly in. Couldn't face the emotionalism of the goodbyes.

Odysseus's dog Argos the same. This is the saddest story. Argos has been waiting for his owner to come back from the Trojan War. Twenty years and not a word. Once upon a time he and Odysseus had hunted together. But now his only function is to wait, lying on piles of dung, infested with fleas. And then suddenly Odysseus reappears, disguised in order to surprise Penelope's suitors. Only Argos recognises him. In his excitement he drops his ears and wags his tail. Odysseus, however, dare not let the dog betray him. 'Dashing a tear from his eyes', he ignores Argos and walks on. Whereupon, in Homer's words, 'Argos passed into the darkness of death, now that he had fulfilled his destiny of faith and seen his master once more after twenty years.'

'Destiny of faith' is not a term that enjoys much currency in our human world. Try saying it to the trivial-minded gasbags and laddish swindlers who govern us, who run down our institutions, fondle small boys, lie about what they know, think destiny is five thousand smackers a day and a motor yacht, and don't know when it's time to quit.

I watch the black Labrador attempt to lift his handsome head to smell the air one last time. But he can't do it. His owner kneels and lays her hand upon him. Then we get up and leave.

So long as there are women laughing, civilisation's safe

IF THERE IS ONE thing theocracies and their variants have difficulty with, it's laughter. If there's another, it's women. Put the two together and the foundations of their states begin to crumble. When the Turkish deputy prime minister made his speech about 'moral corruption' last week, calling for women to be vigilant of their chastity, not to be 'inviting' in their demeanour and, above all, not to laugh in public, he was invoking an ancient neurosis.

Yes, I know Turkey calls itself a secular democracy, but it's a secular democracy with God looking over its shoulder, and it's with God, of course – or at least the Jewish, Christian and Muslim mutations of God – that this fear of a woman's laughter originates. Let the state describe itself how it will; if it is nervous of laughter in general, and women's laughter in particular, it's a theocracy. That this remains the case when the god happens to be Karl Marx, I don't need to remind readers of Josef Skvorecky's *The Engineer of Human Souls* and Milan Kundera's *The Joke*.

In a wonderful flight of speculative fancy in *The Book of Laughter and Forgetting*, Kundera imagines the angel overhearing the Devil laughing and realising what the godly are missing out on. He tries to make a similar sound but can't produce it. He doesn't have the vocal register, but more than that, he doesn't have the critical intelligence. 'Whereas the Devil's laughter pointed up the meaninglessness of things, the angel's shout rejoiced in how rationally organised, well conceived, beautiful, good and sensible everything on earth was.'

Laughter, by this account, is the vigorous expression of our scepticism, our refusal to believe that everything is harmoniously

6

conceived, or that a benevolent agency – God or Big Brother – shapes our ends. Which explains why the angel, the cleric or the apparatchik cannot laugh: there is nothing in their conception of the world to laugh about. Charles Baudelaire dates laughter to the moment of man's fall. Had we behaved in the Garden of Eden as we were meant to, had we settled for being gratefully and serenely supine, as the angel wished, there would have been no reason to laugh. 'Man being there inflicted with no pain, the expression of his face remains unchanged. Neither laughter nor tears are to be seen in the paradise of all delights. They are both children of suffering.'

Worth remembering, while we are in the Garden, that the architect of our fall, and therefore the architect of laughter, was woman. Now is it clear why those who would imprison us in unsmiling paradises of delights are so suspicious of woman? Even where she is not the one doing the laughing, she is the instigator of laughter, enquiring, dissatisfied, critical. The age-old insults that women have had to bear – that they are shrews, termagants, viragos, even that they are sexually insatiable – all testify to man's fear of her power to disparage and discriminate. We don't offer marital guidance in this column, but is it not a matter of common observation that the partner wanting the quiet life is, more often than not, the man? And that the engine for change in a marriage is the woman?

Now unloose laughter in her, and the angels are in turmoil. 'Shame on your immodesty!' they cry, sticking a wig on her, draping her in a floor-length curtain or, to be on the safe side, sealing her in a bin liner. For if laughter denotes a rebellious spirit (we make an exception for that servile laughter that greets comedians on *Live at the Apollo*), it is also an expression of sexual desire and appreciation. And while a man likes a woman to laugh desirously on his say-so, he doesn't want her laughing on someone else's. I am as guilty as other men when it comes to this. As a boy I didn't like my girlfriends laughing at jokes I hadn't made, and today I don't much care for my wife laughing at books I haven't written. I overstate the case for effect. Of course I don't mind, really. And being a modern man with no beliefs, I don't demand that she covers her legs while she's reading. So long as she promises never to find another writer funny again.

We live, it's true, in raucous and unseemly times. Only the other evening, as I was crossing Regent Street, I heard the laughter of a thousand women pouring full-throatedly from a single black cab and felt the tiniest stab of disapproval. Let's be honest: maybe it was also the tiniest stab of envy – for it would have been fun to be in that cab with them – and the tiniest stab of jealousy – for I would have liked to be that laughter's cause: not the butt of it, you understand, but its occasion. What happened next threw all these motives into still more confusion. The cab stopped at the lights, two of the women succeeded in thrusting their heads out of the same window at the same time, and in unison they shouted: 'Show us your willy!'

They did not, let me be absolutely clear, shout 'Show us your willy!' at me. I know this a) because I am not the sort of man to whom women shout that sort of thing, and b) because when I looked interrogatively their way, they did not look affirmatively back. Who they were actually addressing I had no idea. There were, in the vicinity, several men young and presentable enough to arouse the women's curiosity. Ask them what they thought.

What interested me more was the women themselves. Reader, they were not girls out on a hen night. They were mothers, grandmas, materfamiliases. I caught myself tutting. But in other contexts, I remembered, I applaud the unwithered Cleopatra hopping forty paces through the public street, and praise the gap-toothed Wife of Bath for her unfettered appetite. I choked back further disapproval and waved (my arm) in solidarity. So long as there are women laughing – laughing at men, sex, age, propriety, laughing at the very idea that they shouldn't be laughing – we are safe. From one sort of tyranny at least.

Experience is lovelier than innocence

W E TRY TO BE above babies in this column. We don't dislike
them exactly. It's hard to dislike a thing that hasn't yet had
time to form objectionable political opinions or the habit of reading thrillers. It's more that we're afraid of them. What are they
thinking, what do they know about us, why that uncanny scrutiny?
Or it could just be with babies as it is with children in general – if
you never much enjoyed being one yourself, you aren't going to
care for any manifestation of them thereafter. And I was a self-
hating baby.

So I am as indifferent to the royal arrival as I am allowed to be,
what with bells chiming, helicopters circling, fountains spouting
blue water and the media's ceaseless unctioneering. My indifference
wavered for a moment, I confess, when Kate told the cameras she
had found the experience of giving birth 'emotional' and the baby
looked at her with an expression much like his great-grandfather
Philip's. 'Emotional! I should bloody well hope so!' He would no
more have been expecting a treatise on the joy and pains of partu-
rition than I was, but it must have crossed his mind to wonder,
if 'emotional' was the best his mother could muster, what sort of
family he had been born into. This isn't republicanism speaking.
I am no more a republican than I am a royalist. We are all fools
when it comes to what we believe, but few are more foolish than
those who inveigh against royalty for being undemocratic, when
the demos itself can't gorge on it enough. If you have a problem
with the royal family, brother, take it up with their legions of loyal
subjects.

I don't know whether republicans dream of removing the royal
family by diktat, but as things stand they're caught in the bind

of believing in a democracy of which the people are manifestly unworthy. It's the way the 'people' let them down that turns every democrat into a dictator in the end. A paradox for Prince George to chortle over in later years at Eton or Marlborough when they're trying to drill the word 'emotional' out of him.

But enough with babies. While the rest of the country was waiting and wondering last week, I was at a party celebrating my mother-in-law's hundredth birthday. Thou met'st with things new born, I with things dying, except that dying was the last thing on the minds of my mother-in-law's guests, only one of whom could match her in years, though others were coming up fast on the inside lane. Being a hundred takes some getting your mind around, even if you're more than halfway there. Think of it, reader – to be born in 1913, before the First World War had started, before women had the vote, before the Russian Revolution, Nazis, Twitter.

I used to fear the very old in much the same way I fear the very young. And for similar reasons. If we don't know where the young have been, we don't know where the old are going. Both can stare you out of countenance, make you feel you are of no consequence, reduce you to the role of bystander, as though the serious business of life takes place at either end, and you are caught between without a purpose. Isn't that what they are meaning to tell you when they take your hand, the baby with its absent, unfathomable grip, the old with their Ancient Mariner-like urgency – that you are marooned in the middle way, having forgotten what you were, and ignorant yet of what you will be?

Now, as I prepare to join the ranks of the old, I feel quite differently about them. They are, of course – this goes without saying – more fun to be with than the young. Yes, there is some repetition to get over, and a measure of conceit, because they know it's no small achievement to have survived the wreckage of a violent century. They would like a little congratulation. I marvel that the ninety-year-old woman sitting beside me swims in the sea every morning whatever the weather, and that she will be driving back to the Sussex coast when the party's over. But it's when she starts to turn on the charm that I move from admiration to fondness.

We are having an adventure, whispering into each other's ear – I'm the deaf one – recalling a time that never was when we were very close indeed. 'I didn't think we'd get to enjoy another afternoon like this again,' she says, though she knows as well as I do that we haven't enjoyed a comparable afternoon, or indeed any afternoon, before. I don't have to humour her. She knows what's true and what isn't. She is enjoying the fiction, exercising her flirtation muscles, that's all. Checking that they are still in working order. And they are.

A man of 101, erect, ironical and elegant in a fine Savile Row suit, inclines his head to every compliment. He knows he creates a flutter in the women of ninety, while inspiring a no less selfish hope in the rest of us. 'Touch me if you want to,' he says. 'There will be only a nominal charge.'

Meanwhile, my mother-in-law Dena, as queenly as Cleopatra, receives salutations from those who love her. Life beats as fervently in her as it ever did. She greets her friends, looking deeply into their faces as though they share more than they could relate if they lived their lives twice over. So much narrative, so many judgements made and reserved, such wealth of human knowledge. Against the odds, it's memory they try hardest to hold on to. It's memory, they know, that keeps you beautiful. I love being in the press of them, and realise with a pang why it's this beauty I care for over the beauty of a newborn child. Experience is lovelier than innocence.

How to live forever

LET ME SEE IF I've got this straight. If I eat five 80g portions of fruit and vegetables a day, I'll live longer. But if I eat seven 80g portions of fruit and vegetables a day, I'll live longer still. I forget how much longer I was going to live when I was on five 80g portions – that's history now, anyway – but under this new regimen of seven 80g portions of fruit and vegetables a day, I'll reduce my risk of dying of heart disease by 31 per cent and my risk of dying of cancer by 25 per cent, which ought to mean I've increased my chance of living longer by a total of 56 per cent. But that's 56 per cent of what? Don't I need to know at what age I was going to die when I wasn't eating any 80g portions of fruit and vegetables before I can reliably calculate the age I am likely to live to now that I am eating seven?

Or am I simply being measured against someone else – say, you, reader, if you aren't eating the number of vegetables I am? Am I chalking off the years I've got left against the years you haven't? It's not pleasant to think we are competing for life, but that's been the way of it ever since we raced one another out of the primeval soup. At least then, however, we just pushed one another back in and beat our chests. We didn't crow over grams and percentages. Today I can't see anyone peeling an apple without wondering how much longer than me he's got.

But let's suppose – to keep you out of it – that I increase the number of portions of fruit and vegetables I eat a day to fifteen or twenty. And let's suppose further that I up the dosage from 80g to 100g or even 150g. After the rough equivalent of thirty bananas, twenty-five tomatoes, four turnips and two nosebags of swedes daily, could it be that I'm looking at eternal life? This is a serious question with significant demographic and economic consequences for the planet: is it now becoming possible for us to eat our way to immortality?

There was a time when all but the rich could be relied upon to scoff themselves into an early grave. In working-class Manchester, we spooned gravy jugs of grease onto everything we ate at home, and ordered extra of every extra at every restaurant we went to. We couldn't eat chicken curry without an accompaniment of poppadums, rotis, chapatis, stuffed naans, rice, raitas, bhajis, saags, paneers, okra and Bombay potatoes, and we couldn't eat Singapore noodles without a side dish of Singapore noodles.

By curry I mean the first curry of the evening, which we usually put away after getting back from school and before hitting the Ritz. The real curry – the vindaloo we ate between midnight and two in the morning, depending on how the Ritz had gone – came as an extra to itself. We were growing boys. Our mothers were always telling us we looked thin. Hence the cheese-and-pickle sandwiches they stuffed into our satchels to supplement school lunch, which they knew, without seeing it, to be inadequate. In percentage terms, I'd say my chance then of living to the age I am now was 56 per cent less, but don't ask me 56 per cent less than what, or how much further the remaining 44 per cent is going to get me.

If I take more care of myself now, it's as much because there's no one left not to take care of myself *with* as because I want to live forever. The fun's gone. I occasionally see a few of the friends I used to drink wine with, but we spend the first half of the evening trying to decide whether we'll manage to get through a whole bottle between the five of us and, since we know we won't, whether to go for a small carafe or push the boat out and order three glasses which we'll divvy up. And even then there's always one of us who'll want to check that the alcohol content doesn't exceed 11.5 per cent, each half a per cent being equivalent to a year of what's left to us of lives that some would say are no longer worth living.

Smoking's gone the same way, of course, and even yogurt's not the wild indulgence of old. Like everybody else, I went for Greek yogurt whenever it was it became fashionable, but then came the warnings and I changed to low-fat yogurt until that turned out to have too much sugar in it, which suddenly made Greek yogurt all right again, provided it was low-fat Greek yogurt (which meant it didn't taste like Greek yogurt), though here again there was a threat, this time in the form of calcium, too many milligrams of which can reduce your life expectancy by the number of years you've saved by not eating full-fat yogurt.

And now I read that the government is issuing guidelines to restaurants on how big portions should be, in order to reduce the gross weight of the population – a problem that could have been averted had that same population been allowed to die off naturally, as in the old days, as a consequence of all those naans and rotis and never eating a vegetable. How long before someone in the Department of Health wakes up to the fact that the healthier they make us, the longer we will live (up by 56 per cent as I write), and the longer we live, the more rubbish we will want to eat?

We face longer, bleaker lives anyway, with less salt in our salted cod, less fat in our fatty chips, less dough and diameter to our pizza bases and therefore less of the loaded, sloppy toppings that those of us who love pizzas love them for. If it wasn't for the danger I face on a daily basis from mad cyclists – and I only mention this to wind up the mad cyclists who routinely write me hate mail – I'd say I've every chance of making it to 150. Time enough to consume about a million and half grams of fruit and vegetables, though I wouldn't trust my maths.

God is me

S AW GOD LAST WEEK. Not in a sunset or a rainbow, not on Mount Sinai or Uluru, not in Chartres Cathedral or on Glastonbury Tor, and certainly not on the road to Damascus, where these days one is more likely to encounter the devil. No, I saw God at Tate Modern.

If Nicholas Serota, the director of the whole Tate caboodle, thinks I'm talking about him, well, he's not a million miles wide of the mark. It was thanks to his expansive curating, anyway, that I had my big experience, between coffee and a full English breakfast with a 10 per cent discount for Tate members.

It is, of course, the current sell-out Henri Matisse exhibition I'm talking about – Matisse himself infirm and chair-bound, but the art alive as though the wild spirit of an all-creating God blows through every dab and shape of colour. The work is so exceptionally alive, in fact, you half wonder whether the infirmity is essential to it. What we can say for sure, after this, is that there's no better route to spiritual beauty than through an apprehension of mortality.

Which might have been what Matisse was getting at in his famous conversation with Sister Jacques-Marie, the Dominican nun who was closely involved with him in his designs for the Chapel of the Rosary at Vence. Dismayed to hear Matisse talk of making the chapel for his own pleasure, Sister Jacques-Marie reminded him that he had once said he was making it for Almighty God. 'Yes, but that God is me,' he told her.

Matisse and the nun were very close – close enough to share a joke. Rumour had it that she posed nude for him. (Who wouldn't pose nude for Matisse?) We must assume, whether that's true or false, that they would on more than one occasion have discussed the sacred and the profane. And to an artist it is profane to talk of an Almighty God who exists outside the art. 'Yes, but that God is me' is another way of insisting that divinity is in the work or nowhere.

Picasso found it hard to forgive Matisse for working on a chapel. He missed the point. Even the stained-glass windows have no religiosity about them. They celebrate the wonders of the visible world – never so blindingly visible until made so by an artist.

No one should miss this extraordinary exhibition. Ignore the critical unanimity of enthusiasm. I know, I know, agreement kills. Especially when those doing the agreeing are art critics. But this time, reader, miracle of miracles, they are right. And what is more, they are right in the name of art's exhilarating example – the happiness of creation, fecundity, verve and vigour, colour – rather than those footling ironies to which, in the name of conceptualism (the unmade-bed of the embryo artist's mind), Tate Modern has too often granted indulgence.

We have been rude about Tate Modem in this column. A palace of sterility we have called it. But we are happy now to take all that back. Had it never done better than this show, and were it never to do better again, its existence is now justified.

And how clever of the curators to have eschewed cleverness – that curse of the contemporary – and entitled the exhibition simply *Matisse: The Cut-Outs*, with its suggestions of kids messing about at school with scissors and coloured paper. Was ever a show less dauntingly described? And as it is described, so it proceeds, fourteen bursting rooms of such exuberant creation that you discover you are wandering in and out of them – for this is a show to dawdle without aforethought through – in an unaccustomed mood, an unaccustomed expression on your face. Is that a smile? I would not want to make this the once and forever criterion of a good art show, but never have I seen so many people in an art gallery looking happy.

Nor do I want to make it sound as though we were all in the grip of some joyous freedom from exactingness. The greatest art is that of concealing art, and the intellectual life is never better served than when intellectuals speak their profundities in the language of men talking to other men. No artist was ever not an intellectual to some degree, and we'd be fools to suppose that the lightness and immediacy that Matisse achieved with his cut-outs was a triumph of spontaneous or accidental mindlessness. But he was an artist of the greatest tact, and it is artistic tact to hide the means by which you come by your effects and the labours of technique and thought that enable you at last to produce work that seems labour-free.

You can look for hours at a time at those famous blue cut-out nudes, which somehow are as much sculpted as scissored, as though a flat piece of paper has a third dimension that only a great artist can find in it; yet no matter how long you look, you will not discover how this is achieved, how the paper folds back in time as well as space upon itself, and how even the still spaces between the shapes possess the dynamism of movement and change.

Whatever mischief Matisse intended by saying 'God is me', one cannot deny the mystery of creation before these works. The Judaeo-Christian God shaped man from clay, breathed into his nostrils and then expected him to do as he was told. Being cut into life by Matisse's scissors for no other purpose than to express natural vitality and enjoy the simple fact of being strikes me as preferable.

'I have always wished my works to have the lightness and joyous-ness of a springtime which never lets anyone suspect the labours it has cost,' he wrote in 1948. But he worried that a young painter, eager for fame, would see only apparent facility and negligence, and use that as an excuse to skip the labour. The inspiring paradox at the heart of this magnificent show is that you have to toil to achieve lightness and that it's only when you are autumnal that you can create the joyousness of springtime. Ripeness is all.

Sweet boy, that Jihadi John

So how come i'm not the world's most wanted man? I was thin-skinned, sweet-natured, loving – 'a beautiful young man' in every way, my mother remembers – so where did it all go wrong for me? Even my father – a person not given to idle praise – remarked on the gentleness of my disposition. 'Isn't he a bit kind?' I recall him asking my mother when he thought I wasn't listening. 'A bit kind for what?' my mother wanted to know.

I have a faded image of my father shrugging. He didn't like having to explain himself. But I knew what he was getting at. I lacked the qualities of a warrior. We were naive in those days. We didn't understand that a gentle nature was the ideal breeding ground for murderousness. We thought it simply denoted incipient homosexuality.

At school my reputation for being a beautiful person was enhanced by my bookishness, my timidity and by the Gothic-script initials my aunt had embroidered onto my blazer pocket. If ever there was someone who was never going to commit an atrocity – and was therefore, by the inverse logic of these things, bound to go on and commit a whole string of them – it was me. There I sit, in photograph after photograph, just to the right of the headmaster's knees, looking seraphic and isolated – an angel in a line of grinning devils – the quintessential terrorist-to-be aged nine. Some of those photographs even came with my face already encircled so that the newspapers wouldn't have to hunt me out once the extent of my subsequent criminality became known.

I have no memory of banging my head against a goalpost, but then the memory of banging one's head against a goalpost is precisely the sort of memory that banging one's head against a goalpost expunges.

I did, however, once let seventeen goals past me when I was keeping goal for my class team, and the jeering of my fellows might have had an effect comparable to concussion. Shame devoured me anyway, even if oblivion didn't, but why did I not swear, there and then, to make humanity pay for my humiliation? What examples urging otherwise did I attend to? What quiet voice made a coward of me?

There followed, speaking of shame, that sequence of excruciating ignominies which adolescence visits on the hypersensitive – the most productive, in the education of an assassin with a special penchant for the machete, being rejection by girls. It is a strange fact of human nature that the more fervently sentimental we are in our longing to show affection, the more urgent our need to sever people's heads from their shoulders when that affection is not reciprocated.

Considering how often girls rejected me, it remains a mystery that I didn't end up decapitating on what's called an industrial scale. How was it, I must ask again, that other options presented themselves to me? Who suggested I was better off crying over Little Nell or going to the opera?

In the early life of any terrorist deserving of the name is a period working in a lowly capacity during which he shows no interest in politics and is remembered with gratitude by his bosses, who describe him as the best employee they have ever had. Here again I promised much in that I worked my socks off driving a delivery van for Wall's ice cream when I was eighteen and was careful to say nothing about wanting to blow the world to smithereens when I met my fellow drivers at the pie and mash shop in Bolton. Yet for all these advantages I got no nearer to fanaticism than reading English literature at Cambridge.

Here at last, you would have thought, was my opportunity. My moral tutor alienated me by thinking that if my name wasn't Finkleburger it was Grubenstein; my supervisor harassed me by asking for an essay every week and then not liking what I wrote; I ran up bills at the buttery which I was expected to discharge; and fellow students contributed to the atmosphere of bitter disaffection in which I lived by getting better degrees than I did.

Further provoked by that subtle form of persecution known as leaving you alone, I began to walk the streets at the dead of night with my college scarf wrapped menacingly around my face. 'Go home, sir,' the authorities warned me, increasing my sense of beleaguerment. It would have made perfect sense to unleash destruction on that smug university town. So what, I must again ask, stopped me?

It wasn't that there were no extremist lectures to attend. Raymond Williams made a socialist of me. C. S. Lewis a Christian apologist. F. R. Leavis an elitist. But there was still no ideology to hand sufficient to my simmering resentment. Suited by nature and shaped by experience to be a beheader-in-chief, I was denied the opportunity to be anything of the kind by the culture of agreeable mistrust I'd encountered at home, at school, at the Wall's ice-cream depot and at university. Put simply, I'd been ruined: brought up to doubt and question, taught never to follow blindly or believe the world would be a better place the minute I felt better in it.

And where such scepticism has not been instilled? Where education is turned into the very opposite of itself and instead of rebutting fantasy becomes fantasy's proponent? What then? Then, reader, all bets are off. Then, until the impressionable can once again police themselves by breadth of knowledge and elasticity of mind, we must do the policing for them, acting as the intellectual consciences they don't have.

Exposing the easily incited to dogmas of certainty and hate laced with paradisal promises is not the aim of education; teaching to think critically is. 'Let every voice be heard' is a fine sentiment so long as we can trust the discernment of those who listen. But right now – whatever those who believe unconditionally in free speech think – we can't.

All sportsmen die in hotels

L AST WEEK THE CRICKET writer Peter Roebuck died. He is said to have thrown himself out of a hotel window in South Africa. Why Peter Roebuck's death affects me beyond the passing sadness of a shared humanity – every man's death diminishes me, etc. – why I feel quite so diminished by it when I didn't know the man personally or go out of my way to read his articles on cricket, mainly published in Australia where he'd chosen to live – I am unable to explain. But I cannot stop thinking about it.

Could it be because some men carry their destiny around with them, show their fatality in their faces, are cruelly marked not only by who they are but what is destined to happen to them, and if that's so then free will is an illusion? It's easy to be wise after the event, but didn't Tony Hancock always look as though he was going to die before he was fifty with a bottle of vodka by his bed and amphetamines in his fist? Amy Winehouse ditto. In their beginning is their end. And the end of them is written not only on their faces but in their work – the jokes too black, the songs too self-lacerating, in Roebuck's case the too-stern caution, not only of his batting (he captained Somerset before he turned to journalism) but of his precise, never quite animated prose, his stiffness – as it's reported, even by those who got close enough to care for him – both on the field and off it, and the doom-laden complexion of his thoughts.

'To a greater and lesser degree all sportsmen die in hotels,' he wrote after the mysterious death of Bob Woolmer in Jamaica in 2007. 'That night Woolmer went back to his room with its silences and accusing walls, an isolated figure trying to come to terms with futility.'

As a rule, sportswriters overwrite. You will get some of the best journalistic prose on the sports pages of serious newspapers, but you will also get some of the most flowery. You can bet your life that every cricket writer in the business had a go at rendering Woolmer's last hours, but Roebuck's account has the authenticity of someone who knows loneliness well. 'All sportsmen die in hotels' might have been a florid line, but it isn't. Those 'accusing walls' could only have been described by a man who has felt accused by them himself. And 'futility' is a shocking word in that context. The sentence sets us up to expect 'loneliness' or 'defeat'. 'Futility' doesn't merely darken the canvas, it wipes it out. This isn't the cliché of another suitcase in another hall; the futility encompasses sport itself and, by implication, life.

There's a touch of this educated pessimism in all the best sportswriters and in cricket writers most of all. You go to Cambridge if you're Atherton, Pringle or Roebuck, you go to Oxford if you're Vic Marks, and then you give the next twenty years of your life to chasing a little ball. Futility is bound to be a word that crops up from time to time, whether the hotel walls accuse you or they don't.

The walls clearly accused Roebuck more than other men. What they accused him of is immaterial. If you're at all complex as a human being you will feel yourself to be guilty of every crime and omission in the book. Look at photographs of the young Roebuck and you see a shy boy uncomfortable in his skin. Shyness leaves a legacy even when it's overcome. You know your soul to be an awkward thing and you can never forgive it for that. The reason you die in every hotel room you wind up in is that death is all you've ever thought you deserved. I can't imagine Botham, with whom Roebuck famously fell out, lying in his silent hotel bed, trying to come to terms with futility.

Peter Roebuck was too lonely. I never met him but I know he was too lonely. I could tell it from the straw hat he liked to wear, tied, for God's sake, under his chin. A close companion, of either sex, would not have let him leave the house wearing a straw hat tied under his chin. 'You look a prat, Peter,' he or she would have told him. And if he'd persisted they'd have left him. (Perhaps that was his intention.) The persona of his articles, too, was stiff and out of reach. Conversational his style was not. Among the reasons Australians took to him was that he told it like it was, that he had abandoned England and used the word 'us' to mean the Aussies not the Poms, but I think they also sniffed the loner in him; for all their overt gregariousness Australians understand isolation. There was some interior quality in his writing, beneath its pedantic authoritativeness a suggestion that the person he was keeping to the mark was himself.

Roebuck was charged with assault a decade ago. He caned some young men he'd been coaching at his own expense. Discipline, he had warned them, would be part of his regime. It doesn't detract from his philanthropy that it cloaked a strange eroticism. Nobody is purely one thing. The tragedy is that eroticism, for him, had to be cloaked.

A fresh assault charge had been made the night he died. He must have felt the old, accusing futility catching up with him. It's a desperately sad tale.

Did you see what my arm just did?

W HEN IS A NAZI salute not a Nazi salute? When somebody who isn't a Nazi gives it. But how do you decide when somebody's a Nazi – in heart if not in deed – if giving the Nazi salute is not to be seen as indicative? Why would anyone adopt the gestures of a political movement for which they have no sympathy?

Only scratching my ear, or words to that effect, said the footballer Nicolas Anelka, after fisting the *quenelle*, the inverted Nazi salute created by that unfunny French comedian Dieudonné. Some men are born Nazis, some achieve Nazism, and some have Nazism thrust upon them. Remember Dr Strangelove's gloved salute: a man can't always control the direction of his arm.

We exempt the Queen from our ironies. A child will copy anything she is told to copy. And we can't know in what spirit, either, she was encouraged to do so. I gave Nazi salutes with my school friends, making a Führer moustache with a toothbrush long before Basil Fawlty. You can rest assured that we were joking. There were no Jewish Nazis where I grew up in the 1950s. In the case of those egging on the young princess, it's less easy to be certain. Long and deep were the ties that bound British and European aristocracies to the ideology of Nazism.

Funny how class works: you turn your nose up at your own proletariat but allow yourself to be mesmerised by a little vulgarian with a terrible haircut, no dress sense and bad table manners. Jew-hating acquaints us with strange bedfellows. But what if Uncle Edward was making that very observation to amuse his nieces? Hey, kids, did you see what my arm just did. . .?

It's important to remember, Dame Shirley Williams said on *Newsnight* last week – misremembering wildly – that in 1933, when the photograph of the royal salute was taken, Hitler's ambitions were little known; it was still possible to admire him simply as someone who put Germans back to work – no matter that the work was building munitions factories and Dachau.

Oh, the things we don't see when it doesn't suit us to see them. *Mein Kampf* had been published in 1925. Its driving monomania could hardly have been missed by anyone who'd taken the precaution, before giving Hitler wholehearted support, to flick it open, and as early as 1920 he had entertained the National Socialist German Workers Party with descriptions of 'the Jew as parasite' threatening 'the national purity' of the German nation. Not everyone was at the Hofbräuhaus in 1920, just as not everyone was at the General Meeting of the West Midlands Area Conservative Party Centre in Birmingham to hear Enoch Powell give his 'rivers of blood speech', but inflammatory language has wings. Whoever wasn't alarmed by Hitler in 1933 was already a little bit in love with his ideas.

All of which still leaves the Queen in the clear, not least because we wish her to be. We do if we are Jewish, anyway. I don't have the slightest idea what the Queen thinks of Judaism as a faith, whether she numbers Jews among her friends, whether she prefers Roth to Updike, gets Jewish jokes, subscribes to the *Jewish Chronicle*, or wishes her children had found themselves nice Jewish wives and husbands. As for Israel, well, she is yet to go there. But I know she has no radical objection to Jews, and I know she is good for the Jews. How do I know? I just know.

You develop a strong instinct for smelling out your enemies when you've spent a long time running from them. You might not be able to say exactly what you're looking for, but you know it when you see it. And I don't see an enemy in the Queen. There are even moments – I am not referring to any specific face-to-face encounter – when she reminds me of the aunts and grandmothers who pinched my cheeks when I was a child, said something to me in Yiddish – 'Have you come far, *mein Kind*?' it might have been – and gave me a kopek.

It's partly because I see something of my Central European origins in hers that I feel safe breathing the air she breathes. OK, so my ancestors studied sacred texts in muddy hovels in the Carpathians, while hers trod carpeted corridors in some *Schloss* in Saxe-Coburg – we are both still from somewhere else. And precisely because we are from somewhere else, we have the free minds of those grateful not to be living there any more, feel loosened in our ties, and can value the country we've landed in and made our own without believing its purity needs protecting from contamination. No, she won't ever pinch my cheek, give me a kopek and whisper in my ear, 'So how do you find the English, bubbeleh?' But I can imagine she'd quite like to. Queen Victoria had Disraeli. Queen Elizabeth II, had things only fallen out differently, could have had me.

But anyway, the world has changed. It's not the crowned heads of Old Europe who hate us now. If Edward the Impressionable were to raise his arm today, it wouldn't be in fealty to the Nazis but to Hezbollah and Hamas, who openly borrow the salute for its anti-Jewish associations. 'Hamas, Hamas, Jews to the gas,' you will hear sung in the Netherlands and Germany. Which doesn't stop Jeremy Corbyn being Hamas's 'friend'.

How defaming Jews passed from being a pastime of reactionaries to a prerequisite of the hard and not-so-hard left (where it goes by another name) is a matter for further discussion. But the Jew has always been various in his capacity to provoke: now fomenting revolution; now the bedrock of international capitalism; now promising that the meek shall inherit the earth; now grinding the dispossessed under his heel. Thus the salute of extermination passes from fascist to 'freedom fighter', seducing the left as it once seduced the right. Eighty years from now we might be asking whether pictures of a forgotten Labour Party leader hobnobbing with terrorists for whom the murder of Jews is a religious duty could possibly be genuine.

Darts: the last refuge of the serious

THE OLDER GUY WON. In the end, that's all you need to know. The older guy knocked over the younger guy, which means the younger guy will have to wait another year. Thus is natural justice satisfied: wisdom trumps avidity, the brain outwits the body, and the younger guy has the consolation of knowing he'll be the older guy himself one day. Tell me this doesn't beat the Olympics. I defy you: tell me the world isn't a better, fairer, more amusing place for having Phil 'The Power' Taylor, born 1960, destroy 'Mighty' Michael van Gerwen, born 1989.

This, for the uninitiated and benighted, is darts I'm talking about. The World Championships held at Alexandra Palace and shown on Sky TV for what seemed like most of December, with a respectful pause over Christmas. If you wonder why my first column of the new year is so often about darts, it's because I'm usually at home over the holiday period and can't find anything else to watch on television. What's the alternative to darts – *Downton Abbey*? *Call the Midwife*?

Anything 'serious' to watch on television, I should have said. Darts purists might well contest that word 'serious' when it comes to the way Sky packages the World Championships. Do we really need dancing girls flashing their tushes? they will ask. Must players be escorted to the oche by over-tanned promotional girls, bow-legged in white stilettos, who blow toothy kisses to the camera when they leave the stage, under the apparent misapprehension that the event is somehow about them?

The melodramatic introductions, as though John Part vs Dave Chisnall were the equivalent to Muhammad Ali vs George Foreman, the blaring music – 'Chase the Sun' played whenever a player departs to take a leak – the flashing lights, the tanked-up audience shouting, 'Oi! Oi! Oi!', the hysterical commentary in which every game is billed as the greatest ever played – do I call this serious? What's wrong with the actual business – a man aiming to throw seven darts at treble 20, one at treble 19 and one at double 12 – that it must be wrapped to resemble something different?

Ah, reader, I sympathise, but you miss two things. The first is the universal capitulation of sport, along with every other form of popular diversion, to the gaudy. The Olympics were organised along the lines of a rock concert. The same tushes that are flashed at Alexandra Palace are flashed in Mumbai whenever Dhoni hits a six. Even *Strictly Come Dancing*, than which, in its very conception, no light entertainment could be lighter, must lighten the dancing still further with that which isn't dancing – how-much-do-you-want-this interviews, the camp banter of pantomime judges, and Bruce Forsyth mesmerised every time there's a standing ovation, though he of all people should know a television audience will stand and ovate a boiled egg.

The second thing you miss, you who judge the World Darts Championships harshly, is irony. In fact, the inappropriateness of the packaging works in the game's favour. Think of how the mock-heroic satirises the overweening ambition and self-absorption of the hero. Precisely because we know they are not Ali and Foreman, and they know they are not Ali and Foreman, the darts players make their ceremonial entrance with a sort of anti-swagger, conscious of their physical limitations, their mountain bellies, their chubby arms, their unhealthy complexions, in the process flinging our banal expecta-tions of what sportsmen should look like – indeed, what anyone on television should look like – back in our faces. Quite obviously, their sheepish expressions say, as the bulbs explode around them, quite obviously the skills we possess require regimes of dedication that are different from what you're used to applauding. So forget the idea of falling in love with us. Just try concentrating on what we do.

I salute them. We need unfamiliar heroics at any time, but after a year of worshipping at the shrine of speed and muscle, of bodies strung like instruments, it is salutary to be reminded that people have other ambitions, inhabit different shapes, and need not be young and beautiful, or want to dance, to be engrossing.

Seriousness is all. And the size of an ambition is no more a criterion of seriousness than is usefulness. A man might train fleas to jump over matchsticks and be serious. So once the fanfares are concluded and the promo girls have limped off, blowing final kisses at the cameras – in all kindness someone should have told them it was a darts championships they'd been hired to appear on and not *The Only Way Is Essex* – the darts reassert themselves, narrowing ambition to those small bands of cork enclosed by wire.

I have marvelled in the past at the touching contrast between the overflowing bulk of the man throwing and the dainty precision with which he throws. But darts players have shrunk considerably since then – I hope for reasons of health, not vanity – so the contrast is no longer as touching as it was. But the precision itself is still remarkable – such fine judgement, such subtle readjustment. See an arrow fly in slow motion, see how much it arches and how far it deviates, and it is a miracle it ever finds its target. A cheetah can sprint, an antelope can hurdle, an otter can swim. But show me the animal that can hit a treble 20 three times running with three darts.

Yes, the cheetah on the veldt is more beautiful than Phil 'The Power' Taylor at the oche. But beauty, like celebrity, is a fatal distraction. As our powers of concentration wane, we more and more prefer what's ambient to what is. Not so with darts, where neither youthful beauty nor garrulous personality can seduce us from the thing itself – a last refuge of the serious.

The erotic gravitas of George Galloway

NIETZSCHE WASN'T RIGHT ABOUT everything. '*Gott ist tot*,' he told us. Wrong. God is still very much with us. He lives on as a derangement in the minds of people who kill to express their love for Him, or kill to assert His non-existence. If *Gott* were really *tot* we'd hear His name invoked less often. But modern man has to be convinced he's put something behind him – some system of belief, some style in art, some way of looking at the world. So if God isn't dead, who or what is? My candidate is sex. Reader, you read it here first. Sex Is Dead.

We could start in Soho, where chocolate and cupcake shops have replaced the heartbreak peepshows and masochistic parlours in which, for the brief illusion of rapture, young men once threw away their inheritances and their health. But let's start instead with George Galloway and Cristina Odone – the Tristan and Iseult of current affairs broadcasting. Last seen burning up our screens on *Question Time*.

Galloway has since referred to Odone as 'the saintly figure with wandering hands', thereby attesting to the sexual friction between them. That they don't like each other goes without saying, but sex isn't always an expression of liking. The possibility of attraction where there is hostility is a troubling discovery that all men and women who are honest about their emotions make early, what they go on to do with that discovery often determining the sexual course their lives will take.

I know nothing of the sexual course of Cristina's or George's life, though I do recall seeing the latter on his hands and knees lapping milk from a saucer like a cat – unless I dreamed it after eating too much cheese. Maybe I also dreamed his elegant meditation on sexual misunderstanding: 'Not everybody needs to be asked prior to each insertion.'

As for the *gestes de tendresse* exchanged with Odone on *Question Time*, it is worth noting that Galloway had already been softened up by the calm severity exercised by the journalist Jonathan Freedland. Softened up in the sense of being made to look intellectually clumsy and politically foolish, but the encounter could also have acted as a sort of foreplay, rendering him the more susceptible to Odone's 'wandering hands'. She appeared to touch his arm anyway, in the crazed hope of persuading him to a point of view that wasn't his own, whereupon those juices that make men say and do impetuous things flooded Galloway's being. 'Take your hands off me!' he cried. Not everybody needs to be asked prior to each insertion, but no means no.

How salutary, in these morally slack times, to be reminded of the importance of a touch. It was as though we'd been returned to the world of the Victorian novel, only this time it wasn't an outraged maiden saying, 'Unhand me, you bounder!' It was George Galloway.

For returning me to such a world, if for nothing else, I feel indebted to the Respect Member for Bradford West. He is right: a touch can be momentous. It's because a touch matters that readers of Jane Austen all but faint when there is the subtlest intimation of one. I have previously, in this column, confessed to perturbations of the heart when Captain Wentworth, assisting Anne Elliot into her carriage, lays his hand upon her. I don't read Jane Austen to be aroused, but if arousal is what you're after, then Anne Elliot confounded by the abrupt intimacy of Wentworth's intervention offers a thousand times more of it than you will find in any of E. L. James's heroine's lucubrations on the size of her lover's erection. To wit: 'It springs free.' He slips a condom 'onto his considerable length'. (Oh, Sir Jasper, what considerable length you have.) 'Holy cow!' exclaims she, in erotic wonderment.

It isn't only that the author of *Fifty Shades of Grey* lacks the ear, the passion, the wit, the adroitness, the seriousness and the sense of the ridiculous of a Jane Austen – or a Danielle Steel, come to that – it is that she lacks the gravitas of a George Galloway for whom, at least in the instance detailed above, even the smallest physical advance is fraught with significance.

Reader, we are grown too light in the consideration we show our bodies and in the messages we exchange through them. And where there's no weight in the contact, and no seriousness in our interpretation of it, there is no sex worth the discussing. I don't say you have to be desperate to be inflamed by *Fifty Shades of Grey* – though you most certainly have to be sheltered – I say you have to be cowardly. You have to want sex without the sex.

So, to be clear, while I do think explicitness is usually the end of the erotic, which is why Henry James wrote hotter novels than Jackie Collins, it is not in the name of prudishness that I say so. I can take as much filth as the next man or woman. It's possible I can take more. But filth, too, exacts obligations. We talk about pornography as though we know its precise delineations and limits, where it fails as art, at what point it degrades love. But pornography is not a discrete entity. In sex, and so in art, we move in and out of it.

Degradation and even violence visit us in sex, often when we don't expect or welcome them. It can seem sometimes that sex is a little death flirting with the idea of a big one, and who's to say where that flirtation will stop? Writers of true pornography such as de Sade, Bataille or Pauline Réage recognise that their subject lies on the far side of that line, where to deal with sex means to deal with life *in extremis*. They are nothing if not in earnest. Sex dies when it's reduced to lightly perfumed tales of couples locking one another into panda-skin handcuffs bought from Ann Summers. Lovers who take greater risks call this vanilla sex. I wish readers a happy Valentine's Day. But not a vanilla one.

Toast

MEN! I ASK YOU! Be patient: this is neither an attack nor a defence. Of Twitter and Toasters I sing – the baffling nature of man (Wayne and Kevin, not *Homo sapiens*) as evidenced by the latest revelations of their habits, customs, weaknesses and barbarities. Accusations of 'sexism' have been bandied about with such flagrancy this week it has felt like the sixties all over again.

But the word 'sexist' is no longer what it was; it had magical properties then, making every man take a second look at himself, even those who protested their innocence the loudest.

'Sexist? Me! I'll show you bloody sexist!' Now, sexism feels too small a concept for the errands it is sent on. What does it mean to call that man a 'sexist' who tweets threats of rape because his victim made the case for putting Jane Austen on a £10 note?

Sexist! You might as well accuse Fred West of unneighbourliness. When violence of this order has so apparently inoffensive a cause – would he have felt the same had it been Charlotte Brontë on the tenner, or Jane Austen on a fiver? – it's not a catch-all word like 'sexist' we need; it's a whole new science of literary, monetary and social-media psychopathology.

Then, just as we felt we were staring down a pit too deep ever to fathom, came reports of a man calling the fire brigade to free his penis from a pop-up toaster. We are, of course, in the territory of urban legend here. My school friend Malcolm specialised in stories of men trapping their penises – in the neck of a Coke bottle, in a vacuum-cleaner nozzle, an ice bucket, a kitchen tap, a car exhaust, the viewing end of a telescope, the spout of a teapot, an egg slice, a spectacle case, a trombone, raw liver (Malcolm's creativity anticipated Portnoy's by years), a key ring, the strings of a tennis racket, a hole in the road.

Perhaps because he gave us so many ideas, aged eleven, we weren't sure whether to believe him or not. But it was the ferret that finally broke, as it were, the camel's back of our credulity. Why would a man keep a ferret in his trousers? Why would the ferret suddenly decide to lock its jaws, and when the police shot the ferret how could they be sure they hadn't shot the man's penis? Before this barrage of questions Malcolm's inventiveness at last gave way, though he still insists that while the hole in the road was embroidery, the ferret wasn't. And the fire brigade insists the same about the pop-up toaster.

So you tell me, reader, how to begin to understand the appeal of a toaster. Yes, loneliness and desperation will drive a man to try most things, and yes, not all of them will resemble a woman's parts, supposing it is a woman he is missing. But a toaster fails on almost every count. Shape, texture, aperture, accessibility, metaphor – all wrong. Only when it comes to danger – the toaster as femme fatale – can it be said to fit the bill. You turn it on, you make your advances, you wait for it to get hot, and then you are ejected – or, as in the case the firemen attended, you are not – whereupon, burnt, hurt and vowing never to risk such a relationship again, unless of course there's something wrong with you, you beat an ignominious retreat.

That, anyway – and I hope I won't be branded a 'sexist' for it – is the best in the way of empathy for *l'amoureux grillé* I can manage.

As I said, 'Men!'

But the toaster has at least made me think again about Twitter and its misuse. I had thought to argue, when the week began, that if you don't like what pops into your Twitter box – my ignorance of the terminology is both deliberate and defiant – you should close it. You don't leave your front door open, you don't tell everyone where you live, you don't publicise your email address unless you're looking for trouble, and if you have reason to suppose you might be threatened, badgered or abused by phone, you ensure your number is ex-directory.

This isn't cowardice. It's sensible precaution. Before email replaced paper mail I regularly received abusive letters, some brief explosions of apparently motiveless hate, others angry I had found something funny that their senders hadn't, most taking issue with my politics, though I have no politics. One, a card written in spirals of faeces, sperm and blood, promised biblical retribution. So when email became the medium of choice for nutters, I chose not to append my email address to this column. Why invite hate into your life?

I'm not suggesting we play the ostrich. The violence in the human heart doesn't vanish because we look away, but some of it thrives on the knowledge it is being communicated. Social media doesn't create it; it does, though, add to its savour.

Make no mistake: turning the tables might look like striking back, but in the end the public shaming of the troll on Twitter itself is just another way of playing along. So why keep the portals to our privacy wide open? For what? Reader, what is lost if you never tweet again?

And then I remember the toaster. If we are to blame the medium for what's done on it, must we charge the toaster with inciting lust? And are we therefore to forswear toast?

After much consideration, this is my answer: if toasters were suddenly to turn vengeful, showing up in our bedrooms in an elemental rage and issuing threats and curses, then yes, we might indeed decide that toast is bought at too high a price. There's always something else to eat. And some other means of wittering on about it to people we don't know and who want us dead.

In God's name, why?

IT WAS A NIGHT made for eating out. The sun still hot but the glare from the Mediterranean no longer angry, the Promenade des Anglais given over to people perambulating rather than exercising, remembering that their bodies are primarily sites of pleasure, not denial. No more early-morning joggers ruining the golden hour before breakfast with their strenuous example. Now, all was well with the world again, and my only thought a bottle of Bandol. Then I saw her.

I didn't have to stare. I could have looked away. I had a companion to converse fondly with, a menu to study, and a bread roll of the sort that only the French can bake to pull apart, a bread roll that creaks and whimpers the way mandrakes are said to do when you rip them from the ground. But there was something so magnificently heroic about the insouciant carefulness with which she negotiated the steps into the garden, on heels that would have doubled my height had I been wearing them; something so alarming about the upward curl of her lips, as though she'd ordered the surgeon to give her a mouth with which she could blow kisses at her own eyeballs – eyeballs too far apart for her to see in any direction but sideways, like an alligator; something so heartbreaking about the way she tossed her hair, a girl again, prior to sitting herself down on buttocks from which the flesh had been so sedulously suctioned, sliced or dieted away that even over the creaking of the bread you could hear her little bones crunch, that I had no option but to lean over and say something to her.

'*Excusez-moi, madame*, but in the name of God, why?'

Naturally, I didn't say anything of the sort. She was none of my business and a woman has a right to look the way she wants to look. But was it really she who wanted to look like that, or was it the man she'd joined, the man I took to be her husband? It's hard to believe that so many years after *The Female Eunuch* there remain women willing to mutilate themselves to stay in favour with their men. And in truth there was no knowing, on this occasion, for whose behoof this valiant woman had subjected herself to such a drastic assault. But if it was to interest the man, then it had failed. He had been sitting in a sort of rich man's slouch, his feet outstretched in pale pink loafers – no socks – a lazily replete expression on his face, as though he knew life had no new thing to offer him, only more dying sun and flat champagne and, I am afraid to say – all that remodelling notwithstanding – her. He didn't raise his eyes to her when she arrived. Perhaps he knew she wouldn't be able to see him with her repositioned vision anyway. Or perhaps he knew an embrace was out of the question for fear her face would deliquesce in the heat of the propinquity.

She didn't please him, anyway. Reader, she couldn't have pleased him less. If it had been her intention to fool him into thinking she was twenty-one instead of – and I'm guessing conservatively – seventy-one, she had wasted her money and her time. Not impossibly she had wasted her natural beauty too. For if there's madness in a young woman's paying to be disfigured, there is tragedy in an older woman's doing it. We all age differently, I grant you. But it is a cruel fallacy to suppose that the beauty of a girl must surpass the beauty of a woman, that the blankness of expectancy is to be preferred to the marks of knowledge.

This, too, I wanted to lean across and tell my neighbour: a face that bears the history of affection can be a lovely thing; the lines of mirth and sorrow that experience etches are more engrossing – and that can mean more sensually as well as intellectually and spiritually engrossing – than no lines at all; extravagant beauty is not the lot of everyone, at any age, but there is an exquisiteness that even the plainest face can possess by virtue of kindness given and received, by virtue of what the eyes – if you would only leave them alone – have registered, and by virtue of what the lips – if you would let them be themselves – have uttered.

And yet this you have chosen to sacrifice to an illusion of youthful naturalness which resembles youth in not a single aspect and is to nature what Disney's Dumbo is to a living elephant.

Would you not have thought, reader, that sufficient women have traded their dignity and grace for this furious flower of plastic evil that surgeons call a mouth for others to know now what to expect? And don't tell me that beauty is in the eye of the beholder, and that where I see a woman deformed the woman herself sees confidence and allure, for you have only to watch her sit entrapped in her friable cosmetic cage to see that she is mortally unhappy – unable to know how to behave, for she is not a child, whatever her desperation to look like one, and never again to know whether she will be loved for herself or for what's been practised on her. As for him – the man for whom, perhaps, she's done it – then let him show how well he thinks it works by having his paunch and double chin removed to suggest vigour, and his dead unillusioned eyes widened to suggest the sweet ingenuousness of a shepherd boy, ideal companion to his new young Sylvan wife.

I accept it's none of my business. And, for all I know, the silent couple might be wondering why I am so careless of how I look as to be glugging Bandol as though it's the last bottle on the planet and ripping at French bread as though I love making it cry. I grant them their right. But grant me mine. It saddens me, that's all. As the poet said, 'Grow old along with me, the best is yet to be.'

Yet to be, not been.

Fisherman's friend

> In the hold this gear must go,
> Rattling winches, O!
> For mister mate has told me so,
> Rattling winches, O!

I T'S A WHILE SINCE we discussed seafarers and the songs they sing in this column. I'll need to conduct a thorough search of my files but I suspect that while I've touched occasionally on the grog and my noggy, noggy boots, this is the first time I've invoked the rattling winch, O! Clearly, I've been away from the sea too long.

And the reason for this sudden burst of maritime nostalgia? An item in the news about the Fisherman's Friends, a group of Cornish fishermen, lifeboatmen and coastguards who have just landed – 'landed' or, if you like, 'netted': I want you to see I'm still conversant with the idiom – a million-pound recording contract from Universal. Good to hear of anyone who isn't a banker making money at the moment, though no doubt they'll be singing shanties in the City now they know there's a buck in it.

> In the hedge this fund must go
> Rattling rolldowns, O!
> For Warren Buffett's told me so,
> Rattling rolldowns, O!

Port Isaac is where you can hear the Fisherman's Friends perform their repertoire, including 'Rattling Winches', which I initially misheard as Rattling Wenches. (Wishful thinking, I suppose. You think of little else when you're out rattling on a whaling boat on a wild wild sea.) Port Isaac is on the north Cornish coast, just a few miles of blind and winding lane from Boscastle, where I got my grounding in sea shanties twenty years ago and more. There was a fair bit of rivalry between Boscastle and Port Isaac in those days, as I suspect there still is, in the matter of which village is the more ruggedly beautiful, which has the greater history of independence, which smuggled more successfully, which has the better darts and pool teams, and of course which sings the more authentic shanties. So there'll be some sour faces in Boscastle today, is my guess. If I weren't busy proofreading a novel – not a seafaring yarn this time – I'd be down there to give them moral support. It's no joke losing out to a neighbouring village, as I know, having been on the Wellington Hotel pool team and the Cobweb Inn darts team in the days when Port Isaac was devilishly strong in both sports.

They were always slicker in Port Isaac than they were in Boscastle. It was a population thing, partly. While we in Boscastle weighed in with a mere eight hundred inhabitants, a figure widely thought to include family pets, and most of those (pets included) morose, Port Isaac was a seething metropolis of a thousand ebullient faux-Cornish socialites. But it also had to do with our relative places in the popular imagination. Television always preferred to film period dramas in Port Isaac, on account of its looking more conventionally like a smugglers' cove. *Poldark* and all that. And now *Doc Martin*. To probe Boscastle's subtler mysteries you need to get up onto the cliffs, or walk the Valency Valley, a deep, shaded tunnel of ancient vegetation and rivulet where Thomas Hardy courted his first wife. We had the literature and the savagery. Port Isaac was merely picturesque. But you know the public.

So it's all in the saga of their rivalry that in these superficial times the shallower village should have the more successful shanties. Whether ours were more genuine, that's to say more native to the area, is another matter. Most of Cornwall is tainted with Birmingham and Walthamstow now – garage owners and window cleaners who sold their houses in the boom time and migrated west to make crab sandwiches and serve cream teas and chips; and even when you find true Cornish Cornish it's hard to avoid the impression that they're playing at it. When a voluptuous Cornishwoman by the name of Trixie nestles up to you in the snug and calls you 'me 'andsome', is she recalling a Celtic courting ritual hundreds of years old, or is she taking the piss? I divided my time between Wolverhampton and Boscastle for about a decade and never discovered the answer to that. But this I can say: not once did anyone call me 'me 'andsome' in Wolverhampton.

Boscastle needed three pubs to refresh its eight hundred morose souls – Port Isaac, as I recall, had only two – and there was singing in every one of them, though the best singing happened at the bar of the Cobweb. It could break out at any time, depending who was there, but Friday night was when it really happened. Sometimes there'd be recitations or shaggy-dog stories, none of which I much cared for – if I wanted prose I could write my own – and then there'd be the odd Tom Jones favourite, such as 'Green, Green Grass of Home', a song highly inapplicable to Boscastle, which did grandeur, not hospitality, invariably followed by Roger Whittaker's 'The Last Farewell', which is a bit too catchy to be a shanty proper, but we bellowed it like broken-hearted mariners anyway. Then the 'real' locals would turn up, still wet with sea spray (and a little aftershave), still bespattered from the fields, and some still tanned from the oil rigs of the Middle East, at which point mere northern interlopers like me would buy a round of drinks and withdraw from the bar, in the manner of acolytes attending a secret ceremony, and the singing would begin in earnest.

I say they were shanties but many were simply coastal folk songs of uncertain provenance – mainly Irish, I suspected – that suited the mocking melancholy of the Cornish. The one I remember most vividly, perhaps because it was the one above all others that made me feel a stranger under threat, was 'A Bunch of Thyme', an aching, wickedly lilting story of sexual theft, the singer lamenting the bonny bunch of thyme a 'saucy fiddler' had stolen from him. 'For thyme,' we would all join in, 'it is a precious thing. . .'

I always felt they were siding with the fiddler. They were after my wife, of course. 'You got a song, 'Oward?' they asked me once. The bastards! What did they expect – 'Hava Nagila'? So I gave it to

them from the back of my throat – all I'd experienced of the cruel
hardships of the sea.

'Twas on the good ship Venus,
By God you should've seen us. . .

I know other verses if Universal's interested.

Ignorance is Bravo Lima India Sierra Sierra

OK, SO WHAT GREAT novel begins: Alpha Lima Lima Hotel Alpha Papa Papa Yankee Foxtrot Alpha Mike India Lima India Echo Sierra Alpha Romeo Echo Alpha Lima India Kilo Echo – and continues, assuming you are keeping up: Bravo Uniform Tango Alpha November Uniform November Hotel Alpha Papa Papa Yankee Foxtrot Alpha Mike India Lima Yankee India Sierra Uniform November Hotel Alpha Papa Papa Yankee Alpha Foxtrot Tango Echo Romeo India Tango Sierra Oscar Whisky November Foxtrot Alpha Sierra Hotel India Oscar November?

Don't bother deciphering it painstakingly. Just let the whole thing wash over you. What famous opening sentence does the above look and sound like? I'll give you a clue: the novel ends badly, or at least it does if you're more than a little bit in love with the heroine's fur hats and don't particularly like trains.

If you bear in mind that the physicality of words, even when they're in the nature of a code, often take on not just the appearance but the moral atmosphere of the thing they're coding, it should help to notice the suggestiveness of that concentration of Papas. What do you think of when you see Papas? That's right – families. As for the chance concatenation of Uniform, November, Hotel – there you have the narrative in a nutshell. Must I spell it out? Russian soldier. Snow. Clandestine adulterous assignations in a Moscow bed and breakfast.

Whoever hasn't by now guessed Count Vronsky is a dunce. The novel, of course, is *Anna Karenina* – 'All happy families are alike, but an unhappy family is unhappy after its own fashion.' Now you can check, if you've nothing more pressing to do, whether or not I've applied the gobbledegook alphabet correctly.

As for the truth of what Tolstoy says about families, that's another matter. I have always thought that what determines unhappiness in a family is pretty much the same the world over: too many Whiskys in November, too many Tango Foxtrots with Juliet or Oscar.

But this Charlie Oscar Lima Uniform Mike November is not about *Anna Karenina*. It's about the International Radiotelephony Spelling Alphabet and other comparable linguistic devices for avoiding confusion and making oneself understood. My position being that they do neither.

Three days ago – worn out with telling the Internet who I am, where I live and what my password, as opposed to my username, is – I made an airline booking by phone. Having a person to talk to turned out tolerably well. I recommend it. Allowing reasonable health, a person doesn't suddenly crash on you, leaving you to do it all again, which as like as not results in your making the same booking twice, a mistake for which there is no known remedy (as I discovered the time I booked the same seat to Wolverhampton seventeen times) outside of the European Court of Human Rights in Strasbourg, which incidentally had no record of such a place as Wolverhampton. But I can't pretend that having a person to talk to doesn't come with difficulties of its own. The chief of these, in this instance, being his insistence on reading my booking reference back to me phonetically. 'Quebec, X-Ray, Zulu . . .'

'I'll have to stop you there,' I said.

He apologised, assuming he was going too fast for me. I had already given him my age, so he had reason to suppose I lacked most of the organs of cognition. 'That's Qu-e-bec!' he shouted.

I had to stop him again. 'Deafness isn't the problem,' I assured him in a loud and confident voice. 'I'm a writer and a word for me is a plastic entity with distracting associations. So I don't only have the tail of the Q dancing before my eyes, I see the Saint Lawrence River freezing, think of the Algonquin people who gave Quebec its name, hear the clash of languages and cultures, and recall being taken as a boy to see a pageant in Belle Vue commemorating General Wolfe's scaling of the heights of Quebec, where – I mean Belle Vue, not Quebec – I ate a poisoned choc ice and was ill for a fortnight. So you can see why it would have been easier all round if you'd just said Q.'

He wondered whether I experienced similar difficulties X-raying Zulus. A jest he found more amusing than I did.

The truth is, telephony alphabets send me into a panic. All those unfamiliar words in strange conjunction – reminiscent of Dr Johnson's description of metaphysical poetry: 'the most heterogeneous ideas yoked by violence together' – rattled off at such speed that by the time you've worked out the letter denoted by the first, you've missed the following five. That it is intended sadistically on the part of the nerds and pedants who employ it – dreaming of being a pilot bringing down an Airbus A380 in a hurricane or single-handedly preventing or starting World War III – I have not the slightest doubt. The point of a secret language is to exclude those who don't speak it, sometimes to misinform and mislead them, often to flummox them into hasty acquiescence, but always to make them feel inferior.

The God of the Old Testament confounded the language of men, that they might not understand one another's speech. If everyone spoke the same language, He reasoned, there was no knowing what they might get up to. The Radiotelephony Spelling Alphabet, like French and Spanish, was among the weapons He deployed. Twitter was another, and more subtle than all of them on account of its fooling users into thinking they are having a conversation.

You don't argue with God if you know what's good for you. Therefore, I try to live in calm acceptance of the fact that I don't know what anybody's talking about.

Ignorance, as they say, is Bravo Lima India Sierra Sierra.

In the country of the deaf the man with subtitles is king

A FRIEND OF MINE went to the doctor recently, terrified by the sudden appearance of luminescent white spots, like toxic sequins, on his scrotum. After innumerable tests, the doctor wrote to say he had white spots on his scrotum. My friend wondered if the condition had a name. White spots on the scrotum, the doctor told him.

I was reminded of this last week when reading about viewers complaining to the BBC that they couldn't hear a word of what the actors in the new period drama *Jamaica Inn* were saying. After lowering herself deep into the whys and wherefores of what had gone wrong, Philippa Lowthorpe, the director of *Jamaica Inn*, came back up with an explanation that left nothing further to be explained: there was, she said, 'a sound issue'. So 'that's all good then', to borrow a phrase from Ian Fletcher, head of human values in that Beebspeak spoof, *W1A*.

I didn't watch *Jamaica Inn*. I've read the book, seen the movie, caught an earlier TV adaptation and once lived close to Jamaica Inn itself. I'd say that was enough. And if you are going to do wrecking in Cornwall you should have the courage to do its contemporary version. No more standing on the cliff with candles luring ships onto the rocks and then murdering the survivors. I am not being censorious: a lifestyle's a lifestyle, and until Rick Stein opened his seafood restaurant in Padstow, and the Cornish began to export pasties, they had no other way of making an honest living. But things have changed. Not only does the county now enjoy Minority Status, it wrecks differently.

Today, and for all I know this is true of other remote areas of the country, it's not ships that locals target but relationships – marriages, ideally, but courtships and engagements will do as well. First you lure the couple to your village with innocent-looking brochures promising clean air, high seas, beetling cliffs and cream teas, then you beguile them at the bar with tales of mystery and black magic, then you promise to take them out mackerel fishing, but there's room for only one of them on your little boat, and while you're pointing out the bobbing heads of seals to the city wife ('Over yon, maid'), and wooing her with reminiscences of your last great pilchard haul, your own spouse is working over the city husband, calling him 'me 'andsome' and getting him to roll with her in the blackthorn. Within a week one of them will have gone back to Primrose Hill and the other will have found a little cottage to rent overlooking the harbour.

This isn't, it should be said, without its risk of wreckage for the locals themselves. They, too, fall in love, mainly with their own romancing, but otherwise with either of the pair from the metropolis, sometimes even with them both. I've known Cornish men leave the house one morning, without a word, and not be seen again until they return, years later, with a baffled, faraway look in their eyes, like the forsaken merman, incapable of settling back into village life for evermore. Cornishwomen, too, to whom a reputation for emmet-stealing has stuck, who go on walking the cliffs at night, siren-like, in full make-up and high heels, and who at last are spoken of as witches.

Otherwise wreckers' yarns are old hat, whether they have 'sound issues' or they don't. You can overdo the past, not because it's another country but because it's the wrong country. The BBC should try making a series about the way we live now, but without a detective in it, without a mysterious lake, and without a paedophile who has paid his dues to society and deserves to be left alone.

As for making it audible, I am past caring what they do. Because most of what I watch I can't hear, I have taken to making up my own stories to the pictures. Mainly they're stories adapted from late Henry James novels, which are the sort of stories I like – articulate adulteries in English cathedral towns and the lengths to which the betrayed parties go not to show they know. It isn't always easy to match such narratives to shots of midwives wheeling babies in period prams, but if I close my eyes as well I sometimes enjoy success.

The other way is to own up to the problem and get medical advice, though after my friend's experience with his scrotum I'm reluctant to go near a doctor. He'll just tell me I have a sound issue. And I won't hear him. Failing that, he'll send me to have a hearing aid fitted and then, as all people my age know, you're on the slippery slope. First you have a gadget to help you with your sound issue, then a gadget to help you with your water issue, then a gadget to help you with your mobility issue, and the next thing you're in a care home having issues with your carers.

All along the fault lies with the programme makers who either have no interest in words – the picture being everything – or think dialogue is authentic only when it's imperceptible to the naked ear. I can accept that when it's drug takers who are talking, which is why I consented to not understanding a syllable of *The Wire,* and I half go along with it in the case of troubled cops from Louisiana, which is why I was happy to understand only half of what was happening in *True Detective.* It's a truism of detective thrillers anyway: given the banality of most plots, the only real excitement lies in separating one indistinguishable bit of muttering from another.

Otherwise it's subtitles or nothing. Secretly, of course, the entire country is watching everything with subtitles. The success of Scandinavian television is to be attributed to its coming to us with subtitles already attached. May I propose that the BBC should now do that with all its programmes? That way we will eventually be able to do without sound altogether. Which will cut costs and help make up the shortfall when the licence fee goes.

Phoney racists

O F THE WARS WE only pretend to fight, the phoniest is the one against celebrities caught off guard evincing racism. That's if they really are caught, and if they really are off guard, and if they really are celebrities.

Between those appalled by the latest of Jeremy Clarkson's affronts to people of another colour, gender or persuasion, and those who find his slips and sniggers endearing, silly, just Jeremy being Jeremy, or even Jeremy being invigoratingly if bumblingly transgressive – which is clearly how he would like to see himself: a sort of cross between Mel Gibson, Roy 'Chubby' Brown and Don Quixote – lies a yawning chasm of indifference. Do I mean by that that I would wish there to be a yawning chasm of indifference, or do I know of its existence, and even its dimensions, for a fact? Reader, I leave that to you to decide. But I was brought up to believe that if you wished hard enough for something, you would get it.

It is plainly the case, anyway, that even those who are routinely voluble on either side of Clarkson are growing bored. This could be because there have been too many instances of the just Jeremys of the world being just Jeremy, or it could be because there have been too many instances of offended of Primrose Hill being offended of Primrose Hill. Call it mutual fatigue.

But there is a third possibility and that is that we are simply not convinced in our hearts that racially dubious language is sufficient in itself to make the speaker of it a racist. In matters such as this we can use up our vocabulary of disapprobation too quickly. If we are going to call Clarkson a racist, what word does that leave to describe, say, the ideology of Boko Haram? Clarkson appears to want to play around at the edges of offence – baiting the sanctimonious for the fun of it – but if such play amounts to the committing of a hate crime, what do you call the Nairobi mall massacre of infidels?

There is, I know, the continuum theory to contend with. We start by sneaking back an odious designation here, a needling joke there, and soon we are shooting our way through shopping malls. This is the argument of the eternally vigilant, and their wakefulness is to be applauded. But the continuum theory works against them as well. First of all they outlaw words that bear a history of ugly association, and further down the line they are sending round the thought police.

So what are the gradations of racism? Are we racists by virtue of having occasional malodorous thoughts about foreigners? If that's the case, then who shall 'scape whipping? It is fair to say that we should do with such thoughts what we do with comparable invasions from the blackest parts of our souls, and suppress them. But are we not then hypocrites if we accuse others of feeling what we have sometimes felt ourselves? Or does the racism lie not in the thought but the speaking it, or not even then, but in putting the utterance into action? It would take the wisdom of Solomon to decide at which point in that slow sequence – a sequence that might see as much turning back as going forward – the thing we call racism enters.

Should we not do with racism, then, what the wisest of us do with jealousy, envy, pertinacious desire and the like, and accept we are not above any of it, however much we'd wish to be? Not acquiesce in its consequences, but not go hunting it down in others as evidence of their inextinguishable nastiness. Thus, we could say to the latest verbal offender, it is not because we've glimpsed the hem of your bigotries that we are incensed by you – indeed we possess identical undergarments – but because you think we love it when you tease us with the prospect of your showing more. It's not that you're a bit of a racist so much as that you're a bit of a whore.

As for Clarkson, it has always seemed to me that his real crime is to be interested in cars. Not just interested in cars in the way he is, as though they are a definitive badge of masculinity, as though the idea of a man unexcited by cars is inconceivable, as though the din and roar of them must be of universal male appeal, as though driving a car up a slope – sorry, up a hill – represents the *ne plus ultra* of human achievement, but just interested in cars full stop.

This might come as a surprise to cyclists who can't understand why I don't want to be mown down by them at traffic lights, but I detest the car as much as they do. It's just that I detest the bicycle as well. Not the object in itself, which is neutral, but the uses to which it's put. As a general rule, I hold the world to be an even more dangerous and fatuous place than it needs to be so long as there are people in it who idealise a means of transport.

Just get on it and go where you're going. Don't dress for it. Don't smooch with it. Don't see it as an extension of you, or you as an extension of it. A man who doesn't know where he ends and his machine begins is by definition a fool. And a fool on a main road is a menace. As witness what cyclists do when they see a red light – but there I go again.

And a motorist is a cyclist but more so. I say 'motorist' as opposed to driver. A driver employs his vehicle functionally. A motorist has an ideological relationship with his car. In a sane society you'd get eight years for that. But then in a sane society we'd have sent Max Clifford down for lowering the national tone long before we knew what other sins he was committing. And by the same logic, if you must get Clarkson, get him for *Top Gear*.

'Get out of my face!'

So how loud does your voice have to be before someone thinks you're shouting? How sharp your reprimand before it will be described as threatening? And how close do you have to be to someone before you can be accused of being in his face? These and similar questions will be addressed below. But I can tell you the answer to all of them now. And it's the same in every case. Not very.

Anyway, I was curious about this mobile phone I'd been reading about. The BlackBerry Passport. A giant of a phone that would be ideal, I thought, for a man with fading vision, stubby fingers and no interest in selfies. It's possible you can take a selfie with a BlackBerry Passport but it's so heavy you won't be able to hold it up to your face long enough to strike a becoming pose. I should say it 'looks' so heavy because so far I haven't been able to lay hold of one. Indeed, it was in the hope of being able to do just that that I breezed, all innocence, into a Vodafone shop in the vicinity of Covent Garden. I won't be any more specific than that. It's not my intention to encourage copycat visits.

Two assistants were talking to each other at the counter. They didn't look up or ask if they could help me. I found a BlackBerry Passport the size of *War and Peace* glued to a display table and enquired if they had one I could pick up. One of them shook his head. I wondered, in that case, how I could discover how heavy it was and what it felt like in my hand. The other shrugged and said I couldn't. How then, I wondered, did people discover if the phone was suitable to their needs. 'They buy it,' the first assistant said.

I thought I ought to be sure I'd heard what I'd heard. 'So you're telling me,' I said, 'that in order to know whether you want to buy the phone you have to buy it?' 'Yeah,' one of them said. 'But we haven't got any anyway,' the other added.

There's a tide in the affairs of men, and all that. Swept on by that tide I approached the desk and expressed surprise at their way of doing business. I was a Vodafone customer and felt I had a right to expect a certain level of politeness, not to say helpfulness, from Vodafone staff. Were they here to sell phones or weren't they?

It was at this point that a third person, wearing some sort of anorak and sitting at a little table near the counter, told me not to shout. I told him I hadn't at any point raised my voice. I had expressed exasperation, which was not the same thing. 'Don't shout at my staff,' he repeated, though the only person shouting was him.

Since he had in this way declared himself to be a manager – a sub-manager as it turned out – but hadn't stood to address me, I sat to address him. 'If you'd heard the tone in which your staff answered my enquiry,' I said – letting the idea of professional derogation hang in the air between us – 'you would understand why I spoke to them as I did. They were rude; I let them know I didn't like it. I didn't shout.'

'Get out of my face,' he said, getting into mine.

What happened next, how this led to that, how the two original men took turns to say, 'If you know what's good for you you'll get out of this shop,' how the third man threatened to call the police, how I told him to call who he liked, how after no policeman arrived I decided life was too short for this and rose to go – still ignorant as to the configuration of the BlackBerry Passport – all this I will not trouble you with. But as a parting shot, because I felt the event needed a finale, I called the sub-manager a clown. Whether he'd trained to be a clown and failed, or whether his wife had run off with a clown, I had no way of ascertaining, but if he'd been in my face before, he was out the other end of it now. He reared up from the chair in which he'd all along been sitting. 'Come back at six o'clock when I'm not wearing my uniform and say that,' he said.

So there you have it: in the space of ten minutes I'd gone from making a modest enquiry about a phone to being threatened with having my lights punched out. And the cognitive scientist Stephen Pinker tells us that violence in civil society has declined.

I wrote to Vodafone's chief executive, thinking he'd like to know. I was contacted with a number to ring, but it was just customer services – the place you go to complain about your bill. They offered me £30 for my inconvenience. Just think, reader: if I'd gone back to the store at six o'clock and been knocked senseless by the sub-manager, they might have offered me £50.

Whether the person who made the offer believed me when I told him money wasn't the issue, and whether I should have believed him when he told me the case was being investigated, I don't know. But I am not living in suspense.

There are several conclusions to be drawn from this, the more obvious – regarding the part faceless multinational companies play in raising social tension – I leave readers to draw for themselves. But we have reached a pretty pass when the surly, the disobliging and the downright rude believe they have a human right never to be admonished. Of course, no one should be abused, but a rebuke is not abuse. First we couldn't slap a child, then we couldn't tell him off. Now we cannot tell off anybody.

Politeness is a two-way street. We'll be sorry when the public, tired of being treated with contempt and held in queues when it complains, decides to pull the whole lot down.

Raising the age of consent

I'M OUT OF THE country for three weeks and already there's talk of lowering the age of consent. This can't be coincidence. I must assume that, knowing my views on the subject and hoping I'd be gone for even longer, Professor John Ashton, president of the Faculty of Public Health, quickly ups and proposes to David Cameron that we allow fifteen-year-olds to have sex. Not much of a concession, given that most fifteen-year-olds have already had too much, but these things are symbolic, which is why, no matter what is actually going on out there, I'd move in the opposite direction to Professor Ashton and raise the age of consent to thirty-five. Let the fifteen-year-olds in question know what we think, no matter that they'll ignore it.

I am a believer in making unrealistic demands of the young. It's important they confront a challenge. I recall envying school friends whose parents let them sleep with their girlfriends in the spare room – though not as much as I envied them for having girlfriends in the first place – but later noted that these were the boys who went to ruin soonest. No moral compass. No exemplary prohibition.

You might think you want your parents to be your pals, your partners in sexual mischief, but you don't. You want them to be forbidding Noboddadies, silent and invisible, fathers and mothers of jealousy and inhibition, whose commandments you will of course break, but in the breaking of which you come to understand the first pleasure of sex which isn't penetration but disobedience. Here is what we lose when we remove the concept of wrong from sex: secrecy, connivance, terror and, above all, argument. There is more than one attitude to take to sex – and you're a goner as a moral being if you aren't taught that early.

I detect demurrals from the *Health & Efficiency* brigade. Let sex flower naturally, they say. But whoever thinks sex is natural and therefore to be unambiguously encouraged has never seen it, never done it, never thought about it, and never seriously weighed its consequences. I'm not proposing that we din Shakespeare's testy description of lust in action as an 'expense of spirit in a waste of shame' into our children the moment the subject's raised. But I'm grateful to my parents for warning me that I was likely to experience as much disappointment as delight, for cautioning me against impatience, for suggesting there were other things I might do – table tennis was one of them – and for not letting the girlfriends I didn't have sleep with me in the spare room we didn't have either.

We do those we are charged with bringing up no service by pretending to be no older or wiser than they are. To do so only deprives them of precept and example. And don't be fooled by their apparent scorn for such things. They might not know what the words mean but they miss what they denote when it's not on offer. And part of that is a sympathetic but well-reasoned rebuttal of pornography. We can't stop them looking. We used to look ourselves. Many of us are no doubt looking still. How could it be otherwise?

Pornography became inevitable for *Homo sapiens* the moment he turned *sapiens*. We ate of the tree of knowledge and immediately wanted to take dirty photographs. But you can look and know you shouldn't. You can look and gauge the damage that looking does. D. H. Lawrence's denunciations of pornography and 'the masturbation self-enclosure' helped me when I was young – not to give it up but at least to be in a debate with myself about the subject. And that's the parental role: to be the other side of the argument, to make the case for harm in an age where the very idea of harm in the matter of sexuality (a word that is itself part of the problem) has grown dangerously unfashionable.

Thirty-five, then, kids, is when we think you are ready to start. This will come as a shock to you because you believe thirty-five is when you're meant to finish. 'Gross!' you call the thought of people that age perspiring naked in one another's arms. 'Ugh!' you cry,

RAISING THE AGE OF CONSENT

putting your bitten fingers down your baby throats. But all that proves is that you, too, are moralists who lack the words you need to moralise with. Allow anything about sex to disgust or dismay you and you are admitting that the procreative impulse is susceptible to judgement.

We have let you get away with judging us for too long. Time now for the rightful order to be restored. *We* teach *you*. And the single thing you can teach us in return is that teaching is what you hunger for: the gift of our experience. Tell your parents that. Tell them you've got plenty of friends, thank you all the same – remind them that you perform fellatio or similar on most of them – but what you're short of is intelligent authority.

And thirty-five is not as arbitrary as you think. This might surprise you, but in the main people get better at sex as time goes by, not worse. Sure, you lose a little in the way of athleticism, but what you forgo in elasticity of body you gain in flexibility of mind. You notice more. You discover that the slow accrual of mutual fondness adds savour to sensuality. And with luck you will by that time have evolved a sense of the ridiculous, which can be a nuisance during sex but is wonderfully consoling after it.

In the meantime, accept that most of what you think and do you shouldn't. If you don't know that sex is trouble, a pleasure and a plague, no sooner done than regretted, and no sooner regretted than missed – in short, perplexing and unfathomable – you aren't ready for it.

Arrivederci Raffaele

THE DEATH OF AN Italian tailor might not be calamitous in
Catania or Cagliari, but the loss to Soho is immeasurable. We
don't have Italian tailors we can spare here. Each day the London
district loses a little more of its essential self – to developers, gentri-
fiers, scaffolders, diggers of trenches for cables we don't need,
cleaners-up and dumbers-down.

There's a simple arithmetical logic at work. Build more unafford-
able and not always architecturally sympathetic apartments, watch
the rents rise, the tarts leave, the small shops, production offices and
design studios close down, and hey presto, we have another fashionable London suburb indistinguishable from the rest. Given such
depredations, it's cruel of death to want its share as well.

Raffaele Candilio was the alterations tailor my wife and I went
to no matter how large or small the job. He would remodel a suit
or just sew on a button. You would go up the rickety stairs to his
workroom above a Chinese importer of waving cats, and find him
sitting cross-legged on his work table, sewing. Sometimes Pavarotti
would be singing. Not in person, but it was almost as good as.
Other people I have spoken to in the days since he died contest my
description of him. He was never sitting cross-legged on his work
table when they went to see him. Well, we all have our memories.
That's how I see him, anyway: a slight, delicately made man, light
of bone and temperament, easy and weightless in the world, but
precise and sharp – a tailor of genius who floated above the clumsy
inattentiveness of the mundane world.

I loved his workroom and would sometimes take along a garment
that didn't need altering just so I could visit him, listen to Pavarotti
and look at postcards of his native Naples, Rocky Marciano and

58

some football team I didn't recognise pinned to his walls. Nostalgic myself, I am a sucker for other men's nostalgia. So, I think, was he, because while he often had Italian friends visiting him, the small staff he employed appeared to be of every nationality. Whether that meant that songs about returning to Sorrento got to them as well, I can't say. Though you could smell the grief of exile in there, I never saw them cry. At least not until last week.

There, in my mind's eye, he sits on his table, and when I enter with an armload of trousers he makes a quick gesture with his hand, which means that I am to climb over the cardboard boxes in the backroom, draw a simple curtain to cover my modesty and change into whatever I want altering. None of this is necessary. He knows what needs doing, how many inches on or off, just by looking. 'Just estimate it, Mr Candilio,' I say. 'I trust you.' He lets his head fall to one side fatalistically. Yes, I trust him. And yes, he trusts himself. But things go wrong. And customers complain. So just change into your trousers.

In my case, this was partly to prove a point. I believed my legs were longer than he knew them to be. 'Best try them on,' he'd say. And even then I felt I owed it to the dignity of my person and stature to quibble with him over half an inch. 'All right,' he'd concede, changing the chalk mark, but I suspect that when it came to doing the job he trusted his estimate over mine and took the half-inch back off again.

He was an appraiser of appearances, would let you know if he thought something you'd asked him to do would ill become you. Politely – because he had the manners of a gentleman of another time as well as of another place – he would quickly run his eyes over you and give his opinion with the faintest inclination of his head. He had fine, aquiline features and at such a moment you felt you were being looked at by a hawk.

He was interviewed by a national newspaper when Fabio Capello took over as manager of the English football team. Since the Football Association's offices were in Soho Square, the journalist thought it would be a good idea to ask some of Soho's Italian residents what they thought of him. About Capello's managerial skills, Raffaele had little to say. But he liked the suits. 'I have seen Mr Capello on the TV,' he said, 'and I am quite impressed with how he dresses. But then most Italians know how to dress. Without meaning any offence, the same cannot be said of a lot of young English people.'

A critical father, I wouldn't be surprised to learn. Presumably all fathers from Naples are. And perhaps a critical husband as well. Only a couple of weeks ago, in the course of a conversation about the desirable length of a woman's skirts – and no, we weren't being dirty old men, we were simply discussing a dress my wife had brought in for him to lengthen – and no, not at my prim behest – he talked about his own wife's instinctive modesty. He even drew an imaginary line high on his chest, to show her preferred height of neckline.

I stepped away from that conversation out of embarrassment and respect. His wife died a few years ago, and I was inclined to think that there was a sadness about him thereafter. Often I would see him on his own in Soho after work, always elegant and handsome, but a little lost, I thought. But I am a conjugal sentimentalist and am upset by the sight of a once-married man out on his own. No wife to go out with or go home to is no life to speak of. I might, therefore, have invented him forlornly wandering Soho, as some say I invent him, out of the same idealised sorrow, sitting forever cross-legged on his table.

Soho is the poorer, as is everyone who knew and respected and, yes, loved him, whatever the truth of where he sat or what he felt. Another social comfort dropped away. Another good man gone. And with him something irreplaceable – not just industry and skill, but a rare sort of honour.

Rejoice!

So what did mrs Thatcher ever do for us? Gather round, you readers too young to remember, and let me tell you what it was like in those far, dark days before her Coming. Of rubbish gathering uncollected in the streets I sing, of the dead rotting where they fell, of inflation running at such a rate that the only people with money were those who had none, and of the rich taxed so punitively that they would have left the country in droves had there been any reliable means of transport for them to leave by. So why did no one tweet a revolution? Ah, how far away it must all seem. No Twitter, no Facebook, no mobile phones, no iPads. So how did we communicate? Reader, we didn't.

I was teaching at a polytechnic when She became prime minister. Think of it – a polytechnic! If there is one word that sums up the depressed spirit of the 1970s – provincial, grim, strike-bound, maimed, undernourished, unpoetical – it's 'polytechnic'. You can smell the engine oil in the word, as you could smell the engine oil in the country, only none of the engines were running.

I taught – that's when we managed to recruit students – in a bus station adjoining the poly, and I was considered fortunate to be teaching there. 'Fares, please!' other lecturers would twit me, but I took it in my stride. It was better than being punched in the face, which, before 1979, was the prevailing mode of academic discourse in a tertiary institution.

Some of our courses were taught on a traffic island in the middle of the ring road. Given the rubbish, the rats, the piles of unwanted coal and the dead lying in the corridors of the polytechnic, a traffic island wasn't all bad. True, there were no teaching facilities. Not even a blackboard, unless you carried your own. But then we'd sold all the chalk to flying pickets to make ends meet, and few of the students could read anyway. Occasionally a car with no brakes – no cars had brakes before Mrs Thatcher – careered into the class, which would have put pressure on the local hospital had there been one. But so long as no one was seriously injured, accidents were regarded by staff and students alike as a welcome break from the rigours of Humanities 1: The Wit of Arthur Scargill, or Humanities 2: The Wisdom of Arthur Scargill.

When I'd finished teaching I'd go home to a cold-water flat, buying a cabbage for supper on the way. If there were no cabbages I boiled the *Guardian*. Soup's soup. I shared a lavatory with a dozen others, most of them out of work, so it fell to me to replace the bath towel every six months. A rota ensured that no more than three people of the same sex (otherwise no more than two) used the toilet at the same time, and I suppose if I miss anything from those years it's the camaraderie that built up in the course of urinating together.

I had been engaged for about seventeen years but I didn't have the money for a ring. It was our intention to marry before we were seventy but we held out no hope of ever living together. A council flat of our own was a dream it would never have occurred to us to entertain. Few people dreamed before Mrs Thatcher came to power. And no one entertained. Words like 'hospitality', 'lobster bisque', 'lasagne', 'sparkling mineral water', 'Cabernet Sauvignon' and, of course, 'champagne' were unheard of in the early 1970s. My fiancée, Penny – she couldn't afford a second name – would have been pretty had she had teeth. Or hair. But dentists and wigmakers were beyond our means, as were physiotherapists, personal trainers, life coaches, Lacanian psychoanalysts and cleaners. Then lo! – in a shaft of light – She descended, and Penny was illuminated. New teeth, hair that cascaded down her back when she jogged, she no longer walked into buildings now that she had bought her own spectacles instead of waiting to get them on the National Health, and she told me she was leaving me. 'It isn't you,' she explained. 'It's me. I want more for myself.' This, too, we owed to Margaret Thatcher – this 'It isn't you it's me', this 'I want more for myself'.

It's said of Mrs Thatcher that she atomised society, but the truth is she brought us together. If we appeared nicer before, it was only the niceness of deprivation. She showed us how to be companioned in avidity. This was classlessness in action – the rich man at the helm of privatised industry and the poor man with shares in it.

She privatised envy, too, giving everyone a stake. Hitherto, envy had been the closed shop of the poor. Ah, how we envied! What we didn't have we wanted. What others had we wanted. What we didn't have and others didn't have either we wanted even more. This didn't change but it made us feel better to see that envy didn't stop higher up; suddenly those who had everything began to experience covetousness, though they couldn't have said what exactly they coveted. Finally, Thatcherite economics gave it a name. A bigger bonus.

Until Mrs Thatcher unchained the City, industrial blackmail was the prerogative of the unions. In order to get the pay and conditions their members demanded they held the country to ransom. Hence the dead rotting in the streets. Today it's the banker to whom we must capitulate, on pain of his taking his talents somewhere else. Scargill, by this token, would have made an excellent banker.

So, whatever Mrs Thatcher said about society, a big happy society is what we are, joined in universal heartlessness. 'Rejoice!' she famously told us, and that's what the children succoured in her creed are now doing – over her death.

Fanatics only ever read one book

S O HOW FARE OUR investigations into what makes someone want to kill cartoonists? (I'm assuming we know why they want to kill Jews.) Maybe, before pondering the education of a jihadist, we should ask a prior question: what makes a fanatic?

We were given some insight into this on *Newsnight* earlier this week when Evan Davis, growing nicely into his job, interviewed the lawyer, journalist and associate of Edward Snowden, Glenn Greenwald – a man strikingly deficient in the musculature necessary to essay a smile. The subject was surveillance and David Cameron's call for more of it. There are, I accept, differing views on this. I, for example, am for having every member of the human family watched day and night by every possible means because the human family is currently dysfunctional and can't be trusted. But I understand why others don't think as I do. This puts me in a different category of person from Greenwald, who allows no beliefs that conflict with his and attributes those that do to a cowardly subservience to authority.

Leading Greenwald with expert gentleness into the gated hell that is his mind, Davis put the case for differing viewpoints. Nothing could have been more instructive than Greenwald's dead expression – his mouth fixed in the rigor mortis of absolute conviction, his eyes unanimated by the pleasure of conversation or the excitement of controversy. Doubt honours a man, but this was the face of someone whom no ghost of a second thought dares visit. No consciousness of absurdity either. As for the humanity whose civil rights he champions with such icy rigidity, for that he had nothing but contempt. We are merely, if we don't think what he thinks, the playthings of the powerful. This is the terrifying paradox of zealotry: no one hates humanity more than those who believe they know what's best for it.

I don't, I must say, see Greenwald launching rockets any time soon. The ideologue is still a long way from being the terrorist. These, though, are the first steps. Expelling doubt. Refusing contrariety. Hating play. Making oneself the human equivalent of a weapon, implacable, well aimed, reduced to a single function.

Another way of putting this is to say that the fanatic is someone who has only ever read one book. It is right, therefore, to ask not only what the appeal of the story he goes on reading is, but where he heard it, who read it to him first, and where and why it goes on being told. Religions, like cultures, understand themselves through narrative. How we came into the world, what we were created for, what are our triumphs and our losses. These narratives enjoy a fearful pertinacity. They have the capacity to console but also to inflame. There are still people fighting over territory declared holy by their national stories a millennium ago.

So it was heartening to see the French – offenders and offendees, or at least some of them – putting aside their individual stories for an hour. But the anti-immigration demonstrations in Germany were reminders that masses on the move are frightening as well as stirring. A group that has only ever read one book is a fanatic group.

For all the day-long defiance of terror, fear continues to stalk the conversation. Fear for Muslims, for example, and fear of them. May I make a plea, in the name of varied reading – because it's better to read even two books than one – for the right to hold both positions? I don't want to see anti-Muslim demonstrations on the streets. I no more want to see Muslims homogenised and traduced than Jews. But must that mean I cannot ask where the single story beloved of the fanatic is engendered, and if it should turn out that the most moderate Muslim unthinkingly propounds a narrative that fuels the fanatic mind – an anti-Western, anti-Semitic, victim-driven narrative – can I not plead with him to shade it a little, to remember that the best stories liberate us from our pains and grievances into understanding other people's?

We rightly shy from holding communities to immediate and unambiguous account for what their most errant children do, but is it wise, is it honest – reader, does it make the world a better place for any of us – to raise the charge of Islamophobia the moment someone questions the communal atmosphere such errancy might have breathed? At the heart of every narrative of belief is a weak spot of exclusivism and dogma waiting to be exploited by its wilder adherents. Monotheism is a grand conceit, but can we really say that it is innocent of the millions of killings in its name? Danger lurks in the tales we all tell. And whoever goes on telling a tarnished tale is party to its effects.

'Nothing – absolutely zilch – happens without a past,' Robert Fisk wrote recently. But the past is not forever fixed; it too is a story, endlessly spun and woven, told and retold, now this way, now that. A Paris jihadist spoke of turning to terror after seeing Americans torturing Iraqi prisoners on television. It is not to defend such barbarities to say they were but one side of a savage conflict. They too had a past. They did not express the immutable will or character of the American people. A half-truth is a half-lie. The invasion of Iraq, however botched, had a past we falsify if we see it only as a story of Western skulduggery. It is a false tale, falsely told, that Israelis wantonly butcher children in Gaza. It is a false tale, falsely told, that the West is waging war against Islam. Whoever lusts after coherence lusts after lies.

The fanatic craves a single, simple story. Communities of whatever persuasion who provide the pen and paper, ink and plot, should search their hearts. But who are we to talk? We too, in our lurid self-censoriousness, tell madmen tales they love to hear.

Boris and the bikes

AND TODAY'S MORNING STORY is 'The Selfishness of the Long-Distance Cyclist'. You know the plot. Innocent weekend motorist fancies a pootle through central London to feel the wind through his hair, pick up a pizza, show his kids Buckingham Palace, visit a sick relative – there is no end to the pleasant tasks a motorist might set himself on a blowy, autumnal Saturday – in pursuance of any or all of which he puts on his motoring gloves and goggles, adjusts his satnav, and sets off. Only to discover that there is nowhere he can go, that no street is open to him, that diverted buses are causing havoc in every direction, including the shortest way home again, and all because the Tour of Britain, the country's largest professional cycle race – not to be confused with all the lesser, amateur cycle races that close the city every other weekend of the year – is finishing in London with a 'dramatic dash along Whitehall', though how its organisers know that in advance is anybody's guess, unless they have learned of my intention to run out from Horse Guards Parade this afternoon and throw myself, Emily Davison-like, under the wheels of the leaders.

I don't say that unhindered access to the amenities of one's city at the weekends – not just London but any city where runners and cyclists maraud – is of the same historic order of importance as women getting the vote. But now that they have got the vote, now that slavery has been abolished and no child can be bound apprentice before the age of eight or sent up a chimney before the age of twenty-one, now that a man may marry a man and a Jew may join a golf club, we are free to turn our attention to less dramatic but no less far-reaching infringements of our freedoms. And I don't just mean the freedom of city motorists to motor, I mean the freedom of city amblers to amble without being warned off, shooed away, made to wait, held back and hectored by race officials keeping roads and parks and even lakes clear, as they did for days on end last week for no better reason than that a triathlon was in progress. A triathlon, reader! The thrice-cursed triathlon, than which there is no sillier sight in sport, not even counting beach volleyball, synchronised swimming and trampolining, from which you can at least shrink away with your head lowered when you have lost, instead of having to leap from the indecorousness of one into the indignity of the next, in a single unbroken sequentiality of shame.

In Australia they call it the Iron Man. I happen to know this only because I was once strolling along a beach in Broome, thinking my thoughts, when thirty orange men in tiny pea-green bikini bottoms and Esther Williams bathing hats came charging out of the water in my direction, shouting 'Out of the way, dickhead!', which prompted me to ask who they thought they were to be calling me a dickhead, the dickheads, whereupon a race official screamed, 'They're the Iron Men, you galah! Move.' And the next thing I knew they were riding bikes over me on the sand. But one thing I will say for them: at least they didn't close the beach.

Thanks to last week's triathletes, however, I was forced to sit steaming for two hours in a taxi on the way to the London Art Fair, my intention to look at paintings, encourage painters and maybe even add to their meagre earnings, thwarted by the psycho-cycle swimmers' desire to wear hideous clothes and chase after one another to no intelligible end. Don't get me wrong. I am no opponent of sport. Football, cricket, tennis, darts – all these are aired affectionately in these columns. But then no darts tournament has ever necessitated the closure of the city in which I try to live in peace. Darts players know their place. At the oche, in Alexandra Palace or Blackpool Tower. As cricketers know their place is Lord's. If we want to see them that is where we go, if we don't we don't. I don't insist on a poetry reading at Old Trafford while Manchester United are playing, and they don't close Regent's Park to kick a ball around. Thus do we accommodate one another.

But first the marathon runner and now the cyclist have comman-
deered our space. In this they have support at the highest level.
'The Tour of Britain,' says London's Transport Commissioner, 'is
a superb event, further showcasing' (never trust a man who turns
showcase into a verb) 'London's reputation as a city for cycling' – an
assertion as fatuously self-proving as 'The knifing of young men in
deprived areas further showcases London's reputation as a city for
knifing'.

Behind the Commissioner for Transport's transports we can of
course detect the will of Boris, London's Mayor for Bikes. Because
he cycles, he has decreed that we must cycle; because he believes
that cycling is good for him, he has decreed that it shall be good for
us, not only to do ourselves but to tolerate at any cost in others – a
piece of nannying we would not expect from one who in all other
matters opposes the Nanny State.

Beyond bikes, Boris is famous for his classical education. Would
he therefore consider my proposal to close London every weekend
for a year so that actors dressed as Trojan triathletes might wander
at liberty through our roads and parks reading aloud and without
a pause *The Iliad*, *The Odyssey* and *The Aeneid*? To show respect for
which all cyclists must dismount and all runners stand still.

Strictly turn-off

THIS WEEK – THE UNTOLD story of my life in dance. Clear your mind of *Billy Elliot*. Or, if you must, think *Billy Elliot* in reverse – a boy who infuriated his father by refusing to dance and wanting to have boxing lessons instead. Of the dances my father urged on me, I most dreaded the conga, the Russian kazatzka, and the last waltz with whichever great-great-grandmother was still standing. I was too shy to try any of them. Girls might see. Or worse, join me.

But it wasn't just girls I was afraid to dance with, it was the older women in my family as well. To do something as intimate as conga behind a woman I didn't know was bad enough, but to conga behind a woman I did know was worse. In despair with me, my father suggested I forget the conga and just smooch. It was my mother who intervened at this point, saying that she thought smooching with my aunties would be inappropriate. I agreed with her. There's a kind of young man who cannot smooch with a woman without feeling he has to ask her to marry him. And for all my inexperience, I knew you didn't do that with your aunties.

I went through the era of Bill Haley and early Elvis in an agony of incompetence. The kazatzka had been challenging enough, but the jive could kill. I'd accompany my tall friend Malcolm to the Plaza Ballroom, where he would kick his legs so high in the air that everybody had to get off the floor, he thought to watch and admire him, but in truth to avoid injury. Here, hiding in a corner, I would invent stories to explain why I couldn't leave my seat: a slipped disc, ripped ligaments, a bruised heart, torn trousers. One night I saw one of my aunties there, smooching with a man who wasn't my uncle. Had I needed confirmation that dancing was the devil's work, this was it.

And then something wonderful happened. The twist. Whether it was because the twist obviated the need for close contact, or because the corkscrew action suited the configuration of my pelvis, I cannot say, but I took to it at once. Not only could I do it; I taught others to do it. This got me through my first year at university where almost everybody was as wary of moving their bodies as I had been and only I could twist. Undergraduates of both sexes queued outside my college room for lessons. Even the Master wondered if I'd show his wife a few steps. 'There are no steps, Master,' I told him. By the end of Michaelmas term 1961 the twist had swept through the English Faculty of the University of Cambridge. Whatever historians of popular culture in academia say, this was my doing.

From here on my attitude to dancing in general changed. I don't say I ever looked happy or comfortable doing it, and I of course refused to perform any routine whose genesis was the package holiday on the Costa Brava, but at least I never again had to feign angina or torn trousers. All this I mention to explain my vexed attitude to *Strictly Come Dancing*, or 'Strictly' as enthusiasts call it, much as luvvies speak of the 'Dream'. We watch it in our house, anyway, ritualistically, with friends and a grand spread of cheese straws, pizza and red wine. This, I'm told, is called relaxing and is good for me. And as far as the company, the cheese straws, the pizza and the red wine are concerned, I agree.

Nothing beats a merry gathering. It's what we have gathered to watch that's the problem. 'Couldn't we watch it with the television off?' I wonder. But the suggestion has no takers. This is light entertainment, and we all need to be lightly entertained. Demur to that truism and you ruin everybody's night. That was what my father used to take me to task for – ruining everybody's night. I don't doubt that Matthew Arnold's father used to say the same to him. But at least I broke out and learned to twist, which I bet Matthew Arnold never did. Isn't that enough?

And yes, as long as *Strictly Come Dancing* was about people discovering a gift for dancing they never knew they had – an unexpected grace, a fluidity of body and soul previously locked away inside them (think the human corkscrew which the twist told me

I could become) – then it was engaging and at times even touching. But little by little the curse of light entertainment descended on the original conception, lightness begetting lightness as surely as ignorance begets ignorance. I say nothing of the lameness of Bruce Forsyth's jokes, which were apparently part of his charm – a subtlety lost on me – but which promise to continue anyway now he's gone. And nothing, either, of how celebrity has become so debased a concept as to mean somebody of whom no one has heard.

More seriously objectionable is the way the judges, who once demonstrated knowledgeable criticism in action – this is what you're doing wrong, this is how you could do it better, these are the lines and shapes we want to see – have succumbed to the lure of celebrity and declined to pantomimic versions of themselves, gurning, preening, feigning lust, exchanging leers of suggestiveness and innuendo.

In the same collusive spirit we are asked to wonder, when teacher and learner are paired off, whether shenanigans are to be anticipated, whether the spouse seen smiling weakly in the audience as a dancer wraps her legs around the husband's waist, or the wife collapses in a panting heap into her partner's arms, is soon to be made a fool of.

And so, ironically, it falls to me to speak up for dancing as an activity too intrinsically elegant to be demeaned, as movement whose subtle disciplines are worthy of serious respect, and as an art sufficiently sensual in itself not to be in need of lowbrow sexing up.

We accept today that Disney's cartoons of animals in tutus degraded them. Reader, humans can be degraded too.

Who dunnit? The one who dunnit last time

OUT OF THE COUNTRY for ten days, looking at desert, shower-ing in the open air and not watching television. Bliss. Not watching television has much to recommend it anywhere, but when warm winds are winnowing the hairs on your chest and making little floral pinwheels of those between your thighs – let's not be prudish, that's what happens when you walk out of an open-air shower into desert – not watching television feels like a reason to be alive.

It's falling out of the collective passivity that's so good. The not knowing what people are talking about when they use words like 'Apprentice'. But in no time at all, the collective reclaims you on your return, and before you know it, you are eager to know how something or other ended. Bloody *Broadchurch*. Or how something or other began. Bloody *Mad Men*.

My point is general and only happens to be called *Broadchurch*. Prior to going away, I'd watched all but the last episode, mainly for the pleasure of Olivia Colman – with whom I suspect it would be fun to take an outdoor shower – occasionally thinking it was good, occasionally thinking it was poor, but mainly thinking it was above averagely just about all right. It was clear, of course, by episode three who'd done it.

It's always the person who's sufficiently present in the plot for you to know vaguely who he is but is never filmed staring longer than is natural into the middle distance just before a commercial break. And other characters were starting to ask how it is possible not to know what the person you're married to is really like, and it was becomingly glaringly obvious that Olivia Colman didn't know what the person she was married to was really like. Too busy being a detective. Aren't they always? Too busy detecting to detect what's happening in their own lives. Come up with a domestically attentive detective and you've killed the genre. Besides, you don't employ Olivia Colman in the first place unless there's going to be a reason for her to stand sobbing on the sand when all's revealed. There's no point paying for the best tears in the business and then not getting her to shed them. So Olivia Colman's half-anonymous husband it had to be. This is going to be a problem from now on for any whodunnit starring Olivia Colman. The villain is always going to turn out to be the person she shares her home with.

So let's have no more whodunnits. The reason they are never satisfactory is that the resolution doesn't justify the waiting; the answer doesn't live up to the question; the actual reason he dunnit is no match for the millions of reasons someone else might have. Even if you haven't guessed right, it's entirely without human significance that you guessed wrong. There is more drama in not being able to finish the *Independent* cryptic crossword.

The other problem with contemporary whodunnits is that the villains, however would-be complex, are all guilty of versions of the same crime: taking an unhealthy interest in children. Perhaps these things are cyclical, or maybe they reflect something that is happening in the real world, or at least what we fear is happening in the real world, but denouements have suddenly been taken over by paedophiles. The suspicious look like paedophiles but aren't, whereas the guilty don't look like paedophiles but are.

Well, it would seem we do have reason to be anxious, with half the Catholic Church, any number of well-loved TV personalities – when I say well-loved, I don't mean by you or me, reader – and an inexplicable number of classical music teachers under suspicion of paedophiliac offence. Who'd have thought there was so much of it about?

Why child abuse is so prevalent, or was so prevalent a generation ago, since a lot of this is justice playing catch-up; what part authority and celebrity play not only in making children available and susceptible, but in making adults lose their reason; just what the pleasure can be in sex with people below the age of consent and discernment, sex without true reciprocity, sex without adult conversation – now here are questions to build a drama around. But it wouldn't be a whodunnit. It would be a whydunnit or a howdunnit and those are a different kettle of fish. Not a revelation of a secret, or the unmasking of a single sick individual, after which society gets back to normal – i.e. to fornicating with people who are not their spouses but are at least their own age – but a revelation of our natures, after which there is no normal.

Enough with the detection. It's not the uncovering of any predilection that's interesting. It's the predilection itself. Look at *Mad Men*, which threatens to lose itself again in the labyrinth of tracking down Don Draper's secret past. The early episodes of this sometimes superb series were marred by existential hokum, flashbacks to an earlier self, if that was himself – for who's to say where self resides? – name changes, identity crises, lonely half-forgotten infidelities – for who was there to be faithful to? – all filmed in that slightly odd, old-fashioned, halting way that tells you psychology is afoot.

And with the new season we are back on the trail of Don's hunger to make love to women to whom he isn't married – as though that's a weakness that needs explaining – through faded shots of prostitutes in lingerie of another age, and a boy with a weird haircut peering through peepholes in a brothel – the biggest psycho-cliché of them all.

Don't get me wrong. I like a Freudian explanation – but only when Freud's doing the explaining. Otherwise, I want character revealed in action, not exposition, the feel and taste of us – all deranged in some way or another – the here and quite sufficiently mysterious now.

Smiley face

ODD THAT IN PRINCIPLE we care so much about the sanctity of private space, yet have so little regard for it in practice. In Pret A Manger modern Britain, where everyone who sells you a sandwich is your best pal, the concept of distance has gone the way of honorifics.

I have an agreement with Boots the Chemist that they collect my prescription from my doctor and text me when they've dispensed it. I am not ungrateful. The system is efficient and convenient. But I find it intrusive – akin to having a stranger peering into my bedroom window – to be texted by someone I don't know. And the notification isn't businesslike. No 'Dear Mr Jacobson, this is to inform you that your pills are ready for collection. We await your visit with eager apprehension and guarantee you our kind attention at all times. Yours faithfully, The Management.' Instead, they call me Howard. Not even 'Howard, if we may be so bold', just plain, next-door-neighbourish Howard. If I didn't delete so quickly I'd probably discover a yellow smiley face wishing me a great weekend.

Complaining is out of the question. They won't understand the offence. And I don't want to hurt anybody's feelings. Besides, I'm not sure it's wise to mess with a dispenser of poisons. They could put anything in those pills the next time. 'Take 20 of these, 10 times a day on an empty stomach and a bottle of whisky. Sweet dreams, Howard.' Accompanied by an emoticon of a dead man.

I wasn't born into a world in which people made free with Christian names. My friends and I, all of whom aspired to be novelists, addressed one another as *cher maître*. At school I was 'Obson, and I doubted that anyone at Cambridge knew that Jews had

Christian names. My bedmaker called me Sir (and just occasionally Naughty Boy); the college porters did the same, albeit with a snigger. F. R. Leavis called me Jacobson; my moral tutor called me Fagin; the Master called us men and the only girlfriend I ever had at Cambridge called me a name I cannot repeat here. Thus do the educated understand the importance of respecting distance.

When we did not otherwise want to be addressed or disturbed we shut the double doors to our rooms. This was called sporting one's oak. And no one of any breeding knocked on a sported oak. You could be burning in your bed but still no fireman dared transgress against that code. A Cambridge man had the right to perish in inviolate privacy behind his oak. Whether this tradition still persists I have no idea, but I fear for it given that a friend who has a son at Trinity tells me his boy steals Do-not-disturb signs from boutique hotels to hang on his college door. Not the old-fashioned signs politely requesting a little quiet, but the ones that say UP YOURS or GO FUCK YOURSELF, I'M JERKING OFF.

How long before there'll be no need to nick them from the latest bordello B&B because you'll be able to pick them up, three for the price of two, at Boots? 'Dear Howard, this is to let you know that SHOVE IT and SIT ON THIS are now in stock. You'll find them in Alternative Therapies. Have a great weekend. Smiley face.'

How it is that hotels have become sites of gross sexual collusion between hoteliers and guests is a question I leave to sociologists of the hospitality business. But no longer does one need to sign in on a false name and rinse the sheets the morning one leaves. Now, if there's been no congress, you have to fake the signs of it for fear of disappointing the chambermaid. Why else the reproduction of a lascivious Fragonard on the bedhead? Why the fridgeful of energy-boosting drinks? Why the bath oils and body washes whose uses baffle the imaginations of travellers with only business matters on their minds? Why the machine selling fruit-flavoured condoms in the reception area? Why the bar of soap that says *Gettin' jiggy wit' da figgy* and tells innocent users 'we can tell from that grin you've been committing the fifth deadly sin'? What business is it of theirs, and since when was the fifth deadly sin a grinning matter, anyway?

We aren't prudes in this column. We are pleased hotels are more accommodating to the needs of their guests. It's not the obscenity but the familiarity we object to, the assumption that we are all one happy family in facetiousness. Call it the democratisation of the private. This is what you get when the necessary divisions in society are broken down: an end to deference, difference, manners and, above all, gravitas.

A Virgin train I regularly catch to Manchester to see my mother – Mrs Jacobson, to you – has the message 'Hey, good-looking' on the mirror of the toilet. The impertinence aside, what makes Virgin think it falls within its brief to entertain us? You want us to arrive at our destination in a good mood? That's simple: get us there punctually; don't check our tickets at both ends as well as on the train; don't keep asking to see my senior railcard – of course I've got a senior railcard: I am a walking senior railcard – make better sandwiches, and don't run out of them before the train's left Euston.

But that's not all. Over the lavatory bowl is a list of things they would rather we didn't flush – 'nappies, sanitary towels, old mobile phones, unpaid bills, your ex's jumper, hopes, dreams or goldfish'. I'm surprised they lost their nerve and didn't add Richard Branson. For it is he, of course – he and the thousand other Branson clones – we have to blame for our nation's descent into indignity. 'I love,' he says on his Virgin blog, 'when signs and announcements show a little sense of humour.'

Shame, in that case, you don't have one, Dickie.

PS: 'Love when' isn't English usage. You must be spending too much time in your balloon. Have a lovely weekend. Smiley face.

There was a rabbi of Kiev

NOW THAT ANOTHER YOM Kippur has been and gone without my being struck down for my sins – the biggest of them, in some eyes, being my failure to honour the Day of Atonement in the way a Jew is supposed to – I will unfold to you a tale. Call it an expiation for not adequately expiating.

There was a rabbi . . . Jewish parables always begin that way, and as often as not situate the rabbi in Kiev. So: there was a rabbi of Kiev, only he was not a rabbi in the conventional sense, he was rabbi of Radical Scepticism employed by the City Duma's Department of Rationalism to keep an eye out for irrationalism of a specifically Jewish variety. Though known to his friends as Viktor, he always jumped when someone shouted: 'Abram!' This was because Abram was the name his parents had given him. Whenever this happened, Viktor – who had bestowed that name upon himself – fell into a fit of guilt about his parents and prayed for forgiveness from the God in whom they had believed but he did not. Immediately he had finished praying he castigated himself for showing such disrespect to his own non-belief.

Viktor did not keep Shabbes, took no notice of any of Jewish festivals and ate whatever took his fancy. Because lapwing was high on the list of foods proscribed in Leviticus, he would have tucked into lapwing with gusto had he known where to buy it. Food was scarce in Kiev, so it was difficult enough to find ossifrage, let alone lapwing. Snails, however, were a delicacy he indulged. Hare, whether grilled or in a pie, likewise. And as for the bacon he fried in butter every morning, as an accompaniment to blood pudding – so many slices, fried for just the right number of minutes, a little salt, a little pepper, a dash of oyster sauce – why it was almost a religious ritual to him.

But he was troubled by an inconsistency. If he could dine on bacon without a qualm, and pork sausage, and ham hock, and chitterlings – and there was even one dish he adored of which the chief ingredient was pig's rectum – why couldn't he ever eat pork belly? If he saw pork belly on a menu, he needed to drink a glass of water. If he sat next to someone eating pork belly, he had to fight himself from retching. Once, when one of his colleagues ordered pork belly, Viktor announced he would have to leave the table while the food was being consumed.

'Viktor, you must be able to explain this inconsistency,' his colleague demanded. But Viktor was unable to. It wasn't what the pork belly looked or tasted like that was the problem. It was the pairing of the words, the concatenation of sounds – pork and belly. Pork on its own – fine. He loved a pork sandwich with apple sauce. Belly, too, as a discrete entity, presented no problems. He had once eaten yak's belly on a visit to Moldavia and loved it. But put pork and belly together and he was disgusted. It was a foreignness – a transgression even – too far.

So what was it a transgression against? Viktor was damned if he knew.

And thus it was, inversely, with Yom Kippur, that's to say thus it was when it came to ignoring it. Hanukkah, Pesach, Purim – Viktor respected none of them. He saw his co-religionists – except that he was no longer a religionist himself – spruced up for synagogue and shook his head over them. Slaves to custom and superstition! Drones of blind faith! On festivals where it was necessary to be solemn, Viktor took pains to be seen laughing. Where it was necessary to laugh, Viktor wore his longest face. On Yom Kippur, however, he kept out of the way. He saw no reason to apologise for his sins since he was always apologising for his sins. Why set aside a single day to atone for your guilt when you've been atoning for it all year? Indeed, if he had a besetting sin it was being over-conscious of sinning. So he certainly wasn't going to fast. But – and this he knew to be illogical – he wasn't going to be seen not fasting either. No ostentatious banquets at his favourite restaurants on this day. No public retching over another diner's pork belly.

On the Day of Atonement the sun happened to be shining and Viktor decided on a walk. He nodded at some of the Jews he knew – more pallid than ever on account of doing without food – and suddenly, despite having enjoyed a hearty breakfast, he felt hungry. A snack was all he needed. A biscuit or chocolate. He wandered down a side street and found a tobacconist and confectioner's. Here he bought a bar of chocolate. But he hesitated before breaking into it. On this day of all others, he thought, couldn't I at least have done without chocolate?

But that was a superstitious thought and he put it from him. He ate a piece of chocolate, was disappointed in the taste and decided to throw the rest away. What made him decide to throw it in the Dnieper when he could have tossed it over any fence he didn't know. But when he got to the river, he realised he couldn't do it. It looked too much like *tashlich*, or casting your sins upon the water, a ritual Viktor scorned. As though you could drown a sin! He walked on but knew he had to get rid of the remaining chocolate. Why? Did he think he could half atone for half a sin? Did he think he might be half forgiven?

It would seem, he admitted to himself, that I am half superstitious.

Once he got back to his department offices he confessed his recidivism and offered to half resign. At a hurriedly convened meeting of councillors he was fired altogether. You have to make your mind up in this institution, they told him.

There is no moral to this story. But as someone who recently bought a bar of chocolate on Yom Kippur I can vouch for its essential truth.

A pocket manual of blame

'AUNTIE JENNY, WHY ARE the horses' eyes covered?' The questioner was a little girl my wife had taken to the Lord Mayor's Show. 'They are wearing blinkers,' my wife explained, 'so that they can see straight ahead without being distracted by whatever else is happening on either side of them.'

'Like Jeremy Corbyn, you mean,' the little girl didn't think of saying. But I thought it for her later that day while listening to Sami Ramadani address the lessons of the Paris massacres on LBC radio. Just to fill in the blanks: Sami Ramadani is an Iraqi-born senior lecturer in sociology at London Metropolitan University and a leading member of the Stop the War Coalition; the Stop the War Coalition – of which Jeremy Corbyn was chair before accepting the less influential job of leader of the Labour Party – is an organisation dedicated to peace, anti-Western Imperialism and anti-Zionism, though not necessarily in that order; and LBC is a radio station, of especial help to people who can't sleep at night, and therefore of no use at all to Stop the War, whose members sleep the deep untroubled sleep of certitude.

To make it plain where Ramadani is ethically as well as politically, let me tell you that in the immediate aftermath of the Paris atrocities, he tweeted the following: 'ISIS psychopathic terrorists have blood of people in Paris on their hands. Same goes for French govt for backing terrorists in Syria.'

Call anything to mind? That's right, the post-9/11 'butters' informing victims, even as they were leaping from the burning towers, that they were reaping what they'd sowed. That went down so badly at the time you'd think no one would be heartless or foolhardy enough to try it again. The decencies, Mr Ramadani. Observe the decencies. First bury the dead before you start blaming them. The chance to palter with guilt and innocence will come tomorrow. Though I know tomorrow is always too late if you're in the game of playing tit-for-tat with terror.

In fact, Ramadani's tweet is an advance in grossness on that of the 9/11 'butters'. Their 'butting' asked that we acknowledge a chain of consequences leading back from the atrocity to the wrongdoing of the West. Ramadani's 'same goes for the French govt' asks that we see no difference. *Same.* Linger a little on that word. Not even similar, but the *same.* Tweeted no doubt in righteous haste, it is a headlong elision of cause and effect, deflecting blame from the terrorists, minimising their crime, and turning the French into their own murderers.

Take a moment off from being revolted by this tweet, and note a logical flaw in it. If the French are 'backing' terrorists, then how come the terrorists are butchering instead of thanking them? Shurely shome mishtake. Unless ingratitude is to be added to the list of ISIS's crimes.

Here I, and anyone else who heard Sami Ramadani on LBC, enjoy an advantage which others – excluding his students at London Metropolitan University – don't. We lucky few were granted privileged access to the labyrinthine nature of the Grand Conspiracy Theory which, like others in Stop the War, Ramadani espouses. Complicated in the treacherous loyalties it traces, this theory is otherwise simple to describe. The imperialist West is in the wrong whoever it supports, and by this logic is to be blamed for whatever is done against those it opposes. Thus, because they don't back Assad, the French must be assumed to support ISIS, no matter that they're bombing it. And thus, by the same contortion, must Stop the War support the butcher Assad simply because America doesn't.

Imagine being an impressionable student and hearing this. I'm beyond the age of impressionability myself, yet I listened to Ramadani spellbound. He lets loose with fearful gunfire fluency his all-encompassing narrative of alliances that are really enmities, enmities that are really alliances, and evil emanating from a single source, never pausing to think or reconsider, never surprised by a question, never wondering how night can be day or day can be night, because when you know the causes of everything, even the planets dance in terror to your bidding.

The other side of a conspiracy theory is a prelapsarian fantasy of innocence. Those who hold themselves to be aggrieved have just cause for all they do because grievance, in our time, is sacrosanct; the idea that cultures can self-generate rage is not countenanced because it spoils the story.

From Ramadani's history lesson you would never know that Muslim nations were ever imperialists on their own account, ever brawled among themselves or made life hard for others. The bombing of synagogues in Baghdad in the early 1950s? The work of Zionists, you fools. The long campaign of terror carried out by Islamists in Syria in the 1970s and 80s, Syria's support for Hezbollah, the Muslim Brotherhood's uprising in Hama? All a lie because, as Ramadani told Russian television, 'neither Syria nor Iraq had any terrorist organisations before the American invasion of Iraq in 2003'.

A system of thought that accepts no inconsistencies is a frightful thing. Whoever believes he knows why everything is as it is has hold of nothing. But nothing can play havoc. When we look for radicalising narratives, we must ask if Ramadani's is one of them. To the dispossessed and embittered he provides a perfect pocket manual of blame. Simply agree that wherever America goes, you won't, and that whatever the West believes, you shouldn't. Just play follow my leader. Step into line, put on your blinkers, keep pace with the horse in front, and lo! the Lotus Land of absolute conviction is yours without your having ever to think a dissenting thought again. You couldn't enjoy a simpler view of human existence if you went over to ISIS yourself.

Death is Venice

IN VENICE WITH GEORGE Clooney. All right, not 'with' exactly; more 'at the same time as'. And even that is coincidental. The first inkling I had that something more than usually hyperbolic was happening here was an overheard conversation on a vaporetto about the city being struck by 'Rooneymania'.

Funny, I thought. Had Wayne abruptly given up on Manchester United – for which no one could blame him, God knows – and signed for Unione Venezia? The phrase 'the handsomest man on the planet' gave me pause, but who was I to judge Italian taste in men? And as for his marrying a beautiful human rights lawyer, wouldn't Coleen have something to say about that?

Even when my ear corrected 'Rooneymania' to 'Clooneymania' I remained at a loss. Clooney is not a name I encounter much in my line of work and I do what I can not to keep up with the doings of the rich and famous. No *Hello!* falls through my letter box. And all invitations to red-carpet events are returned unanswered. They can beg all they like. This is the cultural equivalent of living as a hermit lives, but without having to relinquish soft mattresses, filet mignon or red wine.

I'm not saying I don't know who George Clooney is. I've seen two or three pleasantly unremarkable films with him in them, and quite like the air of firm-jawed reliability he gives off. He would make someone, I imagine, a nice uncle. And for the same reason – though not of course at the same time – a nice husband. I also have the impression he's short, and shortness is another quality I admire in men, famous or not. So a reliable and avuncular-looking short man had chosen to get married in Venice – excuse my Internet Italian, but *cosi che cosa cazzo*?

The paparazzi clearly do, though in Venice it's hard to tell paparazzi from your ordinary avid tourist. Here, everyone is in a permanently excited state, taking photographs of themselves taking photographs, not quite able to trust the veracity of their own eyes and needing records of their experiences to be sure they've had them. The fake Gucci-bag street sellers have a new line – infinitely extendable selfie sticks which you attach to your phone so that you can stand on one side of the Grand Canal and photograph yourself from the other. Soon, the mobile phone whose virtue used to be its compactness won't be complete without a tripod, a reflection kit and a camera assistant. But at least in Venice the object justifies the labour. Yes, there is too much here for the senses alone to apprehend.

But its virtues are its undoing. Venice has always been a city dying of its own beauty. *Death in Venice* is a tautology. Death *is* Venice. That's what brings visitors back again and again: the allure of putrescence, whether in the creeping damp, the restless church facades – and every church proclaims the majesty of death – the jeering sensuality of Carnival, the disdainful gondoliers, or just the contemptuously atrocious food – an insult so deep that you can only suppose it to be an expression of the city's unconscious desire to kill its visitors.

And maybe not so unconscious. There is only one response here to the proposition that the short man's wedding will draw the world's attention to Venice, and that's a fervent hope it won't. There are already more tourists here than Venice can cope with. Many of them disgorged from giant cruise ships which dwarf the city, pollute the lagoon and lower the tone. Of all tourists, those held in the lowest esteem are tourists let out of cruise ships for an hour in order to satisfy their unaccountable lust for tasteless objects. And the more of them there are, the more tasteless-object shops there have to be. Take away the tourists and Venice's population has been dropping dramatically for decades. 'We are not a city. We are a museum,' one Venetian tells me. A mausoleum would be another word; a charnel house of imported tat.

As the son of someone who sold tat on northern markets – 'swag' we called it – I have mixed emotions about this. There can be a vitality in tat, however cynically produced. We fell in love with much of what we sold, relished its ingenious ugliness as a sort of triumph of the human spirit, and never felt we were taking our customers for a ride. If anything, it bonded us, soulmates in swag. Years later, when assisting at a craft (and semi-swag) centre in Cornwall, I had a confrontation with the National Trust, which ran our village like an occupying army and wanted to control what sort of visitors came through.

'I'm not prepared to see these beautiful cliffs worn away by people who buy witches on broomsticks,' one snooty Trust official told me. 'But you don't mind them being worn away by people who buy National Trust tea cosies,' was my reply.

Tat's tat. Take the long view and what isn't tat? Ruskin thought the Doge's Palace perfection; Goethe couldn't be much bothered with it.

Sitting listening to a Palm Court orchestra playing Andrew Lloyd Webber favourites in St Mark's Square – a square in which I would gladly expire some days, and some days not – I agree with them both. Depends on the light, on what else angles for one's eye, and on one's mood. Depends on whether the inane, idolatrous cries of 'George, George!' come floating in from the canal where Clooney is promenading – if you can promenade on water – with his new wife and their glittering guests.

Gaudy or not, the place continues to die from its foundations up; exquisite and rotten, in the best and worst of taste – like its visitors.

I don't know whether George is thinking about death this minute, but I can't believe he isn't. In the presence of beauty, what other subject is there?

How not to be a knob

SPOILER ALERT: SOME OF what I am about to say I intend ironically. And that includes the previous sentence. Then again, some of what I say I don't intend ironically. And between these extremes of meaning it and not meaning it are likely to be utterances whose status as to truth and sincerity I am unsure of myself.

Here is the joy of writing an essay, as opposed to a manifesto or even an opinion piece. An essay is a process of trying or testing. An experiment in words and thought. Hence those who throng to the armed wing of social media in the hope of destroying what an essayist essays are behaving exactly as Basil Fawlty did when he thrashed his stalled Austin 1100 with a limp branch: they are taking the wrong weapon to the wrong object.

We know why Basil Fawlty was so frustrated, but what ails the Twitter death squads? I leave that to psychologists of mob derangement to determine. I am concerned in this column – that's if I am – a) to educate the deranged in the rudiments of civilised conversation, and b) – altruistically – to prevent them wasting what's left of their lifeblood on causes that aren't causes at all. See a man on his knees screaming his disagreement with the scent of a rose and you want to help. That's what I'm doing.

Sixty-nine would appear to be a fatal age if you're a genius. Joyce Grenfell, who had more claim to being called a genius than many to whom the word is promiscuously applied, died just short of seventy in 1979, which must seem a long time ago to people whose knowledge of past events goes back no further than the launch of Instagram.

She was an actress and comedian, though her comic routines could just as fairly be called short stories. Perhaps the most famous is 'Nursery School' in which she teaches a class of children whose dim-witted naughtiness brings to mind the misdirected delinquency of the chat room. The most beside-the-point of the delinquents is Sidney who, when invited to be a flower of his choice, chooses a horse. 'A horse isn't a flower, Sidney,' Joyce Grenfell tells him, her patience wonderfully tuned to stretch ill doomsday. Followed by, 'No, children, that isn't funny, it's very silly.'

Let that, then, be lesson No. 1 for those who cling like drowning rats to the coat-tails of any writer who can swim: learn to tell the difference between a flower and a horse. Thus, when someone thinks differently from you, that doesn't make him or her a murderer, and it therefore isn't necessary for you to call for the death penalty. Thinking differently from you isn't a crime. Thinking differently from you might, if anything, be a virtue.

Lesson No. 2: A horse is not a flower and Jeremy Clarkson is not a knob because you disagree with him. He might be a knob for other reasons, but he isn't a knob because he has a bone to pick with cyclists and you're a cyclist.

Lesson No. 3: Camilla Long isn't the worst columnist who has ever been because her heart doesn't break into the same number of pieces as yours does when an entertainer dies. Here's a handy rule to follow before calling someone the worst columnist there has ever been: be sure you've read the others. Unless you are only speaking immoderately for the fun of getting up someone's nose. But in that case, ask yourself whether the columnist you can't abide is only speaking immoderately to get up yours.

Lesson No. 4: Don't marvel that publications give space to the particular worst living writer you have your sights fixed on today. It sounds like sour grapes. Of course it *is* sour grapes, but you should try to conceal it. The last thing a person whose only outlet is an online forum should draw attention to is the envy consuming him from the fingers down.

Lesson No. 5: Failing to see the point is not a virtue. The more articles you don't see the point of, the more questions are going to be asked about your perspicacity. You are right that some things are a waste of space; in all likelihood your tweet is one of them.

Lesson No. 6: Don't complain that the media won't stop hounding whoever it is you admire – say, Corbyn, to pluck a name at random. Most public figures, not excepting Corbyn, get a fair crack of the whip somewhere. What you're really complaining about is that *you* don't get a fair crack of the whip *anywhere*. But that won't be bias. It will just mean you're a knob.

Lesson No. 7: Remembering what I said about irony, think twice before buckling up for war. You might be walking into a trap for the literal-minded. As a rule of thumb I'd say that if you don't have a sense of humour you are missing the tone of most of what you read. So why advertise the fact? If you have nothing to do, and are looking for an activity that doesn't require a sense of humour, try colouring in.

Lesson No. 8: A writer who has more words than you have isn't *ipso facto* a show-off. Ditto a writer who has read a couple of books and is otherwise *cultivé*. By bleating about his or her erudition you are merely allowing your own ignorance to embarrass you. It should.

Lesson No. 9: Don't imagine that a word you say is going to make a blind bit of difference. You wouldn't be tweeting poison if you were otherwise able to solicit interest. But if you must fight a losing battle try at least to be sophisticated. Telling a writer you despise that he has his head up his arse will only make him feel good about himself. Better his arse, after all, than yours.

Lesson No. 10: Remember Sidney. Being a horse when you're meant to be a flower isn't funny, it's silly.

The glorious madness of *Wisden*

WHAT A WONDERFUL THING is *Wisden*, that lovely, lozengy, yellow-jacketed, Bible-shaped and Bible-weighted cricketers' almanack, 1,500 pages deep, in which the averages of batsmen and bowlers and wicketkeepers, English and not-English, male and female, living and dead, are collated with a mystic punctiliousness that proves beyond argument the existence of God. You want to see the Divine Watchmaker at work on the mathematics of life? Then read *Wisden*.

If it falls marginally short of retelling the whole story of human existence in statistics, that is only because it records achievements at the cost of failures: number of runs scored but not number of balls missed, number of catches taken but not number of catches dropped, outstanding seasons in schools' cricket but not suicidally dismal ones.

To this degree *Wisden* is essentially a commemoration of success, unlike great novels, which are commemorations of failure. But I would still be inclined to put *Wisden* on my fiction shelves, so fantastical, like a tale from Kafka or Borges, is its illusory narrative of order.

I was guest speaker this week at a dinner to celebrate the 149th edition of *Wisden*, held in the Long Room at Lord's. Though not the sort of memorabilia freak likely to be stirred by candle snuffers and inkwells in the form of W. G. Grace, I am a sucker for rooms with history, for walls hung with portraits of whatever the plural is of *genius loci*, for the company of eminent practitioners, and for a good dinner. So when I was asked to give the speech, I couldn't say no. How else was I ever going to get into the Long Room at Lord's?

Readers unsurprised that I accepted might wonder nonetheless why I was invited. All I can say is that I am known to have a passion for cricket, albeit more of the passive than the active sort. As far as the active side is concerned, I have only once played what could be called a match, and then was out first ball, being simultaneously bowled and adjudged to have fallen on my wicket. This was before the days of the instant replay, which would have shown that I was also out LBW, caught behind and stumped. Whether I illegally handled the ball as well, only I knew for sure. Let's just say I wanted to be out before I was in, fearing what damage the ball could do to a frame as unused to bruising as mine.

What's charming about the fraternity of cricket is that it has a keen sense of the ridiculous and excludes no one. There's probably a page for the likes of me buried somewhere in *Wisden* – batsmen out to the only ball they were ever called upon to play. There I sat, anyway, in the nervous hour before I gave my speech, discussing Cambridge in the early 1960s with Mike Brearley, a man I had long heroised for thinking the Ashes out of Australia's grasp, but never imagined I would one day be exchanging thoughts about F. R. Leavis with. Here, you see, is what's irresistible about cricket, whether you're out first ball or not: it's a game of the mind pretending to be a game of the body.

As I explained when I rose to speak, my more passive lifelong participation in cricket – i.e. listening to it at all hours of the day and night on radio – had, over the years, slipped into a mild form of insanity akin to that described by Dr Johnson in *Rasselas*, when he has an astronomer believe he can control the elements. 'Flood!' he orders the Nile, and the Nile floods. And no argument on the side of pure coincidence can shake him.

Similarly, lying there in my bed in the early hours of the morning, listening to the commentary coming in from Melbourne or Sydney, I would exhort Fred Trueman or Bob Willis to take a wicket and, provided I was concentrating adequately, a wicket was exactly what they took.

Of the forms of superstition that rob the human mind of reason, sporting superstition is at once the most innocent and the least susceptible to cure, so easy is it to persuade yourself that even if you are not controlling the game from your bed entirely, you are still controlling a major part of it. Geoff Boycott didn't always hit a century when I slept with the light on and the dog out, but Ian Chappell was invariably dismissed for a low score when I went to bed without pyjama bottoms.

Believe me, reader, when I tell you that the famous partnership of close to 200 put together by Mike Denness and Keith Fletcher during the 1974–75 tour of Australia was achieved only because I switched from my left side to my right side with every alternate ball Dennis Lillee bowled. In the end it was Max Walker who broke the partnership, and that only happened because I had to go to the toilet.

Whether my pleas to be included in *Wisden* as the unseen force guiding English cricket will be heeded, I won't know until next year's 150th edition. I suspect not. But I think I was able to persuade the majority of people there that you don't have to play the game to be infected by those magnificent numerical obsessions that *Wisden* celebrates. We also serve who turn over in our beds only during *Test Match Special*, now once to the right, now twice to the left . . .

You're going the wrong way, mate

THE GREAT GOD PAN is dead! I was weeping soppily in celebration of another Olympic gold for Team GB when I learned of the death of that formidable intellectual force, the art critic Robert Hughes, and remembered what tears are really for. I can't claim him as a personal friend, though we met occasionally when he came along to editorial meetings of that once fine journal *Modern Painters*, breathing fire, heaping scorn, laughing like Jove, and reminding us by his very presence that there are few higher callings than talking well about art. Some men of stature shrink those they come in contact with; Hughes made everyone around him feel like a god. Olympic sport is all very well, but when Robert Hughes addressed you as 'mate', it was as a welcome to Mount Olympus itself.

He came to Europe in the 1960s on that fabulous boat of my invention which also carried Clive James, Barry Humphries, Germaine Greer, the film director Bruce Beresford, the painter Brett Whiteley and countless more Australians of prodigious gifts. I was on the water at the same time, going the other way. We passed on the equator. That's how I like to tell it anyway.

In fact, they staggered their arrival, as though each was preparing us for the next. What made Australia of the late 1950s such an intellectual hothouse is a subject for another time, as is the reason so many of that generation felt they had to leave it. But, briefly, distance was the cause of both.

In the days before cheap air travel, physical alienation from European culture made Australians determined they would not be alienated from it intellectually, and so they read and looked and listened as no one born in London or Paris felt they had to – if you want to know the location of any art treasure in Italy, you ask an

94

Australian, not an Italian; if you want to know who sings the best *Rigoletto*, similarly – but that same distance created a forlornness (I say nothing of Sir Les Patterson) from which, for many, it was necessary to escape.

Do we yet know how lucky we were to have them on this side of the world? We had our own irreverently clever, establishment-bashing boys at that time, but the Australian contingent brought a combination of wit, rumbustiousness, intellectual scruple and deep seriousness (no matter that it dressed itself as mirth) that the English couldn't match. Their ear for cant and commonplace was sharper than ours, their nose for self-righteousness and hypocrisy keener. They weren't just thinkers – they were pugilists of thought.

Outside the art world, Hughes first became widely known in 1980 with his television series *The Shock of the New*. Has anyone ever looked out of a television screen with more critical menace? It was a series in which the viewer was made ashamed of being stupid. That's to say it was the opposite of most art programmes now. The words flowed, the passion burnt up the screen. He made it manly to look at art, not Sir Kenneth Clark refined and in-the-know, or John Berger ideological, but manly in the democratic sense, engaging our humanity. He hated theory and the linguistic pallor of those who used jargon to shut the uninitiated out of art.

As a critic who talked so well about 'shock', he was expected to love everything the etiolated curatorial class considered 'new', but he fumed against its triviality and cynicism. In a period marked by ignominious intellectual capitulation to dross, he performed Pope's function of excoriating the dunces, but at the same time went on reminding us of what true art looked like, sometimes in the voice of the larrikin, sometimes of the connoisseur, but always wittier than any other art critic, better read, and possessed of infinitely more subtle judgement.

Do I heroise him? Yes, I do. I am unable to heroise Usain Bolt however fast he travels and however beautiful he looks in motion. The macho gurning and showboating for the cameras reduce him. Give me the modest triathlete or wordless pommel horseman any time. But I heroise the man who thinks deep, and looks hard, still more.

Not that Hughes placed himself above the physical life. He was a man's man, a fisherman who drank with gusto. You felt his bulk when he entered a room. The last time I saw him was at a restaurant in London. He had suffered terrible injuries in a road accident in feral north Western Australia and was walking on crutches. I was sitting at a table of writers who'd been speaking earlier that week at feral Hay-on-Wye. Norman Mailer was among them. He, too, had entered the restaurant with the help of a stick.

I don't know which of them saw the other first. Maybe it wasn't a question of visual recognition. Maybe they just sniffed each other's presence, like big cats. How well they were acquainted I have no idea. But they were bound to have met and sparred over the years. And whatever the mutual admiration there was bound, too, to have been the rivalry of alpha males who dealt in grand ideas and spoke like oracles. Mailer rose from the table, anyway, and without the use of his stick made his way to Hughes. Hughes discarded his crutches. Like old soldiers refusing to make anything of their wounds, however grave, they crashed into each other's arms.

It's impossible to heroise without being sentimental. Mailer sentimentalised Muhammad Ali just a little. Maybe for being the Mailer Mailer had never been. In his wonderful book about the colonisation of Australia, *The Fatal Shore*, Hughes, for the same reason, sentimentalised the first wild Irish–Australians who gave the country its character. Thus do high-born aristocrats long to play the low-born rebel. I wouldn't say, though, that he ever sentimentalised Rembrandt or Picasso. You can overdo your admiration for athletes or bushmen, but not for great painters. Or great critics.

Let's introduce ourselves: what's your username?

AT A TIME WHEN there is much to fear, few to trust, and not a damn thing to believe in, may I hold out a flickering torch of hope? I have struck a symbolic blow. I have said no. En oh – NO! Enough is enough. Enough usernames, enough PINs, but above all enough passwords. Now I expect other victims of the relentless march of online passwords to join me in my campaign. Let's all say NO TO PASSWORDS.

I have been chafing against the imposition of the password for some time, but the last straw was an invitation to speak at a literary festival on a date and at an hour I could only discover if I 'accessed' my 'profile' saved under the 'mailings icon' on their 'authors' website'. Don't let the correct use of the apostrophe fool you. Everything else about this invitation is fatuous. 'Access' as a verb is a hateful coinage, invented by computer folk to make the process of looking something up sound busy and scientific. In fact, most of what we can be said to 'access' is either trivial or filthy. When we do call on the Internet to provide a worthwhile service – to find a poem we don't have in any of our anthologies, for example – we don't say we are 'accessing it'. We don't 'access'Thomas Sackville, Earl of Dorset. We look for him, and when we've found him we read him. If anyone should know that, the organisers of a literary festival should.

And what's this about a 'profile'? Do they mean my name? Do they mean the information I require, such as the date and time they would like me to speak? If so, why don't they save us all the bother and just tell me? Friday at 4 p.m., Mr Jacobson, see you there. Anything further – my age, my shoe size, the state of my teeth – I don't need to 'access my profile' to discover because I already know it.

The assumption is, however, that I have nothing better to do than arse around (indeed that I can't wait to arse around) locating the 'mailing icon' ('icon' being another instance of computerese coined to make a childish activity – the equivalent of colouring in – sound like an adult one) in order to gain entry to a place I have not the slightest desire to visit, let alone 'access', namely the 'authors' website'. But even that isn't enough. I have to drop whatever else I'm doing, the novel I'm writing, the Thomas Sackville, Earl of Dorset poem I'm reading, the alms I'm distributing to the needy, and go there 'as soon as possible'.

Is there no end to their impertinence? Reader, no, there isn't. Having chivvied me to go post-haste where no grown man or woman could possibly want to go, they then tell me I cannot go there without a username and password. Given that my username turns out to be my actual name I am compelled to wonder why we need the term username at all. Or is 'username' set to replace Christian and surname? 'Dr Livingstone, I presume.' 'That, sir, is my username, yes.'

Which brings us to the password. And with the request for the password comes that sentence from online hell, 'If you have forgotten your password, you can reset it by following the link on the log-in page.' Ah, reader, how many and how long are the hours we have spent following links to reset a password we see no reason to possess by logging into a log-in page impossible to log into without a password. You want to know why there is so much rage on our streets and unhappiness in our homes? Look no further than the bitter frustration of the passwordless, forever chasing their own tails in pursuit of a key that can only be accessed by the key they're trying to access.

It's possible there are people who love having passwords because passwords remind them of the games they played in primary school, not letting the girls into the boys' toilets until they gave the secret watchword, which might have been schopenhauer17 or weewee2, I can't remember. Or they might love them, as some love putting figures in columns, because they are clerkly by nature. Such people will no doubt have books to keep their passwords in – a little red book for their smartphone passwords, a little blue book for their banking passwords, a little yellow one for adult content and literary festival passwords – and what is more will protect these books from being accessed by the inquisitive by assigning them each a password.

I have a book in which I write usernames, PINs and passwords but never know where I've put it. Since I'm not such a fool as to bank online I don't have any precious secrets in this book and so don't care who reads it. There is nothing I don't want anyone else to read in the aforementioned 'profile' of me either, in which case why do I need a password? In order that no one should have a better idea of the time and day I'm speaking than I do? As for my shoe size, it's a 10, G fitting.

I voiced my objection to all this, anyway. 'Life's too damned short for passwords,' I emailed the person who'd invited me, no matter that she'd asked me to communicate any problems via, of course, their authors' website. She emailed back, explaining how I could get a new password, and telling me the festival was too busy to deal with individual authors except online, though she would be pleased to 'resolve the issue on the phone'. So that would have been two emails and a phone call to tell me what she could have told me in the first place in a single line had she not been too busy to do so.

I haven't made the call. There is no 'issue' to 'resolve'. I don't want a password to speak at a literary festival, that's all. And I don't want to see a literary festival in snivelling thrall to the techno-inanities of nerdspeak. It's time to stand up and be counted. Let's all access the NO icon.

How very dare you

THERE WAS SOMETHING 'HOW very dare you' about Jeremy Corbyn's recent temper tantrum in rebuttal of the charge that the company he kept reflected badly on him. 'The idea that I'm some kind of racist or anti-Semitic person is beyond appalling, disgusting and deeply offensive,' he said.

Alarm bells ring when a politician stands haughty upon his honour. This isn't to say we detect outright dishonesty in the deflection. But it is evasive to answer questions about your judgement with protestations of your probity. How very dare we? Well, since you are putting yourself up for election we have every right to dare you. And if our point is that you don't see racism when it's staring you in the face, then your assurances that you aren't yourself a racist are worthless.

It is avouched on all sides that Jeremy Corbyn is no anti-Semite. How it is possible to guarantee the complexion of another's soul when our own are such mysteries to us, I don't know. But very well – he isn't. Speaking generally, it is easier these days, anyway, to hate Israel rather than Jews, since you get the same frisson with none of the guilt. Besides, anti-Semitism need not be the worst of crimes. Depends on the variety you espouse. Not every anti-Semite is Joseph Goebbels. You can not like Jews much and be no great harm to them.

More serious in a politician riding the wave of a credulous revivalism to high office is a dogma-driven mind, a serene conviction of rectitude, and yes, bad judgement in the matter of the company he keeps. This latter charge, levelled at Corbyn on account of the bigots, deniers and exterminationists he hasn't scrupled to appear with on platforms and at rallies, is often repudiated as guilt by association, as though it is self-evident that a person is never to be held responsible for those he just happens to go on finding himself standing next to, or perchance agreeing with.

But association with a certain order of person, when it is habitual, can be its own offence. 'I am not a criminal but I seem to find myself frequently in criminal company' is a statement that evades more questions than it answers. Corbyn's explanation for denying all knowledge of meeting a notorious advocate of terror and then recalling it when his advisers remembered the occasion for him – a leftist politician, he argued, couldn't be expected to recall every radical with a murderous agenda he encountered – was a careless, not to say comical admission of the habituation I'm talking about. Mix less often with bombers and fanatics, Mr Corbyn, in places where bombers and fanatics are bound to congregate, and the ones you do meet might linger longer in your mind.

His justification for calling Hamas or the IRA his friends is that it's only by talking that peace is achieved. This would be laudable were it not disingenuous. For much depends on what the 'talking' comprises. Doubtless the British government talked secretly to the IRA, but it wasn't being chummy, or expressing sympathy with their aims, that brought them to the table. And if sweet-talking Hamas is to be forgiven for the results it might yield, then by the same logic Corbyn should be cosying up to Benjamin Netanyahu. In fact, the Stop the War Coalition, which Corbyn chairs, is pressing for Netanyahu to be arrested for war crimes when he visits Britain and, at the time of writing, Corbyn is listed to be among those demonstrating against the presence of the Israeli soccer team in Cardiff. To terrorists we speak, to footballers we don't.

Abhorrence for a person's views should not stop conversation, Corbyn insists, unless, it would appear, the person happens to be Israeli. If Corbynites see no moral or intellectual contradiction in that – insisting that Israel is *uniquely* wicked among nations – it isn't only honesty they are lost to but reason itself. For a phobia is a species of madness.

Still I will not call it anti-Semitism. The truism that criticism of Israel does not equate to anti-Semitism is repeated ad nauseam.

Nor, *necessarily*, does it. But those who leave out the 'necessarily' ask for a universal immunity. Refuse it and they trammel you in the 'How very dare you' trap. They are, they say, being blackmailed into silence. The opposite is the truth. It is they who are the black-mailers, intimidating anyone who dares criticise their criticism.

Alone of prejudices, anti-Zionism is sacrosanct. How very dare we distinguish the motivation of one sort from another? Or ques-tion, in any instance, an anti-Zionist's good faith? In fact, what determines whether anti-Zionism is anti-Semitic is the nature of it. Question Israel's conduct of recent wars and you won't find many Jews, in Israel or outside it, who disagree with you. Join Hamas in calling for the destruction of the Jewish state, as the prime insti-gator of all evil, and you're on shakier ground.

In an apparent softening of party tone, Corbyn's warm-up man, the journalist Owen Jones, recently reprimanded the left for its ingrained anti-Semitism. Welcome words, but they will remain only words so long as the Corbynite left – and indeed the not-so-Corbynite left – refuses to acknowledge the degree to which anti-Semitism is snarled up in the before and after of Israelophobia. The Stop the War Coalition is a sort of home to Jew-haters because its hate music about Israel *is* so catchy. It simplifies a complex and heartbreaking conflict, it elides causes and effects, it perpetuates a fable that flatters one side and demonises another, it ignores all instances of intransigence and cruelty but one, inflaming hatred and enabling the very racism it declares itself opposed to.

Let's forget whether or not anti-Semitism is the root of this. It is sufficient that it is the consequence. Face that, Corbyn, or the offence you take at any imputation of prejudice is the hollow hypo-crite's offence, and your protestations of loving peace and justice, no matter who believes them, are as ash.

You can't enjoy Proust or aloo gobi standing up

HERE'S THE BAD NEWS – we are sitting down too much. It would seem that if we want to get to a hundred in any state to enjoy it, we have to do so standing up. Since I earn my living sitting down, this is especially unwelcome news. I happened to be standing up when my wife broke it to me. 'You'd better sit down for this,' she said.

The good news, that curries are lifesavers, thus becomes cruelly ironic. Because who wants to eat a curry standing up? And if you happen to be arthritic – a condition to which curries are thought to offer relief – are you *able* to eat a curry standing up?

Others to whom curries are said to give relief include sufferers from dementia, strokes and bowel cancer. All this before we include the myriad consolations curries have long been known to bring to men who find themselves alone at midnight with nowhere but the Taj Mahal to go to. I speak as one of the consoled.

In the days when I found it easier to stand up, I was living in a place where for ten long years I found myself alone at midnight. It isn't necessary to be geographically specific. Let's just say it was somewhere in the West Midlands, a little to the south of Stafford and a little to the north of Birmingham. Providentially, there was a Taj Mahal on every corner. If you happened to be a visitor to Wolverhampton in the 1970s – blast, I've gone and given it away! – there is a good chance you would have seen me talking to myself in the corner of one or other of those Taj Mahals, just visible against the flock wallpaper whose colour and texture I had grown to resemble.

I had grown to resemble the Taj Mahal intestinally as well. 'You don't appear to have any blood,' the doctor I finally went to see about chronic stomach pains, told me. 'Your veins run with vindaloo.'

In those days there was less of a consensus about the benefits of curry. So his advice was to find somewhere else to eat. 'At midnight?' He took my point. But what about the hot-dog and hamburger stall in the middle of town? I'm glad now, in the absence of any medical evidence to suggest that meat trimmings, saturated fats, sodium nitrate, molten cheese and onions refried in machine oil are good for us, that I stuck with curries. That I survived only goes to show I must have been eating something in the Taj Mahal that agreed with me, whatever the contents of my veins. And we now know what that is. Diferuloylmethane, otherwise known as curcumin, the chemical that makes turmeric the colour of the sun. Diferuloylmethane, the chemical that stops lonely men in a Midlands town from taking their lives.

But I don't suppose you can just nip into your nearest Taj Mahal – which won't be called the Taj Mahal any longer anyway – and ask for extra diferuloylmethane. Who's to say the waiter will even know what it is? And by the time you've talked to him about turmeric, what makes it yellow and the latest medical findings in its favour, you will have annoyed the other diners who've just come out for a curry. My advice is to carry a drum of turmeric everywhere you go, in the way that some people carry artificial sweeteners. There are parts of the world where it is used to stop bleeding, to disinfect wounds, to heal sores, to cure eczema and scabies. So even if you're not a curry eater, there's good reason always to have turmeric about your person.

But if we are healthier standing up, does this mean that turmeric loses its efficacy if we take it sitting down? I am an incorrigible sitter-down to meals, myself. Even in those lonely years when I could have joined the army of midnight peregrinators, crossing and recrossing the ring road eating hot dogs and hamburgers, with scalding onion running down their wrists, I chose to sit in a chair, no matter that a man alone in a chair at midnight waiting for a curry is the saddest of sights.

For of all cuisines, Indian is surely the most intrinsically ceremonial. Only think of the Indian banquets you've enjoyed: starting with tandoori-grilled paneer and spinach cake, with a taste of someone else's chicken tikka pie as the sun begins to set, progressing with no hurry to pan-roasted Kashmiri-chilli halibut, Nepalese bamboo shoot and black-eyed peas, kadai gosht, a side of aloo gobi, every kind of naan and roti, plus a small share of the communal biryani, and finishing off, as the moon comes up, with blood-orange sorbet. Now try telling me you can enjoy such a meal standing up.

Reader, aside from walking, is there really anything we do that isn't more pleasurable sitting down? Reading? Listening to music? Drinking wine? Sleeping? I'd add writing to the list were there not a fad at the moment for writing standing up. Philip Roth does it. Virginia Woolf and Nabokov did it. And Nietzsche lambasted Flaubert for telling Maupassant he wrote better from a chair.

There's an austerity about the idea of writing standing up I don't much care for, as though writing ought to be a penance. The self-flagellating writer can now buy a treadmill desk, enabling him to write running. Why? To add leanness and sinew to his prose? I see how the argument works the other way: you can tell from the flaccidity of style into which Proust sometimes fell, and from his assumption that readers had as much time to kill as he had, that he wrote in bed. But his marvellous, leisurely, unbroken flights of lucidity were also written prone.

In the end it's the idea of writing as though at a pulpit that troubles me. The writer as priest. I prefer him down and dirty. Companionable, comfortable and unfit, a man you'd like to share a vindaloo with. And if that means the diferuloylmethane doesn't kick in and he won't get to a hundred, hard cheese.

Nice porn

PORNOGRAPHY AGAIN. WHEN WE last discussed pornography, we noted how having nothing better to do explains, in part, the hours expended on it. 'The devil finds work for idle hands' – never were wiser words spoken. If it's true that past the age of fervent procreation we rub the itch of sex as much out of tedium as desire, then how much more is pornography – in particular, Internet pornography – the servant of ennui. One bored click of the mouse while we're waiting for our emails and we're in hell.

Once upon a time, when low-quality porn was to be found only in the Venus Bookshop, as like as not situated opposite the cathedral, and high-quality porn was kept under lock and key in the school library, procuring it required not only effort but courage. We had to brave our teachers who would subsequently ask us, in the hearing of the whole class, how we were finding *The One Hundred and Twenty Days of Sodom*. Or we had to sneak down to the Venus Bookshop in a capacious coat, no matter what the weather, and risk the manifest contempt of the proprietor who never failed to draw attention to our purchase, either by commenting loudly on its contents or by wrapping it slowly and ostentatiously in a brown paper bag – the bag being even more a badge of ignominy than the magazine.

Thus were we forced into physical exercise, compelled to negotiate a complex of social relations, and taught shame. And thus, even before settling down to weigh the chances of going blind, did we learn about the consequences of choice. But even leaving aside the ethical advantages of having to forage for our filth, these prolegomena to pornography were advantageous: they gave savour to what we were about; they ratcheted up the excitement; they threw a cloak of secrecy and daring on what has now become mere automatic drudgery.

The child of Internet porn is therefore a loser on every count – introduced to ugliness before he has had time to dream of beauty, denied those preliminaries wherein we weigh our actions, and led to suppose there is no sorrow that cannot be soothed, no blankness that cannot be filled, by watching others perform *soixante-neuf.*

I am pleased to read that that indefatigably optimistic philosopher Alain de Botton is in agreement with me on this. In a press release last week, he noted that Internet pornography reduces our capacity to tolerate anxiety and boredom, exerting its 'maddening pull' in those very moments 'when we feel an irresistible desire to escape from ourselves'. I like the phrase 'maddening pull'. It humanises the impulse, removing blame and reminding us of the universal urgency of the before and the inevitable melancholy of the after. It's only when he promises a different kind of porn, porn that would be 'harnessed to what is noblest in us . . . in which sexual desire would be invited to support, rather than permitted to undermine, our higher values', that I find myself not in agreement with him. Porn that's good to us, nice to us, nice about us, enhancing rather than degrading, life-affirming rather than life-threatening, by definition ceases to be porn. One might as soon ask for tragedy that has a happy ending or alcohol that doesn't make us drunk.

I don't say we shouldn't rethink the way sex is routinely depicted in our society – in *Lady Chatterley's Lover*, Lawrence tried nobly if unsuccessfully to clean up the very language of sexual relations – but you cannot clean up pornography because its province is defilement. However and whenever we go there, and no matter whether it's literary pornography or the perfunctory ins and outs of YouPorn we visit, we go on the understanding that we will witness abasement and – for this is the transaction we all make with pornography – enter into sensations of debased arousal ourselves. In the end, pornography is an act of collusion between the material and the user of it. It is the collusion that is debased, hence our being able to find the images themselves innocuous and even laughable when we aren't in a collusive mood. And it's this collusion that erodes the distinction between classy porn and trashy porn. Pornography is a state of mind: it is nothing less than the willing and necessitous suspension of the very higher values Alain de Botton thinks pornography can be persuaded to make peace with.

In a famous essay on the pornographic imagination, Susan Sontag made the case for some pornographic books counting as literature because they plumb 'extreme forms of human consciousness'. But wherein would lie that extremity if they merely confirmed and flattered our 'higher values'? As a matter of deliberate intention in the pornography we call art, and as a by-product of our collusion in that pornography which does not aspire to art at all, the best and sweetest ideas we have of ourselves, as rational creatures capable of tenderness and love, are trashed.

But the case for pornography is not simply that it derides the decencies. It has, paradoxically, a more energising effect. There's an exhilaration in erotic extremity that arises from its danger. Ordinarily, we harness sex to marriage, family and employment; we accept that we can no more incorporate the fearfulness of sex into domestic life than we can wake every day to the knowledge we take, say, from a Sophoclean tragedy. But 'the temerity of penetration' we find in tragedy – the look into the 'horror of nature', to employ Nietzschean terms – is what we find in pornography, too. We are contrary beings or we are nothing; in the midst of our abundant life, indeed as one of the most powerful expressions of that abundance, pornography revels in wastefulness and destruction.

That being the case, how can it be harnessed to all that's good and noble? Answer: it can't.

The shame that outlives us

OF THE REASONS THERE are to dread death – and no stoic or holy man has yet convinced me there are reasons not to – the most compelling is the shame of it. I don't just mean the shame of illness and bodily deterioration, helplessness, loneliness, reliance on the care and kindness of others, the end of you as a self-determining agent, I mean the simple shame of being mortal, the disgrace of not being able to do a little better than that.

Life is full of humiliations to all but the most insensate, but life petering out like every other, life just giving in to the brute fact of non-life, is the keenest humiliation of all. Small wonder that some cultures have seen a nobility in suicide. Whatever else there is to consider, this way, at least, the time and manner of dying is of your choosing. It is you saying no to life, and not the other way around. You are your own executioner. It's not quite a victory, but it's half a one.

That said, the method of self-slaughter which some settle for appears to steal even that half-victory from them. Before Robin Williams's decision to end his life, we can only bow our heads in respect. It isn't for us to judge. But it's impossible not to wonder why he chose to do it the way he did. Of all the means available, especially to a rich man living in LA, why hanging?

I am no student of the psychology of suicide, but to choose hanging is surely, at some deep level, to ally yourself with criminals. Or, if not that, it is to inflict a final indignity on your person – in your own eyes and in the eyes of those who find you. To choose hanging feels to me like compounding shame with more shame. If all I am is a cadaver, then let it be as a cadaver that I leave life.

But death, as evidenced by the images released by Islamic State – I have not nerved myself to watch the videos – has further ignominies in store for us yet. I say 'us' because faced with such horror we are one human family. Whatever we feel the rest of the time, no man is an island now. Today, the bell tolls for everyone.

So many ignominies here, indeed, that it simultaneously turns the stomach and breaks the heart to itemise them. The preceding torture of your body and your mind; the knowledge of the agony caused to those who love you, for you can be sure they will never know a quiet night again; the public nature of the execution; the vileness of the instrument employed; the anonymous, flat-vowelled barbarism of your executioner, as though he means the act to be at once grand and common or garden, a mockery of itself.

Before Steven Sotloff was executed, there was a picture of him disseminated on the accursed Web, a sideshow to the decapitation of James Foley, which shows one of his captors grabbing him by the back of his shirt, as though he is dead meat already. Yes, let a war start and all life is cheap. And whichever side we are on, we label the other remorseless.

But there is a difference between being one of the casualties of war, no matter how terrible or unforgivable your death, and being a trophy dragged about and held aloft by someone for whom you are as offal. Death is the end of it in all cases, but the ultimate ignominy for any living human being is to be reduced, while the blood is still warm in the body, to a carcass. Forget, for a moment, the politics. There are times when politics are incidental, and the agents of cruelty seem to be answering more a metaphysical necessity than an ideological one.

'Aye, in the catalogue ye go for men,' says Macbeth to those he has hired to murder Banquo – his disgust for them impersonal, almost a disgust for 'bounteous' nature itself. Some bounty that can yield such men!

But I am reminded still more of the shocking final chapter of Kafka's *The Trial*. 'On the evening before K.'s thirty-first birth-day,' it begins, 'two men came to his lodgings. In frock-coats, pallid and plump, with top-hats that were apparently uncollapsible.' To himself, K. admits that he expected different visitors. He is disappointed by fate. 'Tenth-rate old actors they send for me,' he reflects. 'They want to finish me off cheaply.'

We should not be misled by the farcicality. It is integral to the horror. A death at the hands of tenth-rate executioners becomes tenth-rate itself. But what other sort of execution is there?

'Why did they send you, of all people!' he asks as they are escorting him through the streets. More a cry, Kafka notes, than a question. But a cry to whom? God? In this novel, there is no God to cry to. No Judge to meet, no High Court to penetrate. K. thinks of resisting but is instantly reminded of 'flies struggling away from the fly-paper till their little legs were torn off'. Not the only time a character in Kafka is compared to an insect.

The sentences that lead almost laconically to K.'s senseless death are among the most cruel in literature. The tenth-rate actors force K. to the ground, with his head against a boulder, and pass a knife there and back across him in 'an odious ceremonial of courtesy'. Then finally it happens – the knife goes into K.s heart where it's twisted twice. 'With failing eyes K. could still see the two of them, cheek leaning against cheek, watching the final act' – the final act of a farce that is crueller than any tragedy.

K., too, is in the audience, watching himself die. 'Like a dog!' he says. 'It was as if he meant the shame of it to outlive him.'

The shame of the American journalists dying like dogs will outlive us all. If there is or could be a more potent image of the insults our mortality is heir to, of the godlessness of this pitiable planet, may we not live to see it.

Calm down, dear

O F THE PLEASURES INCIDENT to the literary life, one of the most innocent is being able to say – not boastfully, just with quiet satisfaction – that you've read everything a writer has written. It's easier, of course, with some writers than with others. Read *Wuthering Heights* and a few poems and that's Emily Brontë done. Jane Austen isn't too trying either, but don't forget the juvenilia which gives you the opportunity to see that *Tristram Shandy* was important to her only until she grew up. My best effort is every novel by Charles Dickens and ditto, almost, Thomas Hardy. Where I fell down with Hardy was over *A Laodicean*. There were two reasons I stumbled. The first was that I had never heard a good word said about it. The second was the title. *A Laodicean*, for God's sake! A Laodicean, as Hardy intends the term, is someone who blows hot and cold in his convictions – Laodicea having been a byword in the early Catholic Church for religious tepidity. Another title for Hardy's novel, therefore, could have been *The Lukewarm*. Quite a grabber, that. 'If you read no other novel this year, read *The Lukewarm*. It will leave you quivering with indifference.'

It's an unquestioned assumption of our society that lack of enthusiasm is a vice. What we look for in our politicians and sportsmen and thinkers – indeed, in all branches of what we might as well call show business – is zest. Post your attractions on a dating site and you won't get far describing yourself as Passionless from Plumstead. Even 'cool' doesn't really mean apathetic. It isn't cool not to care about anything much, nor is it cool to be a waverer. The cool care passionately, to take just one example, about the sunglasses they wear.

But as an overwrought Wimbledon draws to a close, and World Cup fever reaches its climax, and cruelly misinformed Muslim boys pour out of Swansea hell-bent on avenging something that someone has told them the West has done to them, only to end up killing other Muslim boys similarly misinformed, isn't there a case to be made for half-heartedness? Reader, it isn't just the planet that's overheating. It's us.

I don't speak as one who understands nothing of ideological zeal. As a young academic I waged holy war against colleagues who thought the novels of George Meredith superior to the novels of George Eliot. And when it comes to sport, I am capable of something which, if you can't exactly call it fervour, is in the ballpark of passing interest. For at least two hours after Phil 'The Power' Taylor was knocked out in last year's World Darts Championships I couldn't bring myself to uncork the bottle of expensive Shiraz I'd been saving. But no one actually died in the George Meredith vs George Eliot wars, and I don't wear a shirt with Phil 'The Power' Taylor's name on the back. There's interest and then there's interest.

Why, for example, must those commentating on Wimbledon routinely put the word 'adoring' before the word 'fans'? Not every-one lucky enough to be at Centre Court is a fan of any particular player, let alone an adoring one. Many will simply be enjoying high-quality tennis. Yes, a few will grab gratefully at the sweaty towels or putrid armbands that some players throw into the crowd when they've won, but I saw one of these distasteful items drop into the lap of a dispassionate spectator the other day and his disgust was every bit the equal of what mine would have been in his position. Who are you to suppose I will be grateful for your largesse? his expression said. Who? Well, the commentary team could answer that. 'Royalty watching royalty,' the most sycophantic of them genuflected vocally, as Federer cast an eye in the direction of William and Kate. I am no republican, reader, but do we really need more royalty than we already have?

It was fervour of this servile sort, anyway, that deluded the nation into thinking Andy Murray was going to win Wimbledon again this year after three no more than workmanlike performances against untesting opposition. A cooler appraisal would have told us, and maybe even told Murray, that he was up to his old play-safe, pat-a-cake antics again and would buckle as he used to when the going got tough. Thus does hyperbole, when it's not in the service of scepticism, make fools of us all.

There was, you would have thought, sufficient scepticism about English football not to lead us into a comparably false optimism, yet still 'adoring' fans carted themselves all the way to Brazil wearing shirts with their heroes' names on their backs and expectation agitating hearts which, for all I know, had been calibrated to beat at the same rate as Rooney's. Leaving aside the question of how they could find anyone in the English team to heroise, what is any grown man doing in a football shirt? Come to that, what are adults doing painting their faces the colours of their national flags? Hasn't slavery been abolished? Does the excitement of sport justify subservience?

'Too hot, too hot,' mutters Leontes in *The Winter's Tale*. He isn't watching sport, unless you call imagining your best friend overdoing appreciation of your wife a sport, but he could be describing the current condition of our vocabulary. Just as Murray on form is called 'Magnificent!', so his defeat is greeted with the word 'Surrender!'. Our prime minister, too, cannot suffer a setback that isn't ignominious. 'Humiliation!' the front pages blazed when he was Junckered. Is it no longer possible simply to lose?

Let me be clear: contest excites me too. I am loving watching Wimbledon and the World Cup. I deny no man his gifts. I deny no man his religion either. But the world would be more sensible, the words we use more rational, the wars we fight less unremitting, if we cared a little less. Tomorrow, after watching the men's final on television, I will start Thomas Hardy's *A Laodicean*.

The New Barbarism

WELCOME TO THE NEW Barbarism. I say the New to distinguish it from the Old, whose destructiveness was primarily confined to habits of mind, slips of the tongue, proper nouns, pronouns, modes of address and works of literature that omitted to mention slavery. And I could talk about Our Barbarism to distinguish it from that of ISIS and the Taliban, who have set the standard for thoroughness and celerity when it comes to removing evidence that others think differently from them.

Our Barbarism is more shocking than Their Barbarism because we make a show of difference and tolerance and they don't. And the New Barbarism is more brutal than the Old Barbarism because the words and attitudes policed were hurried out of sight, whereas what faces us now is the blood-stirring spectacle of falling bronze and concrete. Welcome to the Cultural Revolution, Britain 2016, and we don't even have a revolutionary government in power.

Last year looked to be shaping up to be one of the most culturally brutal years in living memory, but it already has a tame look about it. Perhaps we will look back on 2015 as the year of the practice run. What would happen if we tried to get rid of a Nobel Prize-winning scientist on charges of gender facetiousness? Would anyone stand up to us? Nope. What would happen if we tried to ban lectures by people whose views we didn't share? Would anyone stand up to us? Nope. In preparation for the Great Barbarism, the Great Pusillanimity.

Thus empowered, let's turn to Cecil Rhodes, architect of empire, diamond miner, white supremacist and benefactor to Oriel College. You might think the benefactor part would make it tricky, but colleges are soft touches today. We shall see. But the wind is behind those who with a huff and a puff would blow Rhodes down.

Among the many arguments to be made against cultural revolutions is that they are monotonous in spirit and monomaniacal in intention. In this case the monomania is racism. I don't minimise it, but it isn't mankind's only story. What about destroying statues of the sanctimonious and the censorious, the sectarian and the dogmatic, the ideologically driven and the lily-livered? Down, down, with the lot of them.

I am not concerned to salvage Rhodes's reputation. Let him be as bad as those who want his page torn from the book of life insist he is. Most people to whom a statue has been erected are undeserving. Use every man after his desert, and who would 'scape whipping? There's a case for erecting no statues of mortal men at all, though I would argue in their defence that they constitute monumental history lessons and in that regard are of more associative interest than such exercises in conceptual trivia as get a plinth in Trafalgar Square. Speaking of which, how much longer must we tolerate that vainglorious adulterer Nelson on his phallic column? Down with him, too.

That a nation's statuary will reflect beliefs and attitudes that are no longer current or congenial hardly needs arguing. In most instances it doesn't at all imply a continuing reverence. A healthy culture doesn't memorialise only those it agrees with. So when the journalist and broadcaster Bidisha weighs in on the side of the statue-breakers, lecturing the West on its unthinking racism and furiously declaring herself unwilling to see 'our educational institutions decorated with plaques worshipping white racists', she loses the argument. 'Worship'? Does she really mean 'worship'? How many adherents of the cult of Rhodes, one wonders, has she seen lighting candles or genuflecting before his name or image? It tells you something about the fanatic mindset which is revisionist iconoclasm that it must invent an opposing mindset of fanatic reverence to justify itself.

In such cranking up of injury we can detect the influence of Edward Said, the author of *Orientalism*, who ransacked works of

Western art for inscriptions of cultural condescension and contempt and single-handedly turned the study of literature into grievance soup. The day Eng. Lit. morphed into post-colonialism was the day the Lit. part died. Though I suspect even Said would have blenched before the latest expression of aesthetic recoil in which 'survivors', as they melodramatically describe themselves, complain of the 'oppression' of having to walk past an offending statue in a college or a public street. In addition to their original injuriousness, such statues, it is argued, go on revisiting their offence on the injured, forcing them to bear again 'the burden of violence committed on them'.

But soft! By this logic mustn't I, a Jew, tremble every time I pass a place of Christian worship? 'Worship' in its proper meaning, reader – incense, candles, prayers, in service of a religion that for two thousand years has done Jews violence. How long can I be expected to tolerate altar paintings and murals depicting Jews as deicides, baying for the blood of Jesus, or filling their purses with silver earned by betraying him? Why, unless a Jew covers his eyes, he will even see a Judas – the Jew whose name means what it sounds it means – sitting knees parted at the Passover table, failing to conceal that hard-on Jews are known to get whenever they turn a profit. Whoever would look for the inscription of racial stereotyping or evidence of misappropriation in a faith's or culture's artefacts will surely never go home empty-handed, but imagine the burden of violence I bear every time I visit Canterbury or Chartres, knowing I'm in the vicinity of a gargoyle that's the spitting image of my uncle Solly.

My oppression cries out! Must my pain not trump these monuments of stone and plaster? Down with them, I say. The cloud-capp'd towers, the gorgeous palaces, the solemn temples, and finally the great globe itself. Down with everything that isn't me.

Shoot the highwayman

OUR SUBJECT TODAY IS Dr Johnson's hypothetical highway-man. For readers who have forgotten him, here's a reminder. Boswell and Johnson are drinking tea at the home of Dr Taylor, Prebendary of Westminster. Johnson is uncharacteristically silent, 'reading in a variety of books', according to Boswell, 'suddenly throwing down one, and taking up another'. Twenty more triumphant years of Kindling and we will wonder how that would be possible.

Johnson mentions that he means to go to Streatham that night, probably to call on Mrs Thrale. This might explain the agitation of his manner. 'You'll be robbed if you do,' Dr Taylor warns him, 'or you must shoot a highwayman.' Perhaps catching a murderous glint in Johnson's eye, he goes on to say he would rather be robbed than shoot a highwayman.

Human rights hindering direct action, even then.

Johnson is more pragmatic. 'I would rather shoot him in the instant when he is attempting to rob me,' he says – raising the inter-esting side question of whether the author of *Rasselas* and *Lives of the Poets* went about with a pair of pistols concealed in his waist-coat – 'than afterwards swear against him at the Old Bailey.' There is less chance of mistaken identity, that way, he explains. Shoot him in the act and you can be sure you have the right man. 'Besides, we feel less reluctance to take away a man's life, when we are heated by the injury, than to do it at a distance of time, by an oath, after we have cooled.'

'So, Sir,' puts in Boswell, taking the role of Shami Chakrabarti, 'you would rather act from the motive of private passion, than that of publick advantage.'

Comes back Dr Johnson, never a man to miss a joke that punctures high-mindedness, 'Nay, Sir, when I shoot the highwayman I act from both.'

I would have that line framed and placed behind the chair of every judge in the land.

It will now be apparent that while I evoke the hypothetical highwayman, I am looking at Abu Qatada. Not that mistaken identity, or fear that there might be mistaken identity, has played any part in this long-running smash hit comedy of errors – 'The funniest play on in London: don't miss it!' It's to his credit that he has made no attempt to disguise or soften his appearance. He looks what we accuse him of being. Indeed he looks so what we accuse him of being that it's hard to avoid the conclusion that he means to mock us with our melodramatic imaginings.

I trust I will not be construed as suggesting that someone should have taken Abu Qatada's life when he was caught in the act, whatever the act was. But it would certainly have saved time and money. And maybe made the world a safer place. Whoever chose the quick way of silencing Osama bin Laden made a wise decision. It was not a moral decision, but sometimes wisdom must prevail. It could even be argued – and Johnson is on the way to arguing it – that there are times when wisdom, all things considered, seizes the high ground from morality. Whoever saves mankind by an immoral act performs a greater good than he who would see it perish in the name of principle.

The absurdity of giving principle precedence over the humanity which principle exists to serve – because where there is no life there is no call to distinguish between right and wrong – was demonstrated last week by the Court of Appeal's insistence that the possible risk Abu Qatada poses to national security has no relevance to the law on whether sending him home would infringe his human rights. Since the logic of this entails weighing the consequences to Qatada, it breaks down in the matter of not weighing the consequences to us. The key word is 'relevance'. If risk is irrelevant to the letter of a specific law, then there's something wrong with that specific law. For the letter killeth.

As for human rights, we have been round the houses on the subject. Even liberals lacking Johnsonian robustness look uncomfortable when human rights are invoked in the case of Qatada. But a principle is a principle. And there's the problem. Sometimes one overriding principle makes a dog's dinner of another. Human rights is not the first concept to have originated in the highest and most disinterested motives, that compels every civilised person's allegiance, but falls foul of the contradiction at its heart. 'What about *my* human rights?' is a banal, dog-in-a-manger plea, but it asserts a fundamental truth – rule on behalf of one person's rights and you violate someone else's. In this instance, those to whom, by the court's admission, Qatada might very well pose a risk.

Geoffrey Robertson QC argued eloquently on *Newsnight* for the rule of law and the independence of the judiciary, and we agree with him. Something must be set above our private interests, the fury of our passions, the common reasoning of the marketplace and the will of Theresa May. In the end, the cacophony must be silenced. Left or right, bloodthirsty or forgiving, we must all submit to the judgement of those we appoint to reason dispassionately in cases where we, forever 'heated by injury', cannot.

But it isn't only injury, or apprehension of injury, we have to quiet; it's also our sense of the preposterous. And to be told we must protect an advocate of violence and hatred from the risk of torture in the country of his birth outrages both. Principle is a fine thing, but so is common sense. Boswell was a lawyer. The distinction he makes between acting from the motive of private passion and the motive of public good is the law's. And that's the distinction Johnson refutes. 'Nay, Sir, when I shoot the highwayman I act from both.'

Sometimes we just have to shoot the highwayman.

But what if don't want to connect to you?

WHEN I FIRST RECEIVED A message from LinkedIn, telling me a person I'd never heard of wanted to connect to me, how would I like to respond, I resisted all the obvious ways and swatted the request into trash. That, I thought, would be that. But then came the reminders. So-and-so was still waiting to hear.

I won't pretend I felt guilty, but behind the silhouette of the petitioner I recognised the pain. The idea of someone hanging on, anxiously eyeing the mail every morning, wondering if you received the original request, wondering if you've responded yet, wondering if you ever will, is bound to bring back memories of all the rebuffs and repudiations one's suffered – in my case a half a century of unrequitedness. I still recall squatting by the letter box, like a dog waiting for the newspaper to be delivered, knowing in my soul that yet again the reply I craved would not arrive, on that day or indeed on any other, because it never had been, and never would be, written.

But still you wait. Still you beg your parents to get off the phone because you're expecting an urgent message which, again, you know will never come. Still you linger at the end of the lane, wondering if it's the wrong lane, the wrong end, the wrong hour, the wrong day, the wrong life. Rejection is the one constant of human experience. So it wasn't without compunction that I again swatted the request from LinkedIn into trash.

What was LinkedIn anyway? Never having heard it spoken, and possessing no instinct for cyber semiotics, I couldn't make out the word the letters added up to. Link-a-din was how I read it. Like a little bell ringing. Ting-a-ling, Link-a-din. Or maybe it was a Finnish translation of the name of a princess from *One Thousand*

and One Nights. 'Then know,' said the Princess Link-a-din, 'that though I run like a gazelle and have the spirit of a mountain lion, when I do see thee my heart beats like a lamb.'

So some sort of party invitation, was it? Whatever their protestations to the contrary, it's in the nature of such sites to hint at impropriety. I'm guessing now, but I assume that things can get pretty personal in the chat rooms that keep the young awake all night, wondering, wishing, regretting. Did the person who craved my recognition, and was hanging on unto desperation for me to take up Link-a-din's invitation to connect, want to talk dirty to me?

That such was not the case became obvious when those with whom Link-a-din was offering to link me increased in number and eventually became people I already knew. But since I knew them, why the need for the intercession of a third party? Anything they wanted they could simply have asked me for the next time we met. 'Lend me a fiver: how would you like to respond?' Besides which, all my friends were fastidious in the matter of prepositions. That which wasn't euphonious they wouldn't say. And we had perfectly good words already for what we did, none of them requiring prepositions. We met. We conversed. We exchanged ideas. We had never yet 'connected to'.

'Only connect' was E. M. Forster's epigraph to *Howards End*. Not 'Only connect to'.

You can check that, if you have a mind to, by going online. But don't be surprised if you have to scroll through innumerable entries regarding the TV quiz show, presented by Victoria Coren Mitchell, before you get to the novel from whose ashen epigraph it takes its title. This is now the way our culture prioritises. Look up *Steppenwolf* and you'll get the band before the novel. Look up Jesus Christ and you'll get the musical. Look up Princess Link-a-din and you'll get LinkedIn, the business-oriented social network.

Anyway, now I understand what it's for, I remain astonished sane people sign up for it. Sometimes it's best to speak from ignorance: that way you can see the wood without being distracted by the trees. You won't get a rational assessment of a political party from a member, and you won't get a reasoned account of the joys of being 'linked' from somebody who's already 'in'. Attend, therefore, to my uninformed impartiality. Don't go there. Eschew the lot. You announce the poverty of your personal life by signing up to any networking service and you have nothing to gain professionally by linking in with people as unlinked-in as I am. Show some self-respect, for God's sake.

What needs are such services answering? Lawyers – to take a LinkedIn type at random – have never been short of work or behindhand in making useful contacts. Observe lawyers hugger-mugger outside a court and you become aware of the matrix of common aim and influence – class, dress, vocabulary, clubs, eating holes, remunerative ambition – that has served them well since the first man or woman sought to have a wrong redressed.

If you crave more interconnectedness still, it is only because you fear your colleagues might steal a march on you. So get together – outside a court, say – and unanimously agree to quit. There will be withdrawal symptoms, but hang in there. Eventually you'll thank me. That which none of you do, none of you will miss. And untweet yourselves while you are at it. Every hour we hear tweeters remonstrating with the very site they habituate. It's so brutal, they wail. You might as well climb into a boxing ring and complain you've been punched.

'Only de-connect.' Out in the free, uncompromised world of the unlinked no hell-troll can hound the mildest Corbyn sceptic, no sex pest ruin lives with lavish compliment. But if you must stay where you are, confusing work with pleasure, and then getting shirty when someone confuses pleasure with you, expect no pity from the rest of us. Today, let us declare every social and professional networking site a no-cry zone.

Nostril hair and the university

So how did you spend the extra time last week – that leap second inserted into our clocks to keep them in sync with the fickle Earth's rotation? I spent my second wondering how many more it would take to slow down the ageing process. How many leaps before the Earth juddered on its axis and time reversed, as it did for Superman, and I would be able to recall the names of friends again, get out of a chair without groaning, read the number of a bus in time to hail it before it drove past me? How many before the lines of sad experience vanished from my face and the hairs retracted into my nostrils? Which brings me neatly to my theme: nostril hair.

There are two ways we can speak about nostril hair, allowing that some people might not want to speak about it at all. We can speak literally and we can speak figuratively. Allow me to speak literally first.

For my own poor part I go to great lengths to keep my nostrils sightly. I own a mirror for looking upwards, several pairs of scissors with differently curved and blunted points, and a battery-operated razor (the batteries are optional: vanity alone can power it) the shape of a small spaceship. We shouldn't be too hard on vanity. It can be a mark of respect for the world. The day I don't attend to my nostrils is the day I will have forsworn that world and become a different person. Someone otherwise preoccupied. Someone who couldn't care less what anyone thinks of his appearance, someone for whom the material life has lost its appeal. I will have retreated into myself, to that place where eccentricity and maybe even madness reside. Science, perhaps.

The astute reader will by now have worked out that in truth nostril hair is only my sub-theme, and that my real subject is

Tim Hunt, the Nobel Prize-winning scientist who recently made a joking reference to the lachrymosity (were there such a word) of women, in punishment for which University College London expeditiously removed him from the honorary post he held there.

If I say that Tim Hunt is to be numbered among those who don't fanatically barber their nostrils twice a day, I intend no disrespect. I am now addressing nostril hair culturally. Tim Hunt has the air of a man who doesn't put his appearance first, a man who, whether calculatedly or otherwise, inhabits that sphere of extraterrestrial idiosyncrasy whose uniform is a cream linen jacket bought from one of those shops in Piccadilly where they come pre-battered, a fisherman's smock (probably picked up in Cornwall), stained owlish spectacles, a cord that goes around the neck to hang them from (else they'd fall into a laboratory bath) and, yes, figurative tufts of nostril hair.

Among the reasons universities exist is that such men should have a habitat. They are a dying species. When I went to university, there was almost no other way for a don to look. A few military men and dandies were the exception, but even their moustaches and cravats were mildewed and wouldn't have passed muster anywhere but in the Fens. Otherwise, the Scarecrow look from *The Wizard of Oz* prevailed. Bicycle clips, one trouser leg still in the sock, ties unevenly knotted, hair growing out of their ears and from their noses, sometimes in odd fringes above their shirt collars, occasionally in tussocks on their cheeks.

This was the higher carelessness of the academic life. To have turned up to give a lecture any less neglected would have been to put show before sagacity. Nostril hair wasn't simply an inadvertent consequence of collegiate life; it was the very badge of it.

That they held opinions abominable to those of us who tirelessly invigilate the political niceties goes without saying. Here were odd men and women, but mainly men, to all intents still living the monastic life of the thirteenth century. Some were even tonsured like monks and taught in tiny cells where, when they thought no one was listening, they played upon medieval instruments. To them the mundane demands of modernity were a torture.

So what right did we have to expect modern attitudes from them? Of course they were sexists, racists, pederasts, colonialists, anti-Semites. Of course they made jokes which not another living soul found funny. Bigotry was expected and even required of them. There have to be places where people let nostril hair run wild, think differently from the rest of us, implicitly call into question and even deride everything we have made up our minds about, find wisdom through unconventionality, and say a lot of foolish things along the way. Universities are such places. Correction: universities *should* be such places.

Show me a university which is a hotbed of thin-skinned offence-taking, where every unacceptable idea is policed and every person who happens to hold one is hounded out of a job, and I will show you a university that isn't a university but an ideological prison camp and indoctrination centre.

Reaffirming the college's pusillanimous decision to show Tim Hunt the door, the Provost of University College London said: 'Our commitment to gender equality and our support for women in science was and is the ultimate concern.' Wrong, Mr Provost. The right of women to enjoy equal opportunities, receive equal pay and enjoy equal respect to men in science, or anywhere else come to that, is without doubt a matter of high importance. But it is not as high, if we are to talk of 'ultimate concerns', as the freedom to think freely and independently – a freedom which matters as much to women as to men, and without which equality must lose its savour.

Who wants to be equal in an institution which is frightened of the very differences it exists to foster? What shall it profit a man or a woman, if they shall gain the whole world and lose their own soul?

How to be hip

WANNA KNOW HOW TO be hip? After five nights in the hippest of hip hotels in New York's hip Lower East Side, I'm the man to tell you. Never mind why I was there. That's stuff for another conversation. Let's just allow that I was hanging out, doing my shit, being hip.

The first rule of hip is that you don't ring a hip Lower East Side hotel from London and ask if they have tea-making facilities in the room. Of course they don't have tea-making facilities in the room; they don't have any facilities in the room. Bar a bar, that is – in this instance one that's better stocked than Salvatore's. You might not think you want a highball glass of Knob Creek bourbon and a bag of Doritos the minute you wake up, but you do if you're hip. Tea and coffee, if you must, you get in the breakfast room where servers (it's not hip to call them waiters) wear trainers and black tracksuits and look at you with deep suspicion when you request a breakfast menu. What is it you're really seeking? Just ask. They'll have it. 'English breakfast tea,' I say, enunciating my way out of any misunderstanding. English breakfast tea, not to be confused with crack cocaine. They are clean out of teapots so I get a cup with a diaphanous sac of something brown floating in it. I think about shoving it up my nose. As for the bacon bagel I fancy, that they can't do. 'But you serve bagels,' I say. My server nods. 'And you serve bacon.' He nods again. I make a question mark of my body. The hip equivalent of light – let's call it darkness – breaks somewhere in his brain. 'I can give you a bagel and a side of bacon,' he finally says. I settle for that.

From the corner of my eye I catch him watching me putting the bagel around the bacon. He'll be telling the guys he hangs around with about this. It could even catch on. If you are in the Lower East

Side in the next few months and find all the dudes putting bacon between two halves of a bagel, while watching out for the cops, you'll know how it originated.

Back in the room, I resume my search for a cupboard or a drawer. A wardrobe I have. But shelf have I none. Such things are getting hard to find wherever you stay these days. The hotels my father used to take me to when I was a small boy and he was driving a lorry between Manchester and London were marvellously furnished with spaces to put things. I still recall a chest of drawers with separate compartments for cufflinks, collar studs and tiepins. Since then exiguousness has come to be the fashion in the matter of hotel storage. But there's usually somewhere to cram in a sock and maybe a change of undergarment – even if it means removing the Gideon Bible. In hipsville, though, there's absolutely nothing – just the floor of the wardrobe where you'll never be able to find anything because of the exiguousness of the light.

The more hip the hotel, the less light you get. Don't ask me to explain this. It could be that it's not hip ever to see yourself. It could be that you don't mind losing shit if you're hip because possessions don't matter. It could be that the truly hip can see in the dark. I'd ring reception to ask if there's some hidden switch but the phone is more complex than the cockpit of a spaceship and it isn't hip to put instructions in the room. I'd try Skyping on my laptop but that means lying on the floor, because there's no desk or table and no chair that allows me to make a lap to rest my laptop on. If you think this is a cheap hotel you're missing the essence of hip exclusivity. We're in art-world territory here, where less is more, and none is everything. They have to do only one thing to this hotel to make it not just hip but super-hip and that's move the bed out.

Out on the hip streets of Off Soho that get less hip the closer I get to On Soho I see an artisanal juice bar and cake shop that is advertising for 'talented baristas' and happens to have a free seat in the sun. Somebody's Daughter, it's called. I don't recognise the name of the father but the smell's good. I ask the talented barista for a skinny cappuccino – having no fat in my milk accords well with having no light in my room – and a cinnamon pastry. He isn't sure about the cinnamon. He'll have to go check. Ten minutes later word is delivered that if they have a cinnamon pastry they can't find it. That's hip – a cake shop that can't find the cakes. But hipper still is the time it takes to get me my cappuccino.

There are eight, say ten customers sitting out in the sun, waiting for something. There are ten, say twelve talented baristas visible in the kitchen. So how much longer should my cappuccino take? But I've yet to realise that the difference between a talented, hip barista and any old barista is that the talented, hip barista has no talent. After fifteen more minutes I raise an arm. A passing barista says he'll ask. Another arrives – this must be about the sixth not to have served me with anything – and surveys me with laconic contempt. 'We are working on your coffee, sir,' he says.

'Working on it! It's a cappuccino, not the fucking Empire State Building.'

In fact I don't say that. It's not hip. Hip is consenting to getting nothing you really want because there's nothing you really want. I, who never smile, smile.

Peace

'SEA OR SHEEP?' MY wife wanted to know. 'Sheep,' I said. 'No, sea. No, sheep.' This proved her point. I was overworked and tired, I couldn't make a decision, I needed a weekend away looking at something that wasn't a manuscript or a computer. But what did I need to look at – sea or sheep? I was too tired to know.

I pretty much stopped driving a few years ago. This was partly because I had moved into the West End and didn't need to drive, and partly because I was falling prey to road rage. If I didn't stop driving I would kill a cyclist. Throttle one, I mean.

The only time I miss driving now is when the urge to get away, to look at sea or sheep, is upon me. Getting away without a car is tough. You can't just set out and see where you end up: you have to choose a destination and then book taxis, trains, hotels, even sheep. The Internet with its we'll-do-it-for-you dot-coms is said to have made all this easy, but that's a lie. Booking anything on the Internet is Kafkaesque, full of mysterious interrogations and dead ends. After two hours on the Internet you start to wonder who's asking the questions – you or them?

Where are you going, when you are going, what station are you leaving from, when are you coming back – if you knew the answers to any of those you wouldn't be searching the Internet. Find a hotel that doesn't specialise in mystery weekends or hen nights and before any site will tell you if there's a way of reaching it by train you have to register or remember a password or re-register with a new password which turns out to be your old password and is therefore no longer available to you since you're now not the person you were before you re-registered. They want to know your sex, birthday, postcode – which information keeps coming back with the word ERROR flashing in red because you've forgotten to tick a tiny box hidden at the bottom left-hand corner of the page. By the time you've got the information you need to get away you're too worn out to go.

In the end we chose sheep over sea, going for a rural hotel with lily ponds, near enough by train not to have to start our return journey the minute we arrived. No table for dinner until nine o'clock but given the wildlife promised on the hotel website we could always shoot our own if we got hungry.

We arrived at four o'clock, in good time for afternoon tea in the drawing room. All the waiters were busy, pouring tea with one hand behind their back. When we finally got the maître d's attention he noted we hadn't booked. 'We're residents,' I told him. He looked at his watch and shook his head. I told him we'd been told afternoon tea went on until 5.30. 'It takes two hours to bake fresh scones,' he said. I pointed to the scones on everyone else's plates. 'They made a reservation,' he said sadly. I gave him the look I gave cyclists in the days I drove. 'You telling me you have to make a reservation for scones?'

'Calm,' my wife whispered. 'Think sea or sheep.'

'I'm thinking scones,' I said.

The maître d tried to mollify us with biscuits, but brought scones in the end, with rich raspberry jam, Cornish cream and an apology, all of which he served – even the apology – with one hand behind his back.

I calmed down by the Monet lily pond. The gardens were as good as promised. Bunny rabbits played on the lawn, undisturbed by the sound of croquet mallets. At the far end of a magnificent avenue of giant redwood trees an incurious deer chewed grass. 'This is working,' I told my wife, allowing my BlackBerry to quack away unanswered in my pocket. The sun came in and out, fish appeared on the surface of the water, ducks gathered in a circle beneath a bush. Peace!

At nine o'clock we went to take our seats in the restaurant. Nothing doing. Would we please go to the drawing room where we'd be given canapés and shown the menu by one-armed waiters. 'No,' I said. I enumerated my reasons. Hunger, dislike of not being seated at the time I've booked, dislike of eating late, dislike of sitting in low armchairs reading menus and wine lists when I want to be sitting up at a table clinking glasses, dislike of leaving London for relaxation and walking into that hurricane of fuss and obstacle known as 'Fine Dining'.

'If you used both your fucking hands,' I thought of saying, 'you might run a more efficient restaurant.' But I hadn't come to the country to swear.

There was no moving him anyway. So it was back to where we'd earlier had to fight for scones, and the naff ritual of balancing heavy faux-leather menus on our laps and wondering if we were ever going to eat again. Half an hour later we were called for dinner. Soup arrived at the time I normally start getting ready for bed. At 10.45 a waitress offered us desserts. After waiting twenty minutes for them we gave up and left the table. Another waitress pursued us with the offer of coffee in our rooms. 'When – three in the morning!' I exclaimed. She wondered what was wrong. 'Everything. The whole thing's been horrible,' I said, and then was unable to sleep, not because of the late eating but because I thought 'horrible' had been a horrible word to use and was annoyed with myself for having used it. It hadn't been horrible, just fussy and inept, pretending to style where there was none. It confirmed my belief that every hotel in England was a Fawlty Towers at heart. 'We must have been mad trying,' I woke my wife to say.

'Hush!' she said, as we watched the dawn break through the unlined curtains.

We returned to the Monet lily pond in the late morning. The sun came out. Fish showed their backs above the water. Ducks headed for the shade. Far away, a sheep baahed. 'But then again,' I said, closing my eyes.

At that moment two young Australians began setting up a laser version of clay shooting. An amenity for guests. When you hit the clay an electronic buzzer went off. *Zaphbedoyng!*

'Sorry to spoil your view, guys,' the Aussies said.

Should have gone for sea. Should have stayed home. Should have punched a cyclist.

The sweet seductiveness of loss

NO MEAL CAN BE sad, said the critic Mikhail Bakhtin. But then he never dined with me. In anticipation of a meal – supposing we are with the ideal companion at the best table in the perfect restaurant – we might indeed postpone sadness. And maybe even halfway through we will remain in tolerably high spirits, with dessert still to come. But as we near the end of eating we begin to feel anticipatory twinges of anticlimax. Soon it will be over and we'll be wondering why we expected so much. Soon we'll be experiencing that emptiness of spirits which no satisfaction or memory of satisfaction can dispel. Soon we'll be asking why we are alive.

In 'Resolution and Independence', that great despondent William Wordsworth describes the descent from exuberance to wretchedness as a law of the physical universe.

> But, as it sometimes chanceth, from the might
> Of joys in minds that can no further go,
> As high as we have mounted in delight
> In our dejection do we sink as low.

The morning is too beautiful, the sense of natural joy too intense for animation to sustain itself. We sink because we rose. This is how philosophers explain the *tristesse* of sex, how nutritionists explain the slump after gluttony, and how I explain the hollowness that waits on watching tennis day after day.

I am enthralled until the last ball Djokovic hits, and the moment it is over and he is on his knees eating grass I sink into my chair, cannot believe I have spent another fleeting fortnight of the few summers I have left caring about the outcome of contests

I will have forgotten in the blink of an eye, and begin to question my sanity. Only a madman would have murdered time as I just have, and it's no consolation to know there are tens of millions of people out there as mad as I am. If it's bathos you want – and I suspect we are all bathos junkies in the end – nothing gives it to you quite like watching sport. Unless it's playing sport.

Imagine what Djokovic is feeling now. Imagine to what dejection he must have sunk after having mounted in delight so high. I read that he's a devout Christian, so that might help. Since God never puts in an actual appearance, He can't ever be a let-down, and so is bathos-free. Otherwise it would have to be heroin.

Winning itself certainly won't have kept Djokovic high for long. OK, so he's the best tennis player in the world. So what? I recall waking to the realisation that I was the best table-tennis player under seventeen in north Manchester and parts of Bury. The satisfaction lasted for half an hour before I saw into the nothingness of things. So how profound must be the nothingness confronting Djokovic, whose backhand isn't as good as mine was and who hasn't even got Manchester to go home to.

And that's after winning. What happens when you don't? How's Federer feeling just now? Not quite as bad as Andy Murray, and Murray won't be feeling quite as bad as Nadal. Unless he is.

I worry about Murray. There is a particular thing that's not quite happening, and I don't mean winning. I mean apprehending what it is that's not quite happening. He has enough people helping him, I know, but I suspect I have inside knowledge the others don't. I understand the allure of not wanting to win.

That this is a qualification that won't earn me a place on his management team I accept. People who don't know what's best for them don't know what's best for them. But assuming he is a regular reader of the *Independent*, I offer him the following thoughts which he is welcome to print out or transcribe into a notebook of the sort that Vasek Pospisil, his opponent in the quarter-final, kept by his chair and from time to time consulted – without success, admittedly, but we don't know how much more decisively he'd have lost without it.

Court notes for Andy Murray:

To thine own self be true – not. Pop psychology makes much of the need to find ourselves. Ignore it. Find someone else.

Don't be at peace with yourself either. Peace has no place in sport. Sport is war. But don't hold your coaching staff responsible for everything that goes wrong. The thing you're locked into with your mother – blaming her and your various mother-substitutes for every point you lose – is not so much unhealthy (mothers exist to bear our blame) as debilitating. It depletes your energy reserves. Hate your opponents instead.

Face facts. The fastidious Federer scorns you and proves it with every ace he sends down. He doesn't care for the sort of tennis you play and would rub your face in your limitations, winning 6–0, 6–0, 6–0 if he could. Learn contempt from him.

Djokovic is too busy hating Federer to have time to hate you, but he remembers how much he dislikes you whenever you get to two sets apiece, and that secures him the fifth set.

Courtesy is a fine quality in a tennis player provided it is false. I see through the Hibernian cussedness you affect; in reality you're a pussycat. That's the wrong way round: act nice, play nasty is the rule. 'This Duncan hath borne his faculties too meek', and so have you. Be Macbeth instead. Think that's a dagger you see before you.

Don't expect other players to cooperate in your success. Don't wait for them to give you points. Win your own. You have thunderous strokes. It breaks the heart to see you not using them. Softly softly catchee monkey, but you don't want to catchee monkey, you want to breakee monkey's balls. Go to passivity-management classes. And get a second serve. Then you'll be a man, my son. Still sad, but at least a man.

Nellie, I *am* Catherine Earnshaw

PLEASED TO SEE THE new Children's Laureate, Malorie Blackman, coming out of the blocks fighting. Let's get children reading, she says, and let's ensure that black and other minority ethnic children don't turn against history because of too great an emphasis on Nelson and the Tudors. Let's have a few heroes who are culturally easier to identify with. We are in favour, in this column, of getting young people to read, even if we don't think they have to read books especially written for them. Remember, we say, the example of John Stuart Mill, who knew his way through the classics when he was three. Yes, he went on to have a nervous breakdown, but at least he had the classics to help him out of it. Never mind the Prozac, try Plotinus. And we are in favour of a little more Henryless history (and Tudorless television) as well. Too much Tudor and you end up on temazepam. So we are disposed to listen when the new Children's Laureate speaks.

Two statements she has just made strike me as important. The first is: 'I still remember feeling I was totally invisible in the world of literature.' And the second: 'I understand you need to learn about Henry VIII, but when I was young I wanted to learn about something that felt more relevant.'

What a person remembers about being young is not open to controversy. What you felt, you felt. But I have to report differently. Not only didn't I feel invisible in the world of literature, it would not have occurred to me that there was such a feeling to have. I am a few years older than Malorie Blackman, and those years might well have been decisive when it comes to what we think we have a right to feel – I put it like that because feeling is not autonomous: feelings catch on, go in and out of fashion, are determined by external circumstance and ideology – but however it's to be explained, I didn't feel excluded from what I read and nor did my friends. True, we weren't black, but we were Jewish, northern and working class, so if there was an invisibility to feel, we were well placed to feel it.

'Where are the Jews?' It's possible that one of the reasons we refrained from asking that question was that when a Jew did pop up in literature we wished he hadn't. Thanks, Fagin, but no thanks. Quite simply, though, we were perfectly happy to read about people who weren't us. We didn't read to self-identify. We might not have said in so many words that we read for precisely the opposite reason – in order imaginatively to enjoy the company of others, in order to understand what those who were not ourselves were like, in order to feel the world expand around us, in order to go places we didn't routinely go to in our neighbourhoods or in our heads, in order to meet the challenge of difference – but that was what we were doing. We probably wouldn't have said, either, that the best books are inclusive in a way that transcends skin colour, religion or ethnic identity, but we knew they were. Reading felt like a journey out of self, not into it. And if occasionally we thought we saw something specific to us in Hamlet, or Heathcliff, that was interesting but not obligatory.

There's another way of putting this. If I didn't feel invisible, it was because I wasn't. Madame Bovary *c'est moi*, Flaubert declared, invoking the writer's creed. The reader's creed is similar. Jane Eyre *c'est moi*, I felt when I read Charlotte Brontë's great novel at school, and she was no less *moi* because she was a girl. If we should resist the principle of ethnic identity when reading, we should resist the gender principle as well. I was not invisible when I read Jane Eyre a) because the best writers make general what's particular, and b) because I, who had not been taught to go looking for myself missing, honoured the writer/reader compact and found me in characters who weren't me. Did my being a boy make me more Biggles than Little Dorrit? No, it did not. Would I have been more Biggles had Biggles been Jewish? No, I would not.

Our disagreement with Malorie Blackman about history – Tudors aside – is essentially the same. It's not history's job to be relevant to us; it's our job to be relevant to history. I certainly see the argument for schoolchildren to be introduced early to the great issues that bear on racism – the Holocaust and slavery, for example – but that's not because of the special relevance they have for Jews and black people. It's because knowing about them matters to everyone.

I remember where I was when 'relevance' entered the education debate. I remember where I was standing, what window I was looking out of, what bleak landscape I surveyed. That it would come to no good – that it demeaned those it pretended to help by assuming limits to their curiosity; that it denied those it offered to empower, cutting off their access to 'irrelevant' intellectual pleasure and enlightenment; that it was in every essential philistine in that it narrowed the definition of learning to the chance precincts of an individual's class or upbringing – I was certain. The education system I benefited from assumed an equality of eagerness for knowledge, and an equality of right to acquire it. 'Relevance', as the Children's Laureate's urgency to promote a lost literacy proves, has benefited no one.

The answer to a history course that doesn't interest children is not more digestible history; it's better history teaching. A person who has trouble learning to drive isn't advantaged by being taught only how to crash. I applaud your energy and passion, Malorie Blackman, but take the relevance route and you don't educate, you disinherit.

The phoenix and the turtle

ACCORDING TO GILES FODEN, author of *The Last King of Scotland*, what the militant group al-Shabaab, was 'really attacking' when it went on the rampage in Westgate shopping mall, was 'the very idea of capitalism'. A four-year-old boy from Britain, whose mother had already been wounded in the attack, had a different moral take on the massacre. 'You're a very bad man,' he told one of the gunmen. Sometimes you get nearer to the truth if you keep it simple.

Whether the story has grown wings, whether the gunman really was shamed by the boy's words, handed him a bar of chocolate and begged for his forgiveness, saying 'We are not monsters', I'm not in any position to know. It would be nice, though, to think that the little boy had time to say: 'Oh yes you are. And don't give me any of that "what you're really attacking is the very idea of capitalism" crap.'

Ever since Mary Beard responded to 9/11 by saying the Americans had it coming, that the 'civilised world' (her inverted commas) was paying a very high price for refusing to listen to 'terrorists' (again her inverted commas), that there were few people on the planet who 'devised carnage for the sheer hell of it' – thereby setting up a false opposition between mindless carnage and principled carnage – ever since then I have taken a dim view of the argument that very bad men must have a case or they wouldn't be very bad men. What very bad men often have is an inflated sense of grievance, coupled with an unswerving conviction of rectitude, which makes them, if anything, even worse men than if they were acting for the sheer hell of it. May God save us all from terrorists – no inverted commas – with a cause.

It isn't that difficult morally to sort out. A four-year-old can do it. If the killer is firing indiscriminately he's a very bad man. If he's firing discriminately – as in this case firing only at those who don't subscribe to the Muslim faith – he's a bad man doubly cursed. For Allah will no more forgive him than Jesus will. Marx on the other hand . . . but then that's why no man of feeling should be a Marxist.

At the heart of one's outrage on such occasions is a piercing sadness, like a voice from the whirlwind. The innocent die whenever guns are raised, and one could give one's life over to sorrow, imagining how many have been ruined since time began in wars of ideology of no concern or value to anyone but the combatants. Dying in a just cause is cruel enough, but dying because some misbegotten sect misreads history in a way that flatters the ignorance of its members, is crueller still. I thought that was going to be the way of it for all of us after 9/11. And it might be yet. But certainly, at the time, I stood on the balcony of my apartment and saw towers topple before my eyes and waited for the fire to come roaring over the rooftops. And then the question was – did I want my wife to be with me as I burned or was it better for her to be far away, somewhere safe, if anywhere safe was left? Better to burn together, melded into one, rather than one be left behind to mourn?

Call me a melodramatist. Call me a sentimentalist, too, if you think that's the word for me. But it's always the lovers destroyed in an atrocity that I find myself grieving over first. They can be young lovers or they can be old lovers. Just-marrieds on honeymoon or grandma and grandpa taking a golden-wedding holiday in the wrong place. One still alive but as yet ignorant of the other's death is hard enough to bear – how would you do it, you wonder, how would you fare at the moment of being told, or in the thousands of nights that follow, how would you survive a single one of them? – but a beloved pair going together wreaks havoc in me. I have only to discover that they died hand in hand and I'm finished. This time, I read of two who died huddled together, two become one for the final time. Like the Phoenix and the Turtle, either neither. So was there time enough for one to sorrow for the other or for both to sorrow for themselves? And if there was the briefest moment of

THE PHOENIX AND THE TURTLE

clarity, each for each – ah, the pity of it – was there consolation in that? A last confession of devotion in the eyes? Can love do that?

I've been reading lovers' goodbye stories since I was a boy, mooning over them in opera and operetta, as though a goodbye was the thing I had to work hardest on because I knew I'd make such a bad job of it when the time came. But there was a sweetness in the goodbyes I rehearsed with the lights out in my bedroom. The Student Prince kisses his Heidelberg barmaid farewell because duty calls, but at least both of them are left intact and beautiful to love another day.

To be gunned down together, though, is of another order of sadness. We all know love is fragile. Who's to say that lovers who die in one another's arms would even have been together ten years on? So in one way atrocity forces a sort of happy ending on them. But that fragility also measures the callousness of the killings. Love is the antithesis to the ideology in whose name everyone – everyone of the wrong faith on the day, that is – must die.

There are no bad men in the world when we flutter in each other's embrace. And that is why love matters: it's our last illusion.

The wages of indulgence is darts

O F ARROWS AND THE man I sing. It is expected of me. Just as no
year can be considered over for Australians until the fireworks
have illuminated Sydney Harbour, and no year can be said to have
begun for Austrians until the Vienna Philharmonic has played the
'Radetzky March', so must my new-year column be a paean to darts
and those who throw them.

Though I always vow to go along to Alexandra Palace to watch the
World Darts Championships as it were in person and, who knows,
sit at the same table as Prince Harry or Stephen Fry, I am invariably
too clapped out to leave my chair. It's partly this seasonal exhaus-
tion that makes sitting in night after night to watch the arrows fly
on Sky so pleasurable. My worldly task is done. I have survived the
heat o' the sun, I am wrapped against the furious winter's rages,
and I have, in the dying days of the old year, eaten more than twice
my body weight in mince pies and drunk wine enough for Adrian
Lewis and Raymond van Barneveld to have bathed together in –
twice. Home I'm gone, and with my eyes too tired to read, my brain
too charged to function, and nothing else that feels like just reward
for all my labours to watch on television, darts are my wages.

There was a time when dozing in front of the box and waking
only when the hoarse-voiced referee barked 'One hundred and
eighty' marked one out as either a true philistine or a pretend one
like those desperate-not-to-be-stuffy professors of literature who
say they'd rather read Harry Potter than Proust. Today no apology
is necessary. Televised darts is less vulgar than *Strictly Come Dancing*
and more serious than *Newsnight*.

True, there remains the synthetic working men's club atmosphere
to negotiate. Although there are more clerkly, not to say studious,

looking players emerging, the majority still resemble plumbers. I mean no disrespect by that. Given the frequency with which I call out a plumber, I'd be a fool to show the profession anything but the deepest respect. But there's a pedantry incident to plumbing – how many times is it now I've had the mechanics of the 'O' ring explained to me – which is much like the numerological punctiliousness that inflicts darts players if you're insane enough to ask them where they thought they won or lost a game. And it's because something of the mundanely manual still adheres to darts that the players' heroic walk of honour from the green room to the oche is so incongruous. The fanfare begins, the strobes go wild, the crowds roar, hostesses wearing the sort of tinsel dresses that drove me crazy when I was eighteen escort the gladiator into the arena, only he's not a gladiator, he's a plumber.

But change is on the way. In previous years, dancers who might have been on day release from Raymond's Revuebar twerked onstage between matches; now they perform wholesome beach aerobics in order to suggest that this is a sporting event whose ultimate aim is the nation's fitness.

If you think the bodies of the players themselves give the lie to this, you haven't watched for a while. I wouldn't go so far as to say that today's best throwers are the most svelte throwers, but a beer belly is not the sine qua non it was. As is not the beer itself. However much is consumed by spectators, there isn't even a sissy's half-pint glass with a handle to be seen on the little tables where the players fuss with their flights and pour filtered water. It was axiomatic in my pub-darts days that one threw better pissed, but we were playing for fun not glory, and just how often, anyway, pissed or otherwise, did we hit 180?

The mistake which haters of televised darts make is not to see what lovers of it see. And vice versa.

Ambivalence is as essential to the appreciation of darts as it is to the appreciation of Wagner. 'Was I really put on earth to do this?' is a question it behoves humanity to ask, whatever it's doing. An expense of spirit in a waste of shame was how Shakespeare described lust in action, but we don't always wake up the next morning feeling that. We are most rational – as lovers, aesthetes, or just couch potatoes – when we clatter between extremes, punishing ourselves for squandering the gift of life one minute, glorying in the waste the next.

And that, reader, explains why some of us become engrossed in darts. Yes it's trivial, no it isn't. Or rather: yes it's trivial, and therein lies its sublimity. Those tiny points of tungsten, like the light-as-air celluloid ball ping-pong players chase, like Jane Austen's 'little bit of ivory', are metaphors for man's ability to create something out of nothing, to see eternity in a grain of sand, to make a little dartboard an everywhere.

Whoever would be universal must first be particular. Even God had to create the world a bit at a time. The secret of infinity resides in the insignificant. And what could be more insignificant than narrowing one's concentration down to a pinhead and aiming it at a strip of cork no bigger than an ant's eyelash?

Though all darts players must be philosophers at heart, the one who most fully grasps the game's fundamental equivocation is the sixteen-times world champion Phil Taylor. For all the titles he has won and all the studied bluffness of his manner, his eyes remain weighted with the terrible apprehension of defeat. It's not falling from his pedestal he fears, but the chasm of nihilism waiting beneath him.

I follow his progress every year with mounting apprehension. I invest teleologically in his progress. If he loses, I lose; life is emptied of its transitory meaning and I am returned to uncreated matter spinning unavailingly in the void. It's for us, you see – for the illusion of sense and order – that he throws. Pray that when you read this he will still be throwing.

What's Hecuba to you?

O F THE SECULAR MYSTERIES to which I wake with fresh and sometimes angry amazement every day, the queue is the second-most baffling. The first is the fan. Not the fan in the *Lady Windermere* sense. I mean the fan who is an abbreviation of fanatic, that self-abasing follower of a person or a thing whose ardour could in fact do with some of what fans of the other sort provide.

The queue and the fan are of course closely related, in that fans will queue any length of time in any weather to see, touch, watch, hear, read or simply enjoy proximity to the object of their devotion. There is a shop close to where I live, outside which, on certain nights of the month – I've no idea if the transit of the moon determines precisely when – fans of designer skateboards queue from early evening in order – well, in order, I presume – to be among the first to jump on a skateboard when the shop opens in the morning. Why don't they just pop into Hamleys? Or walk?

The same occurs outside trainer stores (where they sell gym shoes – that really is the only way to describe them – that neither you nor I would want to wear), hotels (where someone you and I have never heard of is staying), bookshops (for books neither you nor I would want to read), clubs, theatres, and suddenly, even, town halls and similar buildings suitable for revivalist meetings in Labour constituencies. There is no let-up of excitement either, I am assured, outside the Barbican where Benedict Cumberbatch is being Hamlet, a person (Hamlet, not Cumberbatch) who wanted for nothing, was a fan of nobody, and therefore, we can fairly deduce, never queued in his life. Find all the uses of this world weary, flat, stale and unprofitable, and there is no designer skateboard you would hang around all night to buy, and no celebrity of either sex you are going to sit on wet pavements for two days to get a glimpse of. There's a lot to be said for misanthropy.

I am stern in the matter of being a fan in the fanatic sense, and blame the parents. A proper dose of comic scepticism administered at the right age could stop all that. Listen to your parents shrieking 'Him!' or 'Her!' or, better still, 'That!' with sufficient derision each time you announce the worthless fame-phantom you've grown enamoured of – 'What's Hecuba to you, or you to Hecuba – I'm speaking figuratively – that you should skip school to gawp at her? Fortinbras, you say? That speck of nothing? That stain of hyena's vomit? That bowl of undiluted cat's piss? A dog wouldn't stop to rub his nose in that piece of shit' – and there's just a chance you will start to question your judgement, your self-worth, and your sense of smell. I say just a chance, but just a chance is better than no chance. And it beats having fathers who are still wearing Chelsea shirts in their middle fifties and mothers who queue all night themselves to get a ticket for Justin Bieber, whose name I might just possibly have made up.

I was a supply teacher briefly in another age and whenever I encountered an incidence of mass fandom – more moderate in those days with no social media to inflame it – I would get the whole class to write out 'I am not a slave' a thousand times. I don't say it worked but it made them hate me, and that at least introduced the principle of resistance into their lives. Better to be surly than a serf.

So is this just a roundabout way of saying that I won't be braving the frothing fans to see Sherlock metamorphosing into Hamlet? Not exactly, but no – no, yes, no, as they say – I doubt I will be going. I feel the play is too much mine to have it taken from me by yet another interpretation that might or might not be interesting, but which, for the moment at least, I have no mental space for.

When it comes to Shakespeare, I am a theatre-of-the-mind man. No production beats what you read on the page and go on seeing on the stage behind your eyes long after, though I doubt that Hamlet himself, a lover of plays and a connoisseur of acting styles, would have agreed with me. 'Speak the speech, I pray you, as I pronounced it to you, trippingly on the tongue,' he tells the First Player, not 'Hum it trippingly to yourself'.

And I accept that what lodges a play like *Hamlet* in your imagination – to the degree that you can't remember when you ever didn't know it, or when you ever had a thought that wasn't in some way *Hamlet*-influenced – is not only the attentive reading you give it. Just as knowing a text well will enhance the experience of watching it performed, so might an actor's interpretation change the way you read it the next time. But you can allowably feel you no longer need or want to know how *Hamlet* strikes someone else. You can be as satiated with performance as you can with critical exegesis. Enough exposition. Enough acting. You can want the play to breathe quietly in your arms for a while.

I didn't say expire in your arms. It doesn't kill a work of art to want it left alone temporarily. 'Thou still unravished bride of quietness' was how Keats addressed a Grecian urn at the beginning of that ode that ends with the famous lines about beauty being truth, truth being beauty, and that being that. Which isn't quite saying shut the fuck up, but it is a plea for quiet and reserve. Ours is a noisy culture. We see the bustle of the throng and the size of the queue as proof that's all well in 'the arts', as we disrespectfully call them. But zest and numbers aren't the measure of everything. A little unravished stillness, and not a trainer-wearing, skateboarding, bestseller-carrying fan in sight, can also be a mark of civilised appreciation.

In Leonard Cohen's fedora you too can look like L. S. Lowry

TODAY: TWO LESSONS IN how to wear a hat. My exemplars are the painter L. S. Lowry and the singer-songwriter Leonard Cohen. Dr Johnson said of the metaphysical poets that in them 'the most heterogeneous ideas are yoked by violence together'. We don't hold with violence in this column, nor do we mean to court the cheap controversy of heterogeneity. Lowry and Cohen might, on the face of it, make strange bedfellows, but both took London by storm this week – Cohen at the O2 Arena, Lowry at Tate Britain – and both define themselves by the way they wear a hat.

Leonard Cohen's hat is well known. You'll find sites on the Internet in which aficionados of the singer's wardrobe go head to head, as it were, on the question of whether what he wears is a trilby or a fedora. To the literalists it comes down to the size of the brim and the nature of the crease at the crown, but I am of the party that thinks it's how you wear it that determines what it is. If you are possessed of cool, you will turn a trilby into a fedora. Let's face it, if you are cool, you will turn a knotted handkerchief into a fedora. And Cohen is nothing if not cool. Amazing that one can look cool at seventy-nine, but if he knows how to wear a hat, then a hat knows how to wear him, and a good one can take years off you.

Cool is not a word even his most devoted admirers would use of Lowry. But a giant blown-up photograph of him in a capacious raincoat and a hat that is closer to a pudding than a fedora greets you at the entrance to the Tate show, and there can be no doubt that the hat is a statement of creative intent. Just so you know where I stand, I saw Cohen and Lowry last week, and while I had a good time with Cohen, I had an even better one with Lowry. Make no mistake, this is a magnificent – magnificently conceived and curated – exhibition. You could quibble about the paintings that aren't there – the portraits, the seascapes and landscapes, the late, strange, corseted women – and you could take issue with the Marxist emphasis on him as a critic of industrialism. But to complain of anything is churlish given that it's little short of miraculous that the Tate should have granted so unfashionable (and unfashionably popular) a painter an exhibition at all, given its scale, and given how convincingly, room by room, painting by painting, it makes the case for his genius. Visionary genius, I would say, allowing that you can be a visionary of godlessness, a seer of desolate, whited-out infinities – but that's a matter for another day.

If there was a revivalist atmosphere at the Leonard Cohen concert – people singing along to songs they first heard before their now middle-aged children were born – there was a triumphalist feeling at the Lowry exhibition, where obscure enthusiasts and well-known collectors congratulated one another simply on seeing what they had never thought they'd live to see. 'We did it!' someone who'd been buying Lowrys all his life and didn't own a single painting by anybody else told me, as though he – he and I – had finally come in from the cold. The difference between our enthusiasm and that of Cohen's fans was that while we loved our man's work as much as they loved theirs, we didn't want to be him. Who wants to be a man that wears a hat like that? Whereas to wear a fedora like Cohen. . .

I sat next to a Cohen lookalike at the O2 Arena. Not as aged or as switchblade lean, but wearing his hat identically and given to ironic, deep-throated mumblings. He knew every song by heart, and appeared, at times, as though he had passed over into another reality. Cohen sang what was in my neighbour's soul. I won't say everybody at the concert was transported to this degree, but most were. It was like being at a very sedate, elderly orgy. 'Dance me to the end of love,' Cohen sang, and that was precisely where he took us – to love's very extremities. Cohen's peculiar genius is to have made masochism melodic, and by that means to have turned it into macho. Song after song celebrates erotic surrender. Fine by the man next to me. He yielded up his being. Fine by all the other 20,000 fetishists in the stadium. Sexually speaking, probably the sweetest, least aggressive people on the planet. But the question has to be asked whether art is best served by submitting yourself to it so completely. Can it even be said to be art that you're enjoying when what you are is seduced?

The hat gives the game away. Love me under my fedora, Cohen asks. Ignore me, says Lowry under his shapeless trilby – for I am unlovable – and look instead at what I make. Very Manchester, this unwillingness to whisper sweet nothings. We are plain-speaking, sarcastic, self-denigrating, difficult buggers up there. We'll meet anyone halfway, provided they are plain-speaking, difficult buggers too. For years, it seems to me, it was Lowry's refusal to talk up his work, to give his paintings other than bog-standard titles, to aggrandise, to woo, to seduce us with the charm of paint or the allure of sentiment, that kept him out of the mainstream.

Paradoxically, this reluctance to be idolised should have recommended Lowry to the sternest of contemporary critics – those aestheticians who, after Adorno and Laura Mulvey, cautioned against 'libidinous engagement with the art object'. 'Passionate detachment' was what they preached instead. Precious chance of that when the artist tips his fedora at you. Lowry's charmless titfer, on the other hand, keeps us strictly in our place.

The unhappy wanderer

IT'S A CURIOUS FACT about medical check-ups that you always leave shorter and heavier than when you arrived. 'If I go on losing inches this fast,' I told the doctor the last time he measured me, 'I will soon have disappeared altogether.' 'That's unlikely to happen,' he said, 'so long as you go on gaining pounds at the same rate.'

The vanishing inches I ascribe to faulty equipment, but the accumulated pounds I acknowledge, though what's making them accumulate I have no idea. I understand dieting and occasionally practise it. I get the science of nutrition. Yes, I eat bread and drink wine, but I have cut down on cheese, can take or leave champagne, only eat biscuits on trains, only eat cake at birthdays and no more like chocolates than I like carrots, consumption of which I have also reduced. 'It could be,' the doctor told me, 'that you're happy.'

That was such an astonishing suggestion that I forgot to ask him to explain what the one had to do with the other. Happy? Me! I have been miserable – and have prided myself on being miserable – for as long as I can remember. I was a prodigy of misery when I was small. Strangers commented on it. 'Why the long face?' 'Cheer up, sunshine, it may never happen.' 'Smiles are free, you know, you sour-faced little bastard.'

That last remark was my father's. He hated having a surly son. I think my mother persuaded him it was early-onset adolescence. 'What, in his pram?' But he left me to it and hoped my temperament would lighten by itself. Which it partly did once real adolescence came and went. But I still remained more sullen than sunny, didn't like the feel of my face from the inside, or indeed the look of my face from the outside, when I smiled, and found an echo of my feelings only in sardonic literature and heartbreaking music.

And now, suddenly, according to my doctor, I'm happy. He's right, as it happens, though I'm embarrassed that it shows. I seem to have reversed the normal order of things which is to gurgle away cheerfully when you're an infant and decline into despondency as you start hitting the big numbers. Here is not the place to discuss how this reversal has come about. More interesting is my doctor's contention that happiness puts on weight.

Having pondered it for a while, I think this has a physiological rather than a psychological explanation. When you're happy, you dispense with exercise. I have not spent a great deal of time in gyms or health clubs. Having loathed PE as a boy, it makes no sense to me to embrace it as a man. But whenever I've been in a gym I've been struck by the angry sadness of everyone I see there. The received wisdom has it that running on a treadmill or pressing weights releases endorphins that make us happy, but that's only relative to how unhappy we were to start with. A man with a loving bed-warmed wife to stay wrapped around does not leave the house at seven in the morning to sweat in the company of other men. Unless . . . But that's something else again. Ditto a man with a job he cannot be torn away from. The gym is a place we go to find a simulacrum of happiness, not to compound the happiness we already feel. We are not fools. We can distinguish endorphin-induced bliss from the real thing. No genuinely happy man ever saw the need to exercise.

And walking the same. I have walked a lot in my life. Aged eight, I left home with a Dick Whittington bundle on my shoulder and walked to my grandmother's a mile away. Unhappiness was the cause. My parents had refused to go on paying the fines on my library books. I'd taken out Goethe's *The Sorrows of Young Werther* and André Maurois's *Call No Man Happy* months before and hadn't wanted to return them. I hoped my grandmother would pay the fines for me, though, as I trudged along, I knew in my heart she wouldn't. And once I very nearly walked from Manchester to Cambridge having failed to hitch a single ride. Drivers don't like picking up hikers with sour faces. Since then, I have found it helps to walk off a bout of depression, a severe disappointment, a sudden loss of self-belief, or simply a marriage. More than once, and by more than one wife, I have been accused of 'flouncing' out, but it wasn't a flounce, it was just an irresistible compulsion to walk away from the anguish of conflict, and suffer it on my own. There are Walter Sickert paintings and Thomas Hardy poems that evoke the walled-in suffocation of couples no longer in love; in every case, all parties would have benefited from a walk. I don't say they would have been happier, but walking suits and even explains unhappiness, and so makes for a sort of private harmony of wretchedness.

Some will no doubt maintain that a bracing walk can express high spirits but the fact that they've slipped in the word 'bracing' proves that a walk for them is not a walk for me. There was a popular German song we all made fun of in the 1950s called 'The Happy Wanderer', or *'Der Fröhliche Wanderer'*. 'I love to go a wandering,' it began, and then we'd all join in with 'Val-deri, Val-dera, Val-deri, Val-dera-ha-ha-ha-ha-ha', the false Germanic ha-has giving the lie to the idea that shlepping a knapsack through the Tyrol made you happy.

In fact, all the great wanderers – Cain, Werther, the rejected lover in Schubert's *Winterreise* – were miserable as sin. Walking is motion to feel bad to. Stumble on felicity and you'll never walk again. And that's why the happy put on weight. Why they also lose inches is a question I'm working on.

At least the old aren't young

IT'S A SURE SIGN I'm getting old, according to a study the newspapers are carrying, that I fall asleep in front of the TV. I say 'study', but it's no more than simple answers to simple questions collated by the insurance company Engage Mutual. So what am I doing reading stuff like this at my age? I'm waiting to see my doctor, that's what. And when you're waiting to see your doctor, you read whatever's lying about. I can also tell you, for example, the cost of a six-bedroom, 25-acre property in Chipping Norton, and what Katie Price – or is it Katy Perry, or is it Katie Holmes? – has for breakfast. Nothing. That's what she has for breakfast, not the value of the six-bedroom property in Chipping Norton. Shaming to know such things. Why do we fritter away the hours we spend waiting to see a doctor – hours that could be our last on Earth – on flim-flam? Answer me that, Engage Mutual.

I'm angered by their ice-cream study. Angry with myself for bothering to go through the fifty things that prove I'm past it. Angry with the quietist assumptions that always underpin lists of this sort, as for example that being angry is a sign you're getting old, not that there's something to be angry about. Why is dissatisfaction taken to be a mark of failing powers and patience, when it might just as easily be understood as a proper judgement on a foolish world? Since we know that to be young is to be in a permanent, albeit conformist quarrel with everything and everybody, why is the anger of the aged judged differently? Why is an old man's anger invariably reduced to the status of querulousness?

Take No. 15 on the list: 'Finding you have no idea what young people are talking about' – far from being evidence of decrepitude, might this not be a) good manners, as in minding one's own business; b) seasoned indifference to opinions still at the foetal stage; c) absorption in ideas of one's own, as when William Blake's wife told visitors her husband couldn't receive them because he was in paradise? Absent-mindedness can often be another word for having better things to think about.

Ditto falling asleep in front of the television. I, for one, don't do it because I'm old. I do it because I've lost interest. I never fell asleep during *Borgen* or *The Sopranos*. And when I did start to fall asleep during *Curb Your Enthusiasm*, it was because it had started to be unfunny. In fact, I have always fallen asleep watching television when it's humdrum, which is much of the time. So why don't I do something else? Because the sleep you get in front of TV is of a particularly high order in that it combines active criticism with rest. We speak of the sleep of the just; we should speak also of the sleep of the discerning.

No. 22 of Engage Mutual's fifty symptoms of senescence is 'complaining about the rubbish on television these days'. Thus they have you either way. You're an old fart if you let the pap send you to sleep, and you're an old fart if you make an active stand against it. Which leaves the young where? Either too dumb to notice how dull most television is, or too pusillanimous to complain.

Although the signs of ageing we are told to look out for are of the pipe-and-slippers sort – hating noisy pubs, liking cups of tea, driving slowly, falling asleep after a single glass of wine (messy if you're already asleep watching television), forgetting the names of bands, dressing according to the weather, not knowing any songs in the Top 10 – in fact, there is an implicit rebelliousness here against everything the young, in all their earnest conventionality, never dream of questioning. It isn't retirement that bugs the authors of this study; it's intransigence. The old simply refuse to play along.

Of the accusations devised by capitalism to make the no-longer obedient feel bad about themselves, this is the most heinous: that not agreeing, not accepting, not buying into the manufactured trends of musicolatry – not being good little consumers, in short – mark you out as grumpy old men and women. I don't mean to turn this into a war between the generations. It's miserable enough for the young already without old men like me pointing out their shortcomings, but it does them no favours to treat their slavishness to fads, received opinions, mass delusion, and every other species of regimentation, as manifestations of vigour. Only in body does youth triumph over age. And the old must never begrudge the young abusing those bodies as we enjoyed abusing ours. Thereafter, though, we must teach them to look forward to physical ruination for the consolations it brings: wearing clothes that fit, not being pissed every hour the devil sends, forgetting what you can't be bothered remembering, falling asleep in front of the TV.

But youth and age are only superficially adversaries. In some we call old, youth remains vividly present, just as in some we call young, the fossil is there for all to see. It's naivety, which is no respecter of age, we need to watch. To pass the time in the surgery I began composing a rival list of fifty things that show you are naive. 1: Watching *The Apprentice*. 2: Expressing shock that countries spy on one another. 3: Thinking there'd be no more terrorists if we addressed the causes of terrorism. 4: Having a favourite band. 5: Riding a bicycle in cities. 6: Assuming England are going to win the Ashes hands down . . .

The doctor called me in before I could finish. I mentioned I'd been reading a survey about old age. He got me to try touching my toes. 'Now that's what I call old,' he said.

There's always another Dark Lady

Lovers of shakespeare's sonnets – and who that reads this paper isn't? – will be relieved to learn that the identity of the Dark Lady, supposed addressee of the final twenty-four, has been uncovered. No, not Aemilia Bassano, poetess and lover of Lord Hunsdon, who was a patron of the Lord Chamberlain's Men, for whom Shakespeare wrote and whose mistress, therefore, by the febrile logic of biographical scholarship, he would not have been able to keep his hands off. Nor was she Lucy Negro, the Clerkenwell whore, sometimes called Black Luce but always referred to as 'notorious' – a prime candidate, by the same scholastic logic, for the reason that Shakespeare was often in Clerkenwell.

In the minds of literary biographers, a poet has only to have strolled down a street in early evening for the likelihood to arise of his having sired a family of eight there. Let him have come within half a mile of another man's mistress, whether strumpet, versifier or both, and the chances of his not having had carnal relations with her are minimal. Grant but a tenth of the suppositions made about his sex life and you can see why in Sonnet 110 Shakespeare berated himself for having gone 'here and there' and made himself 'a motley to the view'.

But don't forget that Sonnet 110 predates the Dark Lady sequence and must have been addressed either to the Earl of Pembroke or the Earl of Southampton, though why it couldn't equally have been addressed to Hunsdon, preparatory to Shakespeare's nabbing his concubine, or even John Greene, who kept a disorderly house in Cow Lane, Clerkenwell, which Shakespeare was bound to have passed on his way to meeting Black Luce, I don't know, but the preference of literary biographers for earls probably accounts for it.

The Dark Lady, anyway, according to Dr Aubrey Burl, fellow of the Society of Antiquaries, turns out to have been Aline Florio, wife of John Florio, the translator of Montaigne. This will not come as a surprise to the distinguished Shakespearean Jonathan Bate who, in his book *The Genius of Shakespeare*, published fifteen years ago, cautions against 'reducing the sonnets to their origin' but then reduces them for the hell of it. 'My Dark Lady,' he whispers in the trembling reader's ear, 'is John Florio's wife.' Scholars being nothing if not magnanimous, Professor Bate will be happy to have Dr Burl's belated corroboration.

We won't elaborate here on the reasons adduced by both men for their choice – Aline Florio was someone Shakespeare would have met (and we know where that always led); her husband was old (and we know where that always led); Shakespeare had a thing for witty women and Aline Florio (Bate has to invoke genetics to get this to run) was the sister of a witty man; and she was born of low degree in Somerset, which would explain the darkness of her complexion if not the inconstancy of her nature. Enough. Let the Dark Lady be whoever the Dark Lady was. It is not our affair personally, given that Shakespeare chose it not to be, and it is not our affair aesthetically in that, as Stephen Greenblatt reminds us: 'It would be folly to take [the sonnets] as a kind of confidential diary, a straightforward record of what actually went on.'

Of the misconceptions that continue to bedevil literature, this is among the most obdurate: that it is a record, straightforward or otherwise, of something that actually happened. Even the most sophisticated readers will forget all they know of the difference between literature and life when biography perchance shows its slip. I recall not only a publisher but an agent conscientiously worrying that the end of one of my novels would cause great pain to my two devout but estranged daughters. In fact, I have no daughters, just a son from whom I am not estranged and who is not devout. I take the error as a compliment; my writing, it seemed, was so vivid, that what was imagined could pass as real.

But you would think the case no longer needed to be made, that what is wrought by the imagination vies with actuality, transforming beyond recognition any 'truth' that might have been lurking in its lees. I am not the I of my novels. I am not even the I of these columns. It doesn't matter that there are resemblances. No matter how like the I of reality the I in whose name I write is, he is still a construct. Forgive the apparent self-concern, but in fact it isn't me I'm talking about, any more than we should suppose that the Will in Sonnets 135 and 136, which play ingeniously, if sometimes tiresomely, upon the poet's name – 'Whoever hath her wish, thou hast thy Will, / And Will to boot, and Will in over-plus' – is Shakespeare stripped of art and artifice and coming clean about himself. There is no coming clean in art.

Before he breaks his own rule, Jonathan Bate says we should 'allow the sonnets to rest in a middle space between experience and imagination'. I like the phrase but think he still gives too much to 'experience', which is beyond our reach and business. It's possible that had there been no Dark Lady, had Shakespeare never wandered into Clerkenwell or stolen reechy kisses from the wife of a scholar too busy translating Montaigne to notice, these sonnets about loathing what you love, about believing what you know to be untrue, about the falsity at the very heart of sexual desire, would not have spoken to us with such disquieting force. But there's always another Dark Lady. Isn't that what these poems proclaim: that erotic love is full of pain and contradiction, an eternal search for an anguish one cannot bear and cannot bear to be without? We diminish them by making them the story of an actual affair. We diminish thought, we diminish imagination, and we diminish art.

Bastard

WE TAKE THE GOOD times with the bad in this column. Life isn't all Twitter and terror and porn. In proof whereof I am pleased to share with readers the news that I have been made an honorary Australian. In my heart I've been an honorary Australian a long time, but now it's official.

The title was conferred on me by the Australian High Commissioner, Alexander Downer, at a moving ceremony in London last week. I have a medal to prove it. The only downside is that the honour lasts a mere twelve months. This time next year, someone else will get it and I'll just be any old Pommy bastard again.

Between ourselves, reader, it was being called a Pommy bastard that made me fall for Australia in the first place. Written down, it doesn't have much to recommend it, I grant you, but breathed into your face *in situ* – which might be a sophisticated cocktail lounge peopled by bankers and newspapermen in the middle of Sydney, or an outback bear pit with sawdust on the floor and twenty stockmen in Chelsea boots and ankle socks leering at you from the bar – the phrase 'you Pommy bastard' expresses a warmth, I'd even go so far as to say a sentimentality, it is near impossible to convey to anyone who has never been its recipient.

I'd led a sheltered life before I went to Australia. Until that time no man had poured a flagon of red wine on my head, knocked me to the ground, sat on my chest, called me 'Pommy bastard', then wept into my neck. Time goes slowly while this is happening – slowly enough for you to decide you're going to report the incident to the local constabulary, unless it's the local constabulary that's sitting on your chest, or for you to acknowledge that in some hitherto undiscovered recess of your maleness you're enjoying it. The former denominates you as a 'whingeing Pom' – the worst sort of Pom there is – the latter frees you from ever being referred to as a Pom again. From now on you're just plain 'bastard'. In other words, you're mates, and mateship in Australia can flower quickly into love.

But it isn't love as love is understood in this country. It skips all the usual courtship rituals and doesn't conform to gender stereotypes. It isn't, that's to say, a prelude to another level of intimacy, hetero or otherwise. When, with a watery eye, you call a man a bastard, you aren't looking to take the relationship to another level. This is where you want it to stay, with you calling the bastard a bastard and the bastard calling you a dag – a dag, for the uninitiated, being the dung-matted locks of wool that hang from a sheep's behind. Only someone who knows why it's a compliment to be likened to what's sticking to a sheep's arse will ever make it to be an honorary Australian.

These reminiscences date me somewhat, I accept. Manners are smoother in Australia than they were when I spent time there in the 1960s and 70s. And while I do still have Australian friends I call mate when their wives are in the room and a dag when it's just them and me and all the beer we can drink, I'm beginning to suspect from the half-hearted way they call me bastard in return that they are allowing me this for old times' sake but otherwise indulge it with no one else. So before you go out there and call the first bloke in an Akubra you meet a dag, I'd check that the customs of the country remain as I've described them.

But no matter how much Australia has changed, there remains a nostalgia for the old ways, as I discovered the other night when I publicly thanked the High Commissioner for the honour and riffed briefly along the lines of the previous paragraphs. No sooner did I finish speaking than two hundred Australians called me bastard, eager to reinvest the word with all its old wild gusto. One of those Australians, also there to receive an award, was Kylie Minogue. The moment I returned to my seat she flashed me one of her most dazzling smiles across the table, through the singed ferns and flickering candlelight. 'You bastard!' she said.

Ah, reader, you should have been there.

Australia – and this is why I love the place – is the only country in the world where the word bastard is an endearment. There are obvious reasons for this. Australians don't define themselves by their legitimacy. The more dubious and rough-edged their origins, the prouder they are. A bastard, therefore, is one of them. There was a period when Australians tried to conceal their past in a suburban social primness of the sort Barry Humphries first parodied and subsequently apotheosised, making a Melbourne housewife a figure of the most anarchic mirth – but once that cat was out of the bag, and especially at the margins, in bohemia and in the bush, they rejoiced in whatever was outlandish in their lineage and welcomed every sign of outlandishness in others.

The times we live in are too nice. Allow the wrong word to slip out and you have to grovel in apology. Let a joke get out of hand – and where's the point of a joke if you don't let it get out of hand? – and you'll be terrorised out of ever making a joke again. And the word terrorist itself, remember, is now to be eschewed lest it offend. All of which pusillanimity I refer to only by way of praising the easy give-and-take of Australian manners. We all live better when we make a social virtue out of giving offence.

But enough of this. In just six days, Noam Chomsky has accused me of missing the point – which means I haven't – and Kylie Minogue has called me a bastard – which means I am. What a joyous week it's been!

Scrooge

THERE SHOULD HAVE BEEN snow on the ground and the Salvation Army playing 'Silent Night' outside Waterstones. But you'll have to use your imagination if you want all that. As it was, the evening was mild and the only distinct sound to be heard was that of pedestrians' bones breaking under the wheels of cyclists running lights and riding pavements. I say the 'only' sound, but in fact I'd just learned Joe Cocker had died, so 'With a Little Help from My Friends' was playing in my head. No singer ever sang a song better. Now it was his obituary. And I was just off to the doctor.

We were of the same generation and roughly from the same neck of the woods, Joe Cocker and I, he a wild man from Sheffield, I a wild man from Manchester, though I suspect I read more Charlotte Brontë than he did. Every Saturday night I drove through Sheffield with my father on the way back from Worksop market, and in those days the flames still leapt with hellish allure from the city's steel-works. What if I left school, got a job as a gas fitter, and followed the smell of sulphur? Didn't happen. Jane Eyre won over Cocker. And the fires of Sheffield consumed me not.

There I was, anyway, off to the doctor, packing death as Australians say, because my stomach wasn't feeling right and my father was exactly the age I am now when his stomach did for him. Cocker's going just made it worse. Me next – another feral Northerner who'd lived too hard. Cocker, I imagined, the victim of late nights, blues and cigarettes, and I overdosing on sourdough bread and vintage Cheddar.

The astute reader will have spotted I am pleading extenuating circumstances. For what? Let's say a failure to live up to the spirit of

Christmas. But I had a doctor's appointment and I was, by my own standards of liking to be running early, running late. So when this person tapped me on the shoulder outside Waterstones and said he hoped I didn't mind him accosting me in the street, I had to do battle with impatience.

But he had a nice face. Shy, behind a black beard, self-effacing, untried. I could hardly say: 'Yes, I do mind.' I smiled at him. It felt like a smile from my end anyway, and it must have been encouraging because he went on to say: 'It's just that I'm trying to find a Christmas present for my mother.' And that's when I heard myself reply: 'I haven't got time for this.' In the moment of my brushing him off I saw he was pained. He blurted out an embarrassed apology for troubling me, but I was already down the road before I realised what he'd said, and by the time I began to feel I'd behaved badly he was gone.

I ran in the direction I thought he'd taken but couldn't find him. Unbidden, sounds of moaning issued from my throat. I had to lean against the window of Waterstones. I think I covered my face. One passer-by was good enough to ask me if I was all right. 'I will never be all right again,' I told her, 'and there's nothing you or anyone else can do about it. But thank you for asking.'

So what had happened between me and the shy man in the black beard? Something like this. I hadn't initially taken him for a con man or a beggar but the moment he mentioned his mother I saw a sob story coming. Like everyone, I get hoax emails from people purporting to be friends, saying their passport has been stolen in Vladivostok and they won't be able to get home to visit their dying mother in Limerick unless I send ten thousand pounds immediately. I even fell for such a scam in person many years ago in a Rome railway station. Not for quite so preposterous a sum, it's true, but I should still have figured out that the hustler – who said he was struggling to continue his studies as a nuclear physicist – was too young to have seven children, each in the terminal stage of every disease I'd ever heard of. Reader, what do these people take me for? Whatever else, I wasn't going to fall for that one again. And believe me when I say I was late for my appointment with the gastroenterologist.

But what if this hadn't been a con? I replayed the young man's words. I saw his hurt expression. And I recalled the good impression he'd originally made on me. I even thought I'd noticed he was carrying a roll of wrapping paper. What if he was genuinely looking for a present for his mother and either thought I was of an age to know what mothers liked receiving or – and here was the agonising part – he knew my work and wanted me to accompany him into Waterstones to sign a book for her. You could read this last concern cynically. I didn't want a reader of mine to have a bad opinion of me. True, I didn't. But more than that, I couldn't forgive the rudeness of my rebuff to what I now decided was a perfectly innocent overture: 'Hello, would you be so kind as to sign a book for my mother?' 'Fuck off.'

Fuck off, I might be dying, might have sounded a little better. But it was the season of goodwill, for God's sake. I might just as well have said: 'Fuck off, it's Christmas.'

Then again, since it was Christmas, would it have been so terrible to have given him the little help he wanted whether or not he was pulling a fast one?

Beggars have mothers too. And what did it matter if he didn't? Whoever he was – reader or rascal – I had wronged him. Consumed with shame and sorrow, I stumbled into the consulting rooms. The doctor felt my stomach and talked to me at length, but I couldn't listen. For all I know, I'm dead already.

Is that all there is?

Ireckon I was about eighteen when I discovered despondent hedonism. It was listening to Peggy Lee singing 'Is That All There Is?' that did it. If that's all there is, my friends, then let's bring out the booze and keep dancing.

As a philosophy of life it has much to recommend it. If nothing else it solves the problem, at the heart of monotheism, of what to do next. God created us, now what? Are we just to go on saying thank you? If that's all there is to religion . . .

The Peggy Lee song came back to me, sacrilegiously you might think, during a performance of Haydn's *Creation* in the Great Hall of University College School, London, this week. It was a half-amateur, half-professional affair, though it was the amateur half – the UCS Centenary Choir – that attracted me. It's one of the great joys of Christmas in this country that there's a mass or oratorio being performed somewhere just about every day. And precisely because the choirs are amateur they can be relied on to perform with a marvellous verve. The UCS Haydn was no exception. But were they too thinking, as the concert finished, that they'd glimpsed sublimity and now what?

Haydn's *Creation* begins wonderfully. Darkness broods upon the deep. For a moment we want the universe to stay that way, without form or clatter, undisturbed, uncreated. It is described as chaos, but this is less boisterous than chaos. The spirit of God suddenly moving on the face of the waters is thus unwelcome – an ominous intrusion of divine vandalism – until the orchestra responds explosively to His call for light and we realise that it is better to be alive, even if it's noisy, than to be unborn.

Everything is now thrilling as God busies Himself dividing light from darkness, dispelling spirits whose malignancy hadn't bothered us previously, filling the heavens and inundating those parts of earth destined to be seas. Rain falls, hail, 'the light and flaky snow', and in an exquisite aria the angel Raphael hymns the 'softly purling rivers' and the 'limpid brook'.

Reader, whatever you do or don't believe, these first days of creation are lovely, no matter that no poet has yet been created to describe them. Sometimes undescription is good too. But try telling God that. No sooner has He formed the beasts – the nimble stag, the sinuous worm, the flexible tiger – than He begins to ask Himself if this is all there is. What He's missing is praise. A being who will 'God's power admire'. Enter *Homo sapiens*.

Knowing what we know now, we should have said no then. But the offer was too good to resist: a life of 'incessant bliss' partnered, if you're the man, by a woman of 'softly smiling virgin looks' or, if you're the woman – O lucky virgin, you! – by a man who'll be your guide at 'every step'. But disillusion sets in at once. With nothing to do but extol God's virtues in language that evokes Chief Sitting Bull's – 'Him celebrate, Him magnify!' – Adam and Eve fall to asking if that's all there is.

This is where I come unstuck whenever I visit a synagogue or a church. The Him celebrating. Is that all there is to faith? Saying thanks until you start to choke on the word? The advantage I enjoy over Adam and Eve is that I can walk out and find some booze. They, bored to within an inch of their lives, have to get themselves expelled.

Sin is the natural response to not knowing what to do next, a confession that the grandeur you were promised hasn't eventuated. Smart religions build sin in, so that you will feel your dereliction is in fact another form of faith. I read Graham Greene avidly as a boy, fascinated by the idea that the worse you behaved the holier you were. Now I realise that this is one of religion's solutions to the problem of its inherent tedium.

Another is terrorism. Rather than capitulate to despondent hedonism, let's blow somebody's brains out. The great advantage such extremism enjoys over the soul-searching Western liberalism to which we haltingly subscribe is the promise it holds out to its would-be adherents that they won't ever be left asking what next.

We, the children of Creation, remain locked in the paradigm of enticement and disappointment. Bathos is in our bones. We know no 'softly smiling virgin' awaits us in Paradise when we have killed our hostages. Yet somehow that knowledge leaves us weak instead of strong.

Is it because we fear we cannot offer the young anything like as good a time as ISIS can? Are we secretly envious of those who aren't wondering if that is all there is? Is that why, in our descriptions of ourselves, we act as their recruiting agents?

The gunman who held up the Lindt cafe in Sydney has been described as a 'lone wolf'. Reader, there is no such thing. A man may act alone but no one thinks alone. In the melange of ideologies he expressed before he killed was much he would have found simply by reading the papers we write. If you oppose the West, we will induct you into the hows and whys of hating us, because no one hates the West more than the West hates itself. If you want to make a bomb to blow us up, we will show you how to do it online.

Careless talk costs lives, but we welcome its dissemination on the Internet as the very emblem of our liberty. Though we know we are a lethal species, we forbid invigilation of our menace. To the exhausted liberal who believes in nothing, this at least remains an article of faith: the freedom to say what you like, when you like, where you like. And whoever warns of danger is a fearmonger.

Soon, this faith too will pall and we will ask if that is all there is. Only by then there won't even be a 'that'.

Flyting, sledging, and where to stick your asterisks

TODAY I WRITE on 'SLEDGING Considered As One of the Fine Arts'. Sledging, for those not familiar with the term, is the practice of on-field verbal intimidation much favoured by Australian cricketers though by no means confined to them. Every cricket team sledges, though some do it with more aplomb than others.

As with all aspects of sport, national character is the first determinant of success. The more refined and well mannered the culture, the less accomplished its sledgers. I don't say the corollary follows – I am too fond of Australia to put its love of vilification down to something primitive in the country's psyche – but you only have to read Australia's national poem, 'The Bastard from the Bush' ('Fuck me dead, I'm Foreskin Fred, the Bastard from the Bush'), to see an essential connection between verbal violence and a remote colonial lifestyle.

That said, it's important to place sledging in a tradition of insult-flinging to which even the most sophisticated literature owes a debt. Drama, we are told, originates in the sacrificial, propitiatory rituals of ancient communities. We put on a show for the gods and hope they applaud. Poetry originates in the impulse to exchange insults with fellow mortals. 'Get back to where you come from, that's somewhere in the bush' is how the Captain of the Push responds to the challenge to his authority thrown down by Foreskin Fred. 'May the itching piles torment you, may corns grow on your feet, / May crabs as big as spiders attack your balls a treat. / Then, when you're down and out, and a hopeless bloody wreck, / May you slip back through your arsehole, and break your bloody neck.'

Indistinguishable from the satisfaction of getting your own back, hurling abuse and imagining someone else's suffering is the joy of deploying rhyme and rhythm. We never curse better than we curse in verse. Primary-school playgrounds resound with the scurrilous ditties small children make up about one another. My best friend Martin Cartwright couldn't leave the classroom without hearing 'Farty Marty / Spoils the party'. For years I had to put up with 'Howardy Cowardy Custard / Thinks his pants have rusted'. And a poor religious boy called Manny was yoked with such tireless invention and horrid ingenuity to fanny that his parents had finally to remove him from the school.

Flyting, it's called in Scotland – where poets would formalise the loathing they felt for each other into a contest of invective strictly governed by the laws of poesy. 'Come kiss my Erse' was how the sixteenth-century poet Montgomerie began his assault on the poet Polwart. 'Kiss the Cunt of the Cow,' Polwart retorted in kind. We can perhaps look forward to a resumption of such well-honed hostilities when the campaign for Scottish independence begins in earnest.

At carnival time in Trinidad, some of the country's smartest poets, singers and comedians take to the stage to compete in Extempo War, an off-the-cuff battle of wits in which the grosser they are to one another, the more the audience likes it. Whether the dozens – the game of dissing, snapping and toasting played on the streets of Harlem and St Louis – is an offspring of Extempo War I don't know, but it seems likely. It values the same qualities of quickness of wit and coarse discourtesy.

Another name for it is Ya Mama – unmannerliness to one another's mothers being part of the fun. 'You wanna play the dozens, well, the dozens is a game. But the way I fuck your mother is a goddam shame,' rhymed the comedian George Carlin.

Which is a bit ripe even for the Gabba where the Australian captain, Michael Clarke, was heard to say to say to an English player, 'Get ready for a f****** broken arm.' I resort to asterisks, not because Clarke did, but because that was how most of the papers reported it. Myself, I think asterisks make what he said even worse. Clarke himself has a baby face, so his outburst appeared doubly shocking, but some among his team look as though they were born with asterisks in their mouths.

What concerns me most about this incident, however, is the placing of the expletive. What Flyters, Extempo Warriors and kids in the school playground all know is that word order matters. Put a fucking where a fucking shouldn't be and you take fatally from the affront. 'Get ready for a fucking broken arm' doesn't work for two reasons. 1: It doesn't scan. And 2: The epithet's misaligned; it's not the 'broken' you're meant to be cursing but the 'arm'.

I haven't played much cricket myself. Table tennis was my game. But I was always careful at the table to be precise when I swore. Attentive to both the music and the meaning, I'd have said to my opponent, 'Get ready for a broken fucking arm.' Except that I wouldn't, of course, have said that because it's pretty difficult to break someone's arm with a celluloid ball measuring 40mm in diameter and weighing 2.7g.

This could be the reason so few words are exchanged between players in the course of a game of ping-pong. You look ridiculous issuing threats when you don't have the equipment to carry them out. Or the will, come to that. Somewhere at the back of every table-tennis player's mind is the knowledge that your opponent is as sad as you are. Why compound the lack of self-esteem that made him a table-tennis player in the first place?

So humanity comes into the equation after all. To sledge with style requires a ripe vocabulary, an ear for cadence, a fastidiousness as to the positioning of epithets and respect for your opponent. You want to topple him from high estate to low. You don't want him down and out to start with. Australians don't always get that.

Wasp watching

OF BICYCLISTS AND BUFFOONS I sing. I don't yoke the two by violence together. They yoke themselves. Together they appeared, night after night on the news last week – sometimes separated by a story about football or the latest brutality in the Middle East, but never so far apart that we could miss the vital connection between them. That connection is boredom. Only boredom on a near-universal scale could explain the attraction of either. So it isn't only of bicyclists and buffoons I sing. I sing of bicyclists, buffoons and boredom.

Let's start with the buffoons. The popular-culture paedophile buffoons I'm talking about, who hoodwinked us, in the course of their predations – indeed, as a necessary preliminary to their predations – into finding them diverting. The degree to which buffoonery links them only occurred to me while watching old clips of Cyril Smith hamming it up. A politician, it's true, but he made of politics a popular-culture plaything, just as he made of himself a joker, never off our screens, cropping up in order to mouth fridge-magnet platitudes on chat shows, interposing his bulk between entertainment and the serious business of politics – and how frightening that bulk must have been if you were the unfortunate child who had to cower from it – deploying his lovable Rochdale accent to put an end to nonsense, and laughing all the way to the boys' lavatories like the clown in a fun palace.

We all knew there was something not right about him. All that public doting on his mother. Who else was it who did that? Oh yes, Jimmy Savile. Was it code? I now wonder. Was doting on your mother an earnest of shared interests, a sort of Masonic handshake (meaning no disrespect to Masons), a perverts' Polari for paedophilia? My mother's fine, thank you, nudge nudge. How's yours?

But shouldn't we have been able to do better than just feel something wasn't quite right? You can forgive a child thinking that mirth is always innocent, but it is not forgivable in an adult. Men whose shtick is a rollicking, avuncular, ma-mad incorrigibility, who are more children than adults themselves, men who pull silly faces, emit foolish noises and make themselves friends of the family – isn't it time we woke up to what all that is likely to denote?

I recall a television adaptation of Stephen King's *It* that played with our deep-seated terror of clowns, and I often confuse it with *Killer Klowns from Outer Space*, a film which attributes that terror to the fact that clowns are aliens who long ago invaded and brutalised our planet. Forgive me if I'm confusing both those films with a third that might not even have been made but which plays only in my head. In that one it's the devil who's the clown. Things aren't as they seem with clowns, anyway. We know in the depths of our psychologies that the impulse to make people laugh is close to the impulse to laugh at people, and that both are sadistic. Was Jimmy Savile laughing at us? Was Rolf Harris? Was Cyril Smith?

We will never know, but it's enough to be going on with that they footled with the nation's attention and we let them. Did we have nothing better to do? No. We were bored and so we laughed at Jimmy Savile who wasn't funny and smirked when Rolf Harris swung his extra leg and nodded in amused agreement at the chucklesome Cyril's Smith's sinister sagacity. Life was dull. They brightened it.

That there is no end to what people will do to relieve their boredom was proved by the millions who came out from their cottages in the Yorkshire Dales to watch cyclists in horrible clothes whizz past. It would be easier to understand why people would line the roads to watch a swarm of wasps. I'm told the Yorkshire tourist board is rubbing its hands in anticipation of next year's invasion of visitors who, thanks to the Tour de France, have now seen how beautiful the Dales are. Rivers, valleys, scars, stone cottages, carbon cycling helmets, luminous bib shorts, Oakley Jawbone goggles with scarlet lenses – ah, reader, the loveliness of nature, where every aspect pleases and only pedestrians are vile.

Cyclists think I have it in for them, but I don't. I love cyclists – in their place. That place being France. If every cyclist were to join Le Tour de France, foot soldiers like me would have only buses and juggernauts to worry about in town. No more being told to 'Fuck off!' when you remind a cyclist that red lights are for stopping at and pavements are for walkers. I would make it compulsory: whoever would ride a bike must spend half of every year riding it from Besançon to Pau.

None of which, however, solves the mystery of spectators. More people lined the roads of Yorkshire to see the Tour de France than live there. Cambridge to London the same. And along the Mall the crowds were denser than on VE Day. I don't complain that you could barely move in London if you had other business. I'm used to it. And it would be churlish to put one's own idle interests as a compulsive non-participant before those of athletes who are said to add to the nation's gaiety.

But here's my question: where exactly, if you aren't competing, is the gaiety? Reader, there is little enough to see in a marathon, but in a cycle race there is nothing to see at all. A thousand men indistinguishable except for the colour of their helmets and the tautness of their Lycra speed past, and if you happen to blow your nose they've gone.

But still the crowds gather, wave flags, point phones and cheer. So what are they cheering? There can be only one answer to that. Themselves. They have secured an unrivalled view of something not worth seeing simply for the sake of securing it. They can tweet they were there. At the event. What event? Any event. Because being at an event beats not being at an event.

Oh, boredom, boredom, you old tyrant!

Steady on, Lawrence

ONE OF THE MORE enigmatic statements on the British economy made by Mervyn King before he bowed out was that Jane
Austen was waiting in the wings. Anyone not paying full attention – as I wasn't – might have supposed that King had finally lost
his marbles: were things really that moribund in the City that his
best replacement as Governor of the Bank of England was a long-
dead novelist, no matter how alive her prose? It turned out that
what Jane Austen was waiting in the wings for was the chance to
have her face on the £10 note.

Alien as such a conjunction of literature and filthy lucre is to an
old idealist like me, I applaud the choice. But if that's the tenner
sorted, may I put forward D. H. Lawrence as the new face of our
fiver? This year is not only the 200th anniversary of the publication of *Pride and Prejudice*; it is also the 100th birthday of *Sons and
Lovers*. Lawrence didn't like Jane Austen much, and she probably
wouldn't have cared for him, but there's no law that says the people
on our currency have to get on. As for the conjunction of filthy
lucre and literature being even more inappropriate in the case of
Lawrence, who scarcely earned a penny from his work and scorned
materialism – 'Money poisons you when you've got it, and starves
you when you haven't,' he wrote in *Lady Chatterley's Lover* – well,
there have been stranger marriages. I once owned a D. H. Lawrence
Medal for Promptness that came as a reward for signing up without
delay to a book society and agreeing to take six volumes a year, and
who has ever thought of Lawrence as notable for promptness?

We don't, it seems to me – promptness apart – value Lawrence
as highly as we should. He wrote two, maybe three, of the greatest twentieth-century English novels, countless very fine short

stories, some of the sharpest literary criticism (find me something to beat *Studies in Classic American Literature*), much original poetry, wonderful travel books, essays, journalism, letters, and forget about the paintings. All this before his forty-fifth year. If Jane Austen had genius – and I yield to no one in my admiration for it – then we need another word again for what Lawrence had. It's no surprise he had recourse so often to language whose mysticism makes our prosaic times uneasy: when the well of your creativity is so deep, you must wonder who is speaking inside you and what impulses you are answering. Of such bemusement are prophets made.

Lacking deep wells of creativity ourselves, we scorn the wild words and warnings of such visionary writers, mistrust their fluency and vehemence, fear their long grey beards and glittering eyes, preferring the reserved, spare, well-shaved demeanour of those who work the surfaces of things.

Lawrence is not, for these and other reasons, the ideal writer for a reading group to tackle. This is not the first time I have addressed the phenomenon of the reading group. If anything should give one hope for the continuing vitality of our culture, it's the reading group. People giving up their time, willingly, to exchange informed, animated judgements about works of literature over wine and canapés – reader, I can think of nothing better. It's what passes as informed, animated judgement that's the problem.

Chairing the *Guardian* Reading Group's assault on *Sons and Lovers* recently, Sam Jordison, author of *Sod That!: 103 Things Not to Do Before You Die*, ventures to suggest that reading D. H. Lawrence might be one of them. 'We've already developed quite a rap sheet against Lawrence here on the Reading Group,' he writes, 'and to that growing list . . . I can also add being silly, tedious and sloppy.' Not great critical terms those, I would venture to suggest in return, not least as you must wonder why, if the faults of this novel are so glaringly obvious, readers as astute as Philip Larkin, who found 'nearly every page of it absolutely perfect', and Blake Morrison, who only the other day described it as 'momentous – a great book', failed to spot them.

I don't say we must bow before authority; in the great democracy of reading, our first duty is to report what we find. But we must also face the fact that sometimes all we find is ourselves. That which we call tedious might be no more than the echo of our limited capacity to be interested; that which we call silly no more than a prim refusal to let a writer take us where we are unwilling emotionally or unable intellectually to go.

Jordison cites the following passage from *Sons and Lovers* as evidence of Lawrence's silliness and sloppiness. 'She felt the accuracy with which he caught her, exactly at the right moment, and the exactly proportionate strength of his thrust, and she was afraid. Down to her bowels went the hot wave of fear. She was in his hands. Again, firm and inevitable came the thrust at the right moment. She gripped the rope, almost swooning.'

'That's a description,' says Jordison, 'of Paul pushing Miriam on a rope swing. Steady on!' Steady on, Turner, it's only a bloody sunset! Steady on, Wagner, it's only a ring! But it's not necessary to pursue the Michael Winner Calm Down Dear school of criticism to its philistine conclusion, because Jordison is doubly wrong in this instance – the passage is not a description of Paul pushing Miriam, it's a description of Miriam being pushed. The drama of quivering sexual fearfulness is entirely hers. To accuse Lawrence of overwroughtness when overwroughtness is his subject is like accusing Shakespeare of jealousy for creating Othello.

Reading is a two-way activity: some books fail us, but it happens just as frequently that we fail them. There's silly, sloppy writing out there, but there's silly, sloppy reading too.

Conformity kills

'WE NEED A COUNTER-narrative.' How often have we heard that since 7/7? We need to tell a better story to those young British Muslims for whom bombs and beheadings hold a greater allure than anything we have to offer. Someone's seducing them away with a narrative of lies, so we must seduce them back again with a narrative of truth.

There's a problem with narratives. Most that spring to mind are fictional. And while we like to think it's stories as subtle as *Ulysses* or humane as *Middlemarch* that drive civilisation along, in fact what quickens the popular imagination are simpler tales of goodies and baddies, in which the baddies are always someone else. Artless fairy stories enchant us in our first years and retain their hold on us until our last.

The government's proposed hymn to British values is equally naive. Man wakes up, kisses wife (but not in a homophobic sort of way), reads chapter of Magna Carta aloud to family, goes bareheaded to work, eats humanely killed pork sandwich, practises sundry acts of tolerance, returns home to gin and tonic, prays unfanatically to secular god, and goes to sleep thinking of the royal family. Indubitably, there are worse ways of getting through the tedium of existence, but as a narrative this one's unlikely to prevail against millenarian fantasy and a plentiful supply of virgins. In a battle of facile narratives, the one with more action wins.

But why must it be a choice, anyway, between blowing people up on buses and a docile embrace of British values to which very few Britons of any faith or temper subscribe? Extreme views can kill, but disagreement is the breath of life. Nonconformity has always been one of the great British virtues, and that includes nonconformity to things British. The terrorist isn't a problem because he doesn't conform; he's a problem because he does. It's what he conforms to that makes him dangerous.

That the thing he conforms to is not the spirit of Islam any number of commentators, Muslim and otherwise, have been arguing since 7/7. The point is taken. But that leaves open the question of where, then, we go to understand this particular form of terrorism's nature and motivation. If you're the softly spoken Jeremy Corbyn – and beware softly spoken men, I say; beware the snake who doesn't rattle his whereabouts in the undergrowth – you will argue that the barbarism of the terrorist can only be understood as a response to the barbarism of Western foreign policy. This is the pin-the-tail-on-the-wrong-donkey narrative in which the person who really planted those bombs on the London Underground was Tony Blair.

The writer Mehdi Hasan similarly sprays guilt around and, for good measure, suffering as well. If we think 7/7 was a terrible time for the victims, he wants us to remember who else got it in the neck. When the bombers were identified as British men with names like his, 'a knot tightened at the pit of my stomach', he wrote in the *Guardian*. 'We're screwed,' he told a Muslim friend. Beware the grammar of narrative. Self-concern appears to come too quickly here, trumping the horror of the moment. You're screwed, Mr Hasan? There are dozens dead and hundreds injured and bereaved, and *you're* screwed?

I'd be lying, however, if I didn't admit I understand the reflex. Let a Jew commit an atrocity and I, too, dread the communal consequences. Jews and Muslims share this knowledge: they know how the one is immediately made to stand for the all.

But understanding must work both ways. After 7/7, Mehdi Hasan complains, the Muslim community was subjected to 'unprecedented scrutiny'. But wasn't that an inevitable response to 'unprecedented outrage'? Where else, if not in the Muslim community, were we to look for explanations of a phenomenon that gave itself Islamic credentials and cited Islamic grievance as its motive? Yes, this was an arrogation of religious affiliation the terrorists had no right to claim. And yes, the scrutiny must have been demeaning and frightening for Muslims, the majority of whom should not have had to apologise for what they had not done. But everyone was demeaned and frightened. The dead should not have died for what they had not done either.

Mehdi Hasan's narrative separates the doer from the deed, forever finding baddies somewhere else. The scrutiny to which Muslims were subjected is seen as a driving force of terror, no matter that that scrutiny was itself provoked by terror. In this way is time inverted to change the dynamic of cause and effect, to remove the responsibility for their actions from those who act, and to apportion blame to everyone affected by a crime except the criminal. The British government, Mehdi Hasan continues, still scattershooting culpability, 'helped turn Libya into a playground for jihadists' – as though the playground can be held responsible for the playground bully, as though space creates what happens in it.

As a narrative, this is no more convincing than Cameron's hymn to British values. It might give comfort to people whose favourite fairy story it already is, but it is dangerously alienating of those who prefer more sophisticated reading and dangerously indulgent of those who don't. If a narrative of them-and-us lies at the heart of ISIS's recruitment success, how does the story Jeremy Corbyn and Mehdi Hasan tell slow that recruitment down? Whom will it deter? And whom, on the other side, will it persuade? But that's rhetoric for you: it cares only to hear itself speak. And so we are left still waiting for a story we can all believe in, and meanwhile the butchery goes on.

Happy now?

JUST BACK FROM A few days' holiday in the sun, the intended calming effects of which were vitiated more than a little a) by the fact of there being more sun back home and b) by the hotel's piping music in all its public places – niggling tunes that snagged the ear and sank the heart. Imagine 'The Girl from Ipanema' synthesised through the nostrils of a depressed camel from 8 a.m. until midnight and you have still not approached the torment of it. One particular melancholy repetition of sounds – I suspect Bedouin in origin, for no other reason than that it suggested long uneventful nights in the desert and the disappointments of another insufficiently spiced tagine – entered my brain on the first morning of my stay and remains with me a week later. The word for a tune that lodges in this way is an earworm, said to be borrowed from the German *Ohrwurm*, but it could just as easily be a corruption of earthworm, for that is exactly how it feels – as though an earthworm has invaded your head and is slowly and with a circular motion burrowing through your occipital lobes looking for whatever it is that earthworms eat, all the while humming to itself.

'It is quite a common thing,' Edgar Allan Poe wrote in a story called 'The Imp of the Perverse', 'to be annoyed with the ringing in our ears, or rather in our memories, of some ordinary song, or some unimpressive snatches from an opera.' And that was long before we possessed the technology to disseminate that annoyance simultaneously to millions. It surprises me, I have to say, that we expend so much energy fulminating against surveillance, convinced that governments employ phalanxes of spies (all as airless as Edward Snowden) to catch us doing what we have already posted videos of ourselves doing on Facebook, yet tolerate almost without demur the far less justified (and far more mentally damaging) intrusiveness of music – not just the fact of it wherever we set foot, but the assumption of it as something we cannot live without.

The phenomenon of the earworm is the subject of scholarly investigation at Goldsmiths, University of London, but don't get your hopes up. Far from proving scientifically what common observation teaches, that the earworm is ruinous to our mental health, and recommending that its means of transmission should therefore be proscribed or at least made subject to periodic moratoria – even one month of silence in every three would help – the team at Goldsmiths is uncritical, and might even be said to be upbeat, about its effects. Writing about it in the *Sunday Times* recently, Lauren Stewart, reader in psychology, said of Pharrell Williams's 'Happy' – a bit of earwormery that appears to have been composed with the express intention of being such – that 'it lights up all the areas that matter in the brain'.

It is not for a layman to disagree with a psychologist about which areas in the brain matter, but my brain is my brain and I can say on its behalf that 'Happy' lights up no part of it whatsoever. What, not even when Pharrell Williams gets the world dancing in the streets, spinning on its heels and singing 'Clap along if you feel like happiness is the truth'? No, reader, not even then.

Leaving my own brain out of it, I am not sure I am convinced by Lauren Stewart's argument on behalf of anyone else's. 'The repetition inherent to music like this is enjoyable,' she says – which to my mind immediately raises some of the questions she should be answering about the nature of enjoyment – 'because listening to music causes us to unconsciously make predictions about how a melody will continue. When these predictions are confirmed, the result is a cerebral high that can be as potent as any expected reward.'

If a cerebral high is what you get when you guess correctly where a tune of unsurpassable banality is going next, you might wonder what you have to do to get a cerebral low. But if that's how brains work – getting excited because the next popcorn tastes the same as the last – then that's how brains work, in us as in a hamster, but is it not a wonder, in that case, that we have ever been able to compose or listen to a melody that is *not* a masterwork of predictability?

I wrote with enthusiasm in this column, years ago, about the work being done at Liverpool University by Professor Philip Davis on the demands which reading Shakespeare makes on our brains. Shakespeare is good for the brain because of the strenuous exercise to which reading him subjects it. The more syntactically baffling a Shakespearean line, the more parenthetically distracting his thought, the more grammatically violent his expression, the more work the brain has to do to understand. Wonderful indeed, as registered by the electroencephalogram to which it is wired, are the brain's acts of cognitive athleticism, its leaps and urgent modulations, as it strives to keep up with what's challenging it. No easily attained 'high' here at having the predictable confirmed. What excites the brain in these experiments is precisely what it can't predict. So if we are to talk of parts of the brain 'mattering', surely the parts that Shakespeare reaches matter more.

Fair's fair – Lauren Stewart is addressing an earworm, not *Cymbeline*. And it's not her job to moralise about brains being lit up by drivel. But there are times when even the brain needs ticking off for being easily satisfied. The question of the earworm's function is one she knows she cannot dodge. One theory she is testing is whether it acts as a 'kind of sonic screensaver for the mind', triggering 'vigilance as to our environment'. An entirely unscientific, but better, explanation is that earworms warn us of the perils of listening to Pharrell Williams, of our slavish cerebral willingness to lapse into mental nothingness, of the necessity to free ourselves from the terrible, often cynical, tyranny of the tune.

A self-effacing man

MY WIFE'S UNCLE DIED last week. Her only uncle, which made him special, though he was important to us in other ways too. Everyone who dies is remembered for his sweetness of temper, but that truly described him. We found him hard to locate, so self-effacing was he, so accommodating and yet so locked away, as though by showing concern for others he didn't have to show himself. He was already getting on a bit when I met him, so I missed the deeds and misdeeds of his early and middle years that might have explained him. Right up until his death he had a glamorous companion, a Frenchwoman, herself cloaked in a degree of mystery. They went on cruises together in their eighties and must have cut quite a dash, she black-haired and painted as though for the last cocktail party on the planet, her eyes as jet as Cleopatra's, her ankles as slender as a young girl's, he in a blazer and a yachtsman's trousers, with a touch of David Niven about him, only with a more nautical moustache.

People who'd known him all his life were no less mystified. Did he have a secret life? In international politics? Espionage? Love? Once, as a man of eighty, he flattened a thug a quarter of his age who attacked him in the street. The police warned him against further acts of pensioner ruffianism. We live in insane times. We can no longer flatten thugs with impunity. It's a union thing: only thugs themselves are allowed to do the flattening. But he laughed it off, leaving us to wonder how this elegant, well-mannered elderly gentleman had the strength and know-how to do what he had done. Had he been trained in the martial arts? Could he kill with his little finger if he chose? Was he from Krypton?

He was on the management boards of hospitals, appointing senior staff, dispensing money and advice, counting eminent surgeons among his friends, though none could help him when he needed them most. But there was always a suggestion of some other mission.

Myself, I loved him for the calm he exuded, for his air of being a disinterested amateur in the job of life, for his refusal to sit in judgement on anybody, and because his being my wife's uncle rubbed off on me. I like other people's relatives, which isn't to say I don't like my own, but about other people's you experience none of the vexed loyalties of consanguinity. In his company I too felt an amateur in the job of life. Had I been closer to him in age I'd have enjoyed going cruising with him, sipping cocktails while his Frenchwoman beat her eyelashes at the captain.

His final illness was shockingly sudden but mercifully brief. He'd been in hospital about three weeks when my wife rang to say he'd asked for me. He was deteriorating but insistent and she felt I should get over right away. Why me in particular? Perhaps to tell me to love and look after his niece. But he knew I already did. Perhaps he wanted everybody close to him around his bed, the more especially as his partner was ill in another hospital herself, a separation which, the longer it continued, was taking on a tragic complexion.

He began making scribbling signals in the air the minute I arrived. His voice was gone, his throat ruined by the cancer. He was wired up to a barrage of screens that monitored every breath he struggled to take. The day before, he'd worn everybody out by persisting in raising an arm and lowering it again, pointing to the nurse and growling out a word that seemed to begin with an H. 'Helpful?' we'd tried. 'Hopeful? Hospital? Happy? No, not happy – hateful, heartfelt, hopeless?'

He'd grown exasperated with our stupidity. 'H – h – hi – hi . . .'

'Him,' we tried, 'hill, hymn, hirsute, hibiscus, hispid?'

He raised his arm again, pointed to the nurse, and then made a moustache with his other hand.

'Hilary? Hildegarde? Hitler? Hitler!'

He smiled, nodded, and fell back on his pillows.

His nurse was as bossy as Hitler, was his point. A joke. All that effort for a joke. My father had been the same when he was dying.

Making one more joke was all he cared about. Hearing laughter one last time. Men and their jokes! Some men will go to hell for a joke.

We knew, anyway, that whatever he wanted me to write about was going to be hard to decipher. We must have spent three hours on it. Eventually we made out the word 'police' and the word 'destruction'. That he could get out 'destruction' after the trouble he'd had (or we'd had) with 'Hitler' only went to show how fiercely he felt about whatever he believed had been destroyed. His health? Himself? We didn't doubt it. But then why 'police'? There are no cancer police. There is no one who will apprehend and punish cancer for you, and if there were such a person he'd probably tell you to leave it alone, that cancer, too, has human rights. So did he feel he'd been the object of criminal neglect? If so – and neglect is always possible in an age of hurried doctors and crowded hospitals, and he a man who knew about hospitals – it didn't tally with the praise he'd been expressing earlier for the care he had received. What then was I to say to the police? Who or what had been destroyed? And why did he need a writer to tell them?

Seeing me bemused, he sought another word. 'Am-mo. A-am-amo.' He settled on that. 'Am-mo.'

Amo, amas, amat? Was he trying to tell us who he loved? We thought we knew who he loved. No, he shook his head violently, rattling the tubes in which he was enmeshed. 'Amo, ammmo . . .'

Ammo. Ah – ammunition! Those gathered around him exchanged looks. Was the truth finally about to come out? Was I to tell the police about the ammunition, before it destroyed half of London? But whose ammunition, and where was it?

He gave up on us and fell asleep. Three hours later, he died. Leaving me with a job to do, but not knowing what. I expect to go on wondering forever. Amo. Ammo. Or was he teasing to the end? 'Am only joking' – was that he was saying? 'Am only pulling your leg.'

We know nothing. Neither of our going hence nor our coming hither. My wife's uncle was the only person I've ever met who seemed contented with that thought. The loveliest of men, mystery or no mystery.

When enough's enough

THOUGH NEVER MUCH GIVEN to heroising, I did, when I was sixteen, heroise a Regency dandy who killed himself because he could no longer be bothered doing up his buttons. I would act likewise when the time came, I thought. Wasn't I half bored to death already? I saw myself writing the suicide note and then being too bored to finish it. 'Goodb . . .' I'd write. I imagined with satisfaction my friends and family puzzling over what I was trying to tell them.

By what means my existential dandy did himself in, I can no more remember than I can his name, but I like to think he died swallowing buttons. A good suicide should be death by what you no longer want to live to do. Or know about.

So if you're up to here with loud music, you should put on your worst clothes, talk your way into a club for fourteen-year-olds and go to sleep by one of the speakers. If you can't any longer live in a world of mad cyclists, just wait at a traffic junction for the lights to say it's safe to cross, and cross. If you've exhausted your interest in the rituals of dining, reading reviews, making reservations and checking bills to see if service is included, book a table in Mayfair and choke publicly on caviar, refusing with your last words to leave a tip. Alternatively, fill the bath with Krug, float your duck and go under. Sex the same – though the precise manner of death by sex must be left to individual predilection. I know how I want to go – that's all I'm saying.

This hasn't been a good week for dying by whatever means. We don't need to have known much about Peaches Geldof while she was alive to feel the infinite sadness of her in death. This is a story of unimaginable grief all round, tragic in a way that makes us reach for analogies beyond the accidents of personality and profession. To speak of the House of Atreus might be going too far, but it does seem as though, here again, the gods have some score to settle.

That Peaches Geldof gave birth to a son on what would have been the anniversary of her mother's birthday and that she chose to call him – strangely for a boy – Phaedra, only adds to the sense of fatality. 'It's all in the saga,' as D. H. Lawrence wrote when he heard that Rupert Brooke had died. 'O God, O God, it is all too much of a piece: it is like madness.'

If we didn't already know how damaging to a child is the prema-ture death of a parent, especially if that death smacks of recklessness or despair, we certainly know it now. To say we don't belong to ourselves is not to say anything original or even necessarily true. But have children and your life is no longer yours to play with. Whether that should make me reconsider my admiration for the dandy who could no longer be bothered dressing must depend on his paternal status. But I assume him to have been without offspring. If he'd had a child he would surely have got him to help with the buttons.

As for the eighty-nine-year-old woman who recently killed herself at the Dignitas assisted suicide clinic, and identified herself simply as Anne, the question doesn't apply. She had no child on whom the fact of a mother's not wanting to live would lie forever like a curse. Which leaves us free to consider the virtue of her actions without the distraction of consequence. And you won't be surprised to hear me say, reader, after what I have said already, that her decision to put an end to a life that no longer interested her strikes me as entirely admirable. Upsetting – for it is no small thing to feel that existence has lost its savour – but impressive in its clear-sightedness, its lack of fuss and its independence of spirit. This was the Roman way, before Christianity rhapsodised the indignity of suffering.

It is not our business to agree with her or not. The world is full of people who will tell you they have never experienced a day's boredom in their life, from which one can only conclude that they have never experienced a day's imaginativeness either. Their opin-ions are irrelevant anyway. Distaste for life is a private matter. It is impertinent to list all the activities you enjoy, all the fun times you have, all the useful contributions to society you make and all the bollocks you enjoy watching on television, as though another person must want to live as you do. It also risks a stinging reproof. 'What, you call what you have a life?'

Anne's point was that she had lived interestingly and indeed 'adventurously' already – she had been a Royal Navy engineer and, after that, an art teacher – but at eighty-nine found life alien and dull. One can pick and choose from the menu of instances of contemporary pointlessness she left behind. Yes, right about the robotic nature of the modern world, with screens replacing genuine interaction, but no, a supermarket ready-meal needn't be so terrible. What's important, though, is that we have people who swim against the current, no matter that the effort finally wears them out. Where everybody is an enthusiast, we should make heroes of those who, on principle, demur.

I wish I'd known Anne and that she'd lived a little longer so we could have discussed the outpouring of celebrity Twitter grief for Peaches Geldof. The vanity, the banality, the trivialising. Nothing betrays an inert heart like an inert commiseration. 'Our thoughts are with X or Y,' the famous for nothing very much in particular proclaimed like automata, proving that their thoughts, if indeed they had any, were somewhere else entirely. And then – speaking of the mundanity of the modern – there was Lord Sugar's immortal contribution to the vocabulary of feeling: 'Peaches Geldof dies aged 25. What happen there??? That's a shock.'

How to confront the august mystery of death – 'What happen there???'

Now tell me that Anne was wrong.

The world turned upside down

'EARLIER THIS WEEK, NASUWT general secretary Chris Keates told delegates . . .' It doesn't trip off the tongue, does it? 'Delegates' is one of those words you can't hear without immediately seeing the face of Arthur Scargill, and the name Chris Keates suffers from an intrinsic bathos, like Kevin Coleridge or Sydney Shakespeare, but it's the acronym that's the real problem. NASUWT – it doesn't look or sound like anything you want to belong to.

I wish they'd give themselves their full title – National Association of Schoolmasters Forward Slash Union of Women Teachers. The pedantry is appropriate, and the word 'schoolmaster' in particular is rich in associations if you're old enough to remember when that was what a teacher was – a forbidding personage who assumed responsibility for your education, a master in that he'd mastered his subject, and a master in that he mastered you. Schoolmistress the same, though there are other associations to contend with once you invoke 'mistress'.

The business of mastering came up at last week's NASUWT conference. Just who is mastering whom these days? The teacher who'd been interviewed for a job by pupils and rejected because she reminded one of them of Humpty-Dumpty made the headlines, of course. One's first response was to take it for an April Fool joke. 'Schoolkids given say in the one thing they know bugger all about: their education – April Fool!' And certainly many of the other horror stories have an apocryphal feel to them. Pupils on an interviewing panel asking a teacher to sing Michael Jackson's 'Bad'; another hopeful being asked what he would do to impress the judges of *Britain's Got Talent*; pupils marking teachers for the way they dress, their friendliness, their willingness to exchange emails. Impossible, surely? But then again not.

Whatever the accuracy of specific complaints, there is no reason to dispute the general point that teaching has been turned upside down, that those who are there to learn are deciding the futures of those they are there to learn from, that youth is sitting in judgement on age, that ignorance has become the arbiter of knowledge. The Christian world used to permit this topsy-turvy-dom once a year at Carnival, when the beggar would be king and restraint would bend the knee to licence. Then we'd return the next day to the way the society functions best. We have forgotten the back to normality part; when it comes to education, at least, we want it to be Carnival all the time.

Blame the twentieth century. It was then that learning lost its crown. There is nothing to know, libertarian philosophers of education insisted. Knowledge did not exist. Knowledge was illusory at worst, relative at best, and either way the tool of those who would colonise the minds of the young and the subservient. It was the friend of hierarchy, the ally of hegemony, the tool of patriarchy, and therefore to be resisted as we resist all other tyrannies, never mind that belief in the relativity of knowledge is the greatest tyranny of them all.

Though it appears stringent in its scepticism, relativism is sentimental at heart, favouring the simple over the complex, the savage over the man of social accomplishment, and the child over the adult. But like all sentimentalities, it ends up depriving those it pretends to serve. Was any savage yet made happy by the patronage of the sophisticated? Was any child empowered by being indulged for all it didn't know?

NASUWT is right to be enraged, though it could, it seems to me, be angrier still. Quite simply it should refuse as a union to allow any of its members to be subjected under any circumstances to the uninformed judgement of a child. The baby does not interview prospective mothers. It does not get to select the breast that suits it. Let me give NASUWT a new motto and a new acronym to remember it by. SASU – Suck and Shut Up.

That any other ordering must humiliate the teacher hardly needs to be argued. Teaching is already a demeaned profession.

Why it matters to us to denigrate teachers is a question for the social psychologist, but it is without doubt a further expression of our superstitious fear of knowledge. Once upon a time we called those possessed of knowledge necromancers and witches, and burned them at the stake; now we employ our children to bring them low.

But it is our children we are punishing. Insist that learning must be fun and the child loses out on the invaluable experience of learning not being fun. Indulge them in their desire to have teachers who remind them of Cheryl Cole and call them 'pet' and they might skip home with smiles on their little faces, but they won't have begun to scale that high and arduous hill on which wisdom resides.

Are we afraid they will encounter teachers they don't like? We should pray for teachers they don't like. An alien presence at the blackboard helps break down the hateful fallacy that you read and think primarily to find out who you are and wave hello to your own reflection. As though an education is nothing but the primrose path to you. In fact the opposite is the truth – we learn in order to be liberated from ourselves.

The classroom is neither a collective nor a focus group. We fail entirely of our educational responsibility to children every time we pretend we are partners in the learning business. There is no such equality when it comes to knowledge. If this means that the child is sometimes bored and sometimes afraid, no matter. Boredom and fear are mulch to the imagination. And a child's perception of its own experience changes anyway. The teacher who seemed inaccessible suddenly makes sense; the teacher who wanted to be your friend now looks a clown.

And then, years later, it will all look different again – those teachers from whom you said you got nothing resurface in your thoughts, you recall something they said, maybe no more than a scrap of information, maybe a whole way of thinking. They are not just characters in the drama of your life, changing and unfolding long after your last physical contact with them, they are the shifting determinants of your intelligence. This is the privilege of an education over which, in your best interests, you were not permitted any say.

What is it we fear? Brainwashing? Indoctrination? Reader, no one was ever brainwashed by exposure to a good teacher so long as there are other good teachers down the corridor. Where children are subjected to unremitting mediocrity, the last thing they need are teachers chosen in mediocrity's image.

Down and out in Covent Garden

You know you are grown sentimental when you start counting the cygnets on the duck pond in the park to be sure none has perished since you counted last. None has, you will be pleased to hear. Eight last week, and eight this. Each the colour of egg yolk dipped in pale ale. I can't describe their softness because neither of the swans guarding them will let me get close enough to take a cygnet in my hand and stroke it.

They bite the air fiercely when nosy coots or marauding mallards swim into their space, and they arch their necks at me and hiss if I show more than a passing interest in their families. In an age in which parents force-feed their babies hamburgers and blow cigarette smoke into their faces, there are things to learn from the jealous parenting of swans.

But that could just be me being sentimental again. For all I know, swans do terrible things to their cygnets when I'm not watching. A pet rabbit, for which my father made a capacious hutch, and over whom I made much fuss when I was eight or nine, took it into her head to eat a couple of her babies one night. I didn't witness the crime. I simply found them gone in the morning, the only evidence they had ever existed a bit of mangled gristle, a flurry of bunny hair, and mummy rabbit twitching her nose prettily, as though butter wouldn't melt. Sentimentality works by our seeing only what we want to see.

This was brought home to me forcibly twice recently when leaving the Royal Opera House wet-eyed – first for Mimi and then for Violetta, victims of operatic tuberculosis both – only to have to pick my way between the homeless camped out in their cardboard boxes in Covent Garden. It's a rude shock. Inconsiderate of them to disturb the deep emotionalism of my evenings this way. Couldn't they at least wait until we opera-goers have left the area before they turn in for the night?

If you want an image for a cruelly divided society, you won't find a better one. But what is one to do? I don't mean politically. Politically it's easy to salve one's conscience, no matter that salving it rarely makes the problem go away. You join the Labour Party, write articles attacking the privileged, give the money you spend on opera tickets to homeless charities, and vow never to go to anything that can be considered elitist again. What isn't for everybody shouldn't be for anybody: the world's opera houses are the reasons we have cardboard cities. Weep. Occupy. Destroy. Fine, if these resolutions make you feel better, but they aren't answers to my question. What do you do? What do you do at the very moment of stepping from deeply affecting music and pretend suffering into misery which no great composer has laboured over and no singer rendered exquisite?

There are, I accept, questions to be asked of me. Inequity apart, what am I doing hopping from *La Bohème* to *La Traviata* in such quick succession that I am barely over the death of one consumptive woman before I am grieving for the next? Is there not enough real suffering out there that I must go in search of the make-believe variety? Just what kind of itch am I rubbing?

Philosophers have put their minds for centuries to the reasons-why of art. In our time, the argument that we come out of the fires of art more finely tempered, more civilised, the better humanly for where we've been, gets short shrift. We've always known about the wealthy who weep over depictions of the poor while treating those in their employ like dogs. For as long as there have been theatres, people have sobbed their hearts out watching scenes of domestic suffering, the like of which they will be the cause the minute they get home. But more recent accounts of Rudolf Hess crying at operas put on by Jewish prisoners he wouldn't scruple to send to the gas chambers an hour later have focused our minds, not only on the disconnect between life and art, but on the contribution sentimentality makes to the sensibilities of monsters. How can we defend art when art lovers stoked the ovens? You can see why some said that after Auschwitz poetry had better hold its tongue.

Yet poetry is still being read and written, and we do, despite everything that's happened, continue going to the opera even if we can no longer pretend we will be better people for it. But do we have to be? Isn't it enough that for the brief time we are in our seats we are not our commonplace selves, we submit to unfamiliar emotions, glimpse what we might have been, if not what we actually are or ever will be?

Much depends, of course, on what we're watching. If I am honest, I go to that schmaltzfest *La Bohème* more to indulge the sentimental self I discovered at about the time my rabbit ate its family than to escape it. *La Traviata* is a different kettle of fish: people sing because there is no other way of expressing what they feel; the orchestra swells now with sympathy, now with contrary emotions, and in the choruses we hear a deep communal lamentation.

It helps if you have the great Sonya Yoncheva interpreting Violetta's rage and sorrow but, whoever's singing, you have to be made of stone not to be engulfed by grief watching her short, tumultuous life ebb away. All right, so you're breaking the heart of a real-life Violetta even as you're applauding a pretend one – that only goes to show how brazenly versatile a species we are, how infinite in faculty, in apprehension like a god, in action the very devil.

But all's not lost: just because I'll be eating braised cygnets tonight doesn't mean I wasn't genuinely anxious for their safety when I counted them on the duck pond this morning.

The star is fallen

THERE WAS SOMETHING OF Zelig – Woody Allen's nobody who turns up at every event in recent history – about the deaf sign-language interpreter at Nelson Mandela's memorial service, who, in the view of experts and amateurs alike, talked 'gibberish' with his hands. I didn't watch the service on television, having had enough of all the easily bought, hushed-tone reverence – which is not the same as having had enough of Mandela – but it was plain enough on YouTube, from his frozen eyes and inexpressive jazz hands, that he wasn't doing the business. He has since blamed it on schizophrenia. Which could have been Zelig's defence as well.

Leaving aside the insult to the deaf, you have to admire him. Though he has apparently performed this function for the ANC before – could it be that there is something they don't want the deaf to know? – it still takes courage to appear before the world quite so ill-equipped for what you are employed to do. Yes, I know Cameron was there as well, but that's somehow different.

I'd be surprised, anyway, if a film starring Tom Hanks as a sign-language interpreter who doesn't know how to hand-sign isn't already in production. If I were not otherwise engaged I'd be working on the novel. It's an irresistible metaphor for our times: you and I unable to communicate except through a mediator who, out of whatever motive, passes gobbledegook between us. Another word for this is television.

But there's something else about this fiasco that strikes me. It pertains to the event. I don't say the occasion was fatally marred by the farcical, for all that the crowd booed Jacob Zuma, the audio systems failed (so it wasn't only the deaf who missed out), and the attention of the world's press was distracted by the Danish prime minister's 'selfie' – a marvellous act of solipsistic bathos in the midst of this celebration of selflessness, the fact of Helle Thorning-Schmidt being married to Neil Kinnock's son somehow compounding the absurdity. And I certainly don't mean that a memorial service for Nelson Mandela in particular was bound to breed indignities. But the moment we forget our innate buffoonery and elevate men to the status of gods, we invite the gods to slap us down. If we want to make ourselves laughing stocks we have only to overreach.

This isn't a piece about Mandela. The world doesn't need another one of those. But view him how you like, he was a flesh-and-blood man, not a deity. Believers will have to forgive me when I say the same about Jesus. It does neither a disservice to keep the supernatural out of their achievements. Goodness is harder for men than it is for gods. It's the admixture of the ordinary and the exceptional, reminding us of how much there always is to overcome, that makes us respect them. The sight of Mandela laughing with the Spice Girls is one I would expunge from my memory if I could, but whether he posed with them in hard-nosed compliance to the realpolitik of the trashy world we live in, or because he had the bad taste actually to like the Spice Girls, such worldliness throws his real virtues into relief. Were he alive today, Jesus would surely pose with Tulisa on his way to chasing the money-changers from the City.

We deify at our peril. 'There was no one like Lawrence before or since,' wrote the art patron Mabel Dodge Luhan of D. H. Lawrence. 'His genius lay in his capacity for being . . .' Let's stop it there. I yield to no one in my admiration for Lawrence's work, but when I hear of his, or anyone else's, 'capacity for being' I'm with the gods of mischief on Parnassus. Quietly they wait, and then when death strikes those we aggrandise, so do they. And if not at the moment of death itself, then at a memorial service or an exhumation.

Lawrence's remains were exhumed in 1935, five years after his death. What happened to them is uncertain, but there's no dignity however the tale's told. One version has them incinerated in Marseille, and the ashes handed over to Captain Angelo Ravagli, the one-time lover of Lawrence's wife. Whether you believe that Ravagli transported them to Taos in New Mexico, where devotees were waiting to receive them, or dumped them outside Marseille to avoid transportation costs, finally posting over some other ashes altogether, depends on how demeaning you want this story to be.

Some ashes turn up in New Mexico, anyway, where, according to one account, they fall into the hands of the poet Witter Bynner who drinks them in his cocktails in the hope of imbibing Lawrence's 'capacity for being'. Otherwise they get finally to Taos and become objects of fierce contention between Mabel Dodge Luhan and Lawrence's widow, Frieda, the latter finally carting them off in a wheelbarrow of wet cement, into which she drops ash from her own cigarette, saying something along the lines of 'let's see the bastards try to nick them now'. And this to the remains of a man whose personal symbol was the phoenix.

The great Roman soldier and lover Antony – a man forever writing his own epitaph – fares little better at Shakespeare's hands. Imagining how he will be disgraced by Caesar if he's captured, he begs those who think him godlike to finish him off in the grand manner, but they are unobliging. 'The star is fall'n.' 'And time is at his period,' proclaim a couple of poetically minded soldiers, contemplating the mess Antony has made of killing himself. Having delivered the eulogy, they scarper. Denied a heroic finish, Antony is carted wounded around the stage before being heaved up for a final kiss from Cleopatra. It lacks only a sign-language interpreter to explain it all in 'gibberish'.

Advice to a young artist: Don't be yourself

M Y THIRTEENTH NOVEL WAS published on Thursday. Throw in non-fiction and that's eighteen publication days. You'd think I'd be relaxed about the whole business by now. Ho-hum, another bloody book . . . what's for lunch? But it doesn't seem to work like that for me. I still go on thinking the world will look physically different on publication day – splendour in the grass, glory in the flower, an overarching rainbow of jubilation. And even more unreasonably, I still go on thinking I will look different too. A new spring in my step, a new insouciance. But the world wakes, as it has for eighteen books, with its usual cruel indifference, and I remain the fretful novelist of old.

So why, exactly, the fretting? I think it's the necessary condition of making something that requires approval. If one wrote for oneself, happy in the act of creation alone, there'd be none of this. To lose oneself in making art – all questions of quality apart – is an incomparable way of living life. Never mind self-expression. The truly wonderful thing about being a painter, a writer or a musician is escaping self. You light the touchpaper, step back, and watch the pages or the canvas explode.

People ask writers where they get their ideas. The answer is – from the work. Start with an idea and you're dead in the water. Inspiration doesn't precede the work, it finds itself in it. Down you go into the deep dark tunnel which is writing, wondering when, if ever, you will find the light, and so long as you are down there, unsure, perplexed, not someone you recognise, not anyone at all, just a thing that burrows, you are happy. But then, alas, the light, at which moment you see what you have done, declare it good, like God on the morning of the sixth day, and from then on start wondering if others will see what you have done as well. Call this the corruption of art, when the letting it make you is over, when noise and self obtrude on silence and mystery, and the mechanical side – vanity, reward, applause – takes control.

The best writerly advice I've ever heard was Kingsley Amis's. As soon as you've finished one book, start another. That way you get the better of disappointment. Fall out of love with the book that's done (and probably won't succeed) and fall in love immediately with another. For infidelity mends a broken heart. The other justification for this is that it keeps you in the domain of art, still tunnelling in the dark, far from the treacherous blandishments of public notice. Do this and publication days will come and go as chaff before the wind. That's the theory. But the flesh is weak and up we come, in spite of art, to collect our wage among the living.

The other thing I have against publication day is the morbidity it engenders. Another book, another two years gone, another three hundred pages closer to the grave. In order to dispel such thoughts I cast my mind back to the moment when my first novel was accepted. Time has passed but at least I'm a little less green now than I was then. There, as I choose to remember it, I stand, looking in perplexity from the poet Dennis Enright to the biographer Jeremy Lewis, guardians in those days of the fiction portals of Chatto & Windus, wondering why they were looking in perplexity at each other, all three of us lost for words, because they hadn't quite said yes, so I couldn't quite say thank you. In the end, they told me that what was needed was an outside arbiter of taste, someone who could confirm or otherwise what they did or didn't think of what I'd written – in other words, an agent – and when I asked where one went for one of those, they pointed with their thumbs and said, 'Upstairs.'

Up the single flight I therefore went, knocked on the door of Mark Hamilton of A. M. Heath, mentioned who'd sent me (though I think he guessed), left my manuscript, and returned seven days later as he told me to. Enright and Lewis were waiting for me. Perhaps they'd been there all week. They watched me mount the stairs and watched me come back down again. 'Well?' Enright asked. 'He seems to like it,' I said. 'Wonderful!' exclaimed Lewis, pumping my hand. And that was that. Publishing as it used to be. One building, one flight of steps, few words, small advance.

So yes, I'm less green but not less all the other things. Indeed, the shock of coming up from the tunnel is even greater this time than before. I'm not sure whether that's because I was down a little longer, or was led a little deeper, or because the beckoning spirits were not ones with whom I was familiar. They joked with me and jossed me less for one thing. And there were more women among them than men.

Prufrock heard the mermaids singing each to each but didn't think they would sing to him. That's faintness of heart speaking. The mermaids will sing to anyone who'll listen. But what determines which voices a writer will listen to and why he will suddenly listen to new ones? I have no answer to that. Maybe he just gets tired of those who normally keep him company. I heard women's voices, anyway, as I wrote J, and let them take me wherever they wanted to go. And when they told me to shut up for a change, I did their bidding.

Among the reasons that the title of this novel is J with two strokes across it, like a musical notation, or as though the letter is being smoked the way a tramp smokes a fag end he's found in a rubbish bin, is that it's a hushed story about hushed events. Unowned memories hang in the narrative like photographs taken by one doesn't know whom. Never trust the teller, D. H. Lawrence said, trust the tale. So don't look to me to tell you what I've done. I'm still rubbing my eyes against the light.

Cropper

I FEAR IT MUST attest to the essential morbidity of this column that almost the only time I refer to *Coronation Street* is when someone dies on it. Last time it was the fragile Alma, who departed in a becomingly confused state listening to Perry Como. We should all shuffle off as peacefully, though I've chosen Richard Tauber singing 'Goodnight Vienna'. If I make it through that I want the same singer singing '*Dein ist mein ganzes Herz*' to Marlene Dietrich, and if I'm still alive then, it's obviously going to be a long night and I'll need the *St Matthew Passion*. In this instance, the death on the *Street h*asn't happened yet but, barring divine intervention, will have before you are able, reader, to send flowers.

This isn't a spoiler. Not only has Hayley Cropper's death been dramatically imminent for some time, it has become second-page news in the popular press because the actress playing Hayley believes as fervently in assisted suicide as her character. The furore is of the usual uneducated sort. How dare they show children the way to suicide before the watershed! I would worry more, myself, that we show children the way to intellectual suicide whenever we let them watch Simon Cowell, but anti-euthanasia campaigners have a narrow understanding of what a life is.

Those who express pious concern about sex and swearing on the box the same: we violate the minds of the young with every manner of crassness and triviality, and then worry lest a profanity offend their hearing. Suffer the little children to gibber, so long as they grow up unsullied of ear and chaste of body – which they won't anyway.

Hayley, notwithstanding, is off. And if she does go the way she promises to, in charge of her own final hours, a whole person in the arms of the strange man she loves, we should salute her. But I'm not sure I'll be able to watch. Too painful.

That this has a lot to do with Julie Hesmondhalgh's acting – that I am going to miss her shadow puppetry as much as I'm going to miss her shadow puppet – I don't doubt. She has been the best thing in *Coronation Street*, along with David Neilson who plays her husband Roy, for years. And to be the best thing in *Coronation Street* is to be the best thing in any British soap opera – a verdict I reach, admittedly, without having seen all the others, but I have my finger on the pulse and what I know I know.

The premise of their relationship is somewhat convoluted – Hayley, a pre-operative transgender male to female, and sometime friend, incidentally, to the Alma who died listening to Perry Como (an early intimation of mortality), meets Roy who isn't a pre-operative anything but carries a shopping bag and could be said to be in need of a boost to his self-image of some sort, though it's Hayley who goes to Amsterdam (an early intimation of her free-thinking ways) for what I used to think was called realignment but is actually called reassignment surgery.

Roy's coming to terms with this, to say nothing of Hayley's coming to terms with Roy (a humourlessly honourable pedant with a thing for model railways), has kept the writers of *Coronation Street* busy for the past fifteen years, masterfully steering the story out of the shallows of macabre curiosity into the deeper waters of an abiding and now tragic affection between two gauche and unglamorous people.

Detective dramas have come and gone on television recently, most of them overpraised. Too many lakes, too many dead children, too many wrongly accused paedophiles, and of course too many detectives. For my money, the tale of Hayley and Roy Cropper has knocked them all for six. And if you think Olivia Colman and Benedict Cumberbatch could have done it better, think again.

(Just an aside, but given our national obsession with the Old Harrovian Benedict Cumberbatch, to say nothing of such Old Etonians as Dominic West, Damian Lewis, Tom Hiddleston, Eddie Redmayne, Henry Faber and God knows how many more, isn't it time we English stopped complaining about the Etonian complexion of the Cabinet and admitted that the minute a public schoolboy opens his mouth or shows us his dimple we go weak at the knees? Britons never never never shall be slaves? Pull the other one.)

But acting alone doesn't account for my reluctance to watch Hayley die. No matter how well Julie Hesmondhalgh goes on to perform as Medea or Lady Macbeth, I doubt I will feel about them as I feel for Hayley. This is the point in a conversation about soap operas where the subject of catharsis invariably crops up, the classical view that art should purge us of immediate emotion and return us to life, restored to calm.

The justification for art lies in its being at once real and unreal: us but not us, us with the space to reflect on what we are, us as our own study and not the helpless victims of being – a familiarity tempered by remoteness that is beyond the reach of soap operas, partly because of the illusion of intimacy they create night after night, sometimes for years on end, and partly because they refuse both the artificiality of theatre and the fictionality of novels – even novels read out of the misbegotten impulse to 'identify'.

I don't mean this to be a qualitative distinction. *Coronation Street* is better written than many a play and film I've seen recently. But it isn't in its nature to free us from the raw immediacy of experience, to position us simultaneously within suffering and outside it.

So Hayley will have to die without me because I can't bear the naked, unmediated sadness of it.

Tenho saudades tuas

L ET'S GET THE ENVY question out of the way. Yes, I would like it to have been me the 15,000 Madrileños, or better still Madrileñas, turned up at the Bernabéu Stadium to welcome to their club. Ever since I attended a bullfight on a school trip to Barcelona I have smelt blood in the sand, tasted *churros* from a sugared paper bag, and heard the crowd chanting my name. *'Oward! 'Oward!* Never mind that I am not fleet of foot or brave of heart – am I not a matador, a *galactico*, in my soul?

And yes, all right yes, I would rather that the £300,000 (or is it merely euros?) Gareth Bale will be earning at Real Madrid every week – come rain or shine, regardless of whether he plays or sits on the bench, regardless of whether he scores or falls over in front of goal, regardless, in fact, of all contingencies including the collapse of the Spanish economy and the impoverishment of his Spanish fans – went to me.

I don't say I am more or equally deserving; I don't say I am deserving at all; I would simply relish being loved – and let's not pretend that money is not now the prime signifier of popular affection – to the tune of four nicely presented semi-detached houses in Prestwich, north Manchester, per month.

Think of that – forty-eight a year, a round five hundred if Gareth Bale goes on to play at Real Madrid for a decade. I don't actually want five hundred houses in Prestwich (though I can think of a few people I'd like to give an avenue or crescent of them to), but then neither, I suppose, does Gareth Bale. It's just nice to know that you can buy up a suburb if you are of a mind to.

But neither money nor acclaim is what this is about. It's Gareth Bale's linguistic virtuosity I envy. 'Hello, it's a dream for me to play for Real Madrid,' he said, smiling that still-wet-behind-the-ears, Welsh, mother's-boy smile of his. 'Thank you for the great welcome. Go Madrid!' Only he said it in Spanish. Reader, two whole sentences of Spanish! '*Es un sueño para mí jugar en el Real Madrid, gracias. Gracias por esta gran acogida. Hola Madrid!*' What wouldn't a British prime minister give to be able to speak two whole sentences of Spanish? What wouldn't I give to be able to say '*Hola Madrid!*' and receive a *gran acogida* for it?

I don't know where Bale was educated but my school was hot on languages. I studied French to A level, Spanish to O level, German for a year, Latin for the whole time I was there, and had to do an Italian paper at university. And to show for this polyglottery, what do I have? A deep, disturbing resentment of Gareth Bale. '*Hala Madrid!*' he said, the little shit, and I am green with envy. In fact, thanks to my Spanish teacher, I pronounce it far better than Gareth Bale does. I know to slide my tongue between my lips, roll a bit of spit around and fill my mouth with ths. *Mathrith. Mathrith*, is how you say it, Garethth. But the difference is that he stood up there and delivered it and I am not able to. Too self-conscious.

To my ear, and no doubt to everybody else's, I sounded a prat speaking a foreign language as a teenager and as a consequence everything I learned was turned by the corrosive power of embarrassment into forgetfulness. I shamed myself into lingual oblivion. Now, I can read a line or two of Dante but can't order a cappuccino in Italy without making the shape of a cup with my hands, imitating the sound of a Gaggia machine, and then deciding I'm not thirsty after all.

And yet I am not a xenoglossophobe. From the earliest age I somehow needed, and knew, foreign words and expressions and peppered my conversation with them. *Plus ça change*, I apparently told my mother at around about the time she was trying to wean me on to the bottle. '*Tenho saudades tuas,*' I used to write to my grandmother when I was away on holiday, knowing that 'Miss you, Nanna' inadequately rendered my desolation. And I have rarely been able to go a day since without having recourse to *Schadenfreude*. How else to universalise the daily satisfactions one takes in the misfortunes of others?

Nothing to inspire *Schadenfreude* in Gareth Bale's progress, however. Which might be why questions of the morality of his transfer fee and salary are asked. Money and morality are uncomfortable bedfellows. That money is the root of all evil we know until we make a bit. But cynicism shouldn't stop us asking how good a thing it is, in tough times, for huge amounts to go to a few people, allowing that one way or another it's always the poor who finance them.

Real Madrid will recoup its investment many times over, we are told, by marketing the kitsch that goes with sporting celebrity, which means parents who can ill afford it having to buy their offspring shirts with Gareth's name and number on it. And grown men, who can't afford it either, will do the same – though they have only their own inanity to blame. If a tattoo is the last resort of the desperate, how lost to self-respect must you be to wear a shirt with someone else's name on it?

My imagination falters at the moment of wanting, let alone buying, let alone wearing such a thing. I had my idols as a boy, but I still wouldn't have been seen dead with the words *Mrs Gaskell* or *F. R. Leavis* on my back. And if I saw someone else wearing a shirt emblazoned with the name *'Oward*, how would I feel? Reader, that's *eine rhetorische Frage*.

Preacher man

YOU'VE GOT TO HAND it to Jesus. He didn't settle for the easy part of being a rabbi, turning up to charity fundraisers or telling folksy parables about the wise man of Minsk to bored bar mitzvah boys. He went out, in Matthew's words, 'to cities', or wandered by the seashore where 'great multitudes were gathered unto him'. I have started to do the same. 'Lecturing', I call it. Addressing people in the streets on matters of practical morality, dress sense, litter – that sort of thing.

'That's not lecturing,' my wife tells me. 'That's preaching.'

'Preaching! Why is it preaching when all I am trying to do is warn young women that if they go on wearing six-inch heels they'll be lame by the time they're forty, that's if they haven't already walked underneath a truck while tweeting about Robbie Williams, an interest in whom is not compatible with live brain activity?'

'There you go again,' my wife says.

I recently saw a woman drop a scarf in Trafalgar Square. It was bright red and lay like a splash of blood coughed up by one of the lions. I bent to pick it up but I'm a slow bender and by the time I was upright she was halfway across the square. I took off after her, shouting 'Madame!' – a word she'd probably never heard before – then tried 'Miss!', 'Lady!', 'Mrs Woman!' (an expression from my father's market days), and finally '*Izvineetye*, your babushka!' on the reasonable assumption she was of the same nationality as everyone else currently traipsing around London.

No response. If anything, her pace quickened. My bad luck that she was the only woman in Trafalgar Square not wearing six-inch heels. I had to run to catch her in the end. I tapped her on the shoulder. When she turned I saw that she was wearing headphones.

Now I have been careful about inveighing against the wearing of headphones in public places ever since a person apparently wired up to the usual musical inanities walked blindly into me, stopped in amazement and, before I could dress him down, told me that by wonderful coincidence he was listening to my latest novel on audiobook. I let him off with a caution.

But on this occasion I could think of nothing but the madness of making yourself so deaf to the world that if someone tells you are on fire, you can't hear. Not waiting for her to remove the cans, I took her arm and told of the risks she faced.

'It isn't only that you won't know when you've lost something,' I shouted, 'but when the driver of that bus over there suffers cardiac arrest you won't hear it careering towards you; you won't hear the mad cyclist (not that there's any other kind) ringing his puny bell and abusing you for being a pedestrian; you won't hear air-raid sirens, bells tolling, buildings being blown up by terrorists, a plane falling out of the sky. . .

'Apart from which, why seal yourself away like this, why deny yourself a faculty, why shut your ears to the multifarious sounds of the city, the very carnival of existence itself, for the sake of a tune you've listened to a thousand times already? Do you have no conception of quiet? Is it really inconceivable to you that your head might want to think its own thoughts unmolested by the monotonous beat of a band you should be ashamed to have heard of let alone to call your favourite? Little Mix! Are you quite mad? I like your scarf by the way.'

Though she had no English I didn't doubt that had there been a policeman close to hand she'd have summoned him.

And then a family of Italians stops me on Haymarket and asks the way to Abercrombie & Fitch. There are four of them, mother, father, and two daughters aged somewhere between six and thirty. They are well dressed, in possession of a *bella figura* apiece, the mother swathed in furs, and wheeling suitcases.

I want to ask them why they aren't in a taxi. Why people cart luggage through the streets of London when there are plenty of taxis, and taxi drivers know where Abercrombie & Fitch is, I don't understand. Are they saving money? If they want to do that why don't they buy cheaper tickets for *Charlie and the Chocolate Factory* or *Mamma Mia!*, or better still no tickets at all. They must know people who have sat through these trumperies. Are their lives perceptibly better for the experience? Do they have an inner glow? And there is something else they can do to make their time in London more pleasant, to avoid having to schlep through the West End wheeling cases, wondering where Abercrombie & Fitch is – they can not bother going there.

'Aberzombie & Filch,' I joke to my wife whenever we pass the shop in question. She is not amused. What I mean is that the young are being stolen from by a cynical fashion industry that turns its customers into zombies. Tourists wearing the expressions of the undead queue outside Aberzombie & Filch in all weathers in order to take photographs of themselves queuing to buy identical T-shirts and gawp at half-undressed California boys with muscled torsos. 'You can get that at home without queuing,' I tell my wife, who still isn't amused.

I refuse, anyway, to show the Italian family where the shop is on the grounds that their daughters should not be encouraged in their avidity, their conventionality, and their *Grazia*-driven concupiscence. 'Why not take a taxi to the Wigmore Hall instead,' I say, 'or Hatchards where you can buy your girls a novel each by Dickens and return them to their innocence?'

I don't know if that's preaching, but if it is, someone has to do it.

American buffalo

THE FIRST TIME I met David Mamet he was wearing a red shirt and black braces and playing honky-tonk piano. I had expected no less. He was in London to promote a novel, had spoken in interviews about the new play he was working on, the film he'd just finished, the children's books he'd recently written and illustrated, and the research he was undertaking into Jewish mysticism. He *had* to be playing the honky-tonk piano when I met him.

Had they put a piano in the green room of the Southbank Centre especially for him? He was a big star; they would give him what he wanted. Myself, I asked politely for a sparkling mineral water but said still would do if that was all they could lay their hands on. We were due to go onstage together, to talk about writing, being funny, being Jewish, being men. At the eleventh hour, though it had loomed large in the transatlantic briefing, he decided he didn't want to talk about being Jewish. He wasn't, he said, a performing monkey. I wished I had the courage to say the same, but as the chairman was more interested in the Jewish part than any other, there'd have been nowhere to go had I too refused to play the monkey. So there we were, onstage in front of a packed house of Mamet fans, with me throwing my hands about, making jokes about my Manchester upbringing, anti-Semitism yes and no, Cambridge, Dr Leavis and Talmudic exegesis, and Mamet sitting silent.

He grew interested in Leavis whom he claimed never to have heard of, so I gave him a short seminar on the subject. Occasionally he jotted something down. The word 'cretin' maybe. Afterwards we signed a few books. No one seemed to have minded. Simply seeing Mamet was apparently enough.

As for me, I was completely smitten with the man. I knew his prose works better than his plays – a number of his essays and a powerful novel about the lynching of a Jew in Georgia in 1915. He was as bolshie as they come. Bristling with principles, some loopy perhaps, but others of a sort we would all bristle with if we had the balls. And he played honky-tonky piano. I wanted him for my father.

I saw him one more time for lunch, when we argued over Dickens. He couldn't be doing with the comic names. I reminded him of the morality-play tradition Dickens partly inherited. He reckoned the problem was the English. We thought things were funny that weren't. I told him the Americans thought things weren't funny that were. I felt him going off me. We promised to correspond but of course didn't.

I haven't seen anything he's done recently, though word that his views have been growing ever more extreme has reached me. I set no store by that. He's a writer, not a politician – a writer ought to be contrary and in a samey sort of world any contrariety looks extreme. I don't doubt, either, that he plays with seeing how far he can go: it's a way of showing that strictly speaking a writer should have no views – views are not what art's about – but since you ask, and if all you really want to hear is the same left-leaning, liberal-humane mishmash of pre-prepared attitudinising, get ready to be disappointed. I also know that 'extreme' is code for being over-supportive of Israel.

Mamet has been forgiven many things for his art – the bolshi-ness, the macho posing, the gun-toting backwoodsman politics, but being over-supportive of Israel strains the loyalty of even his most ardent fans. Odd, isn't it, that while we in the arts pride ourselves on disparities of understanding, of thinking the unthinkable, of going, intellectually, where no one has gone before, we elect certain subjects to be sacrosanct (though we don't believe in the sacred), inviolable (though we rate violation to be the artist's first vocation), unsusceptible to difference (though difference is the prime justifi-cation for what we do). When it comes to Israel, we must all think the same.

In an interview with the *Financial Times* last week, Mamet prodded away at the prevailing pieties, attacking Obama and praising Sarah Palin (how's that for going where you don't expect an artist to go), dismissing global warming, heading dangerously, if anything, to a too-predictable jettisoning of pinko commonplace. Not that it matters: he's an artist and no one's going to vote for him. But while his interviewer took all this on with good grace, he stumbled before what Mamet had to say about anti-Zionism and anti-Semitism. The great no-no of our times is to say that anti-Zionism is anti-Semitism by another name. In fact very few people argue that it is, but in a sophistical twist which itself perfectly illustrates the meaning of the word *chutzpah*, the anti-Zionist paints himself a victim of a crime that has not been committed. Where once he argued that he was not necessarily an anti-Semite, he now insists he cannot possibly be an anti-Semite precisely for the reason that disreputable people say he is. We are but a hair's breadth from seeing it argued that anti-Zionist is *ipso facto* an expression of love for Jews.

Asked the question – is the one necessarily the other? – Mamet pauses, bites the air, and then, emitting a 'grunt of relief . . . throws caution to the wind'. It's a dramatic description and should be interpreted as drama. Why the preliminary caution? And why the relief? Because Mamet, like the rest of us, lives in a moral world inundated by sophistries of the sort I have just described. And for once, the joy of it, the joy of letting his interlocutor have it with both barrels. That the interlocutor should dare to say he considers Mamet's calling anti-Zionism by its worst name 'offensive', and this after Mamet has delivered a broadside against British anti-Semitism, is a measure of how deeply the conventional wisdom is embedded. If Mamet is even only infinitesimally right about the 'ineradicable taint of anti-Semitism in the British' and 'the anti-Semitic filth' he finds in the work of many contemporary British novelists and playwrights, it is not for his interviewer to be 'offended'. Offended where, pray? Offended how? You want to turn the tables on those you offend? Purloin his offence.

That said, while I can think of a few routinely anti-Semitic British playwrights, I must say I'm not sure who the filthy British novelists are. For all I know he might mean me. Americans can read one in the wrong spirit. But that doesn't matter. Here is someone speaking against the murderous orthodoxy of the times. Agreement is the last thing he's angling for.

Norovirus

YOU WANT TO KNOW how to get through the rest of the winter norovirus-free? Don't handle anything. This advice, I accept, will be harder for some to follow than others. To me – because I grew up to be a universal non-handler, not touching other people, alien food, animals or myself – it's second nature. That I was a precociously fastidious boy I ascribe primarily to a confused under-standing of Jewish hygiene laws: if it was sinful to go near some things, but impossible to remember in the heat of living which, the most sensible plan of action was to go near nothing. Otherwise I put it down to my family's revulsion – probably acquired over centuries of being treated like dirt in Eastern European shtetls – from filth.

Though we lived in a house in Manchester big enough for us all to enjoy a degree of privacy, we congregated in the living room. Whoever needed to make use of the bathroom or the lavatory would slip away without making reference to it, though his absence was immediately noticed. There were two sorts of contamination we feared: viral and aural. Distance and doors protected us from the latter; against the former we waged an unending war of disinfectant and ingenious precaution.

What we most went in terror of, to be precise, were drains, sinks, pipes, plugholes, toilet bowls, anything, that is, through which waste matter was dispatched and therefore through which waste matter could be regurgitated. Just because you hadn't seen the regurgitation process with your own eyes didn't mean it hadn't happened. In the night, for example, or while you were out of the house. Back it all came. And whoever doubts that toilet traffic can be two-way should try sitting on an outback dunny in far North

Queensland and waiting for the blue frogs to come leaping back up through the plumbing. In Manchester, from where I confess we would have re-migrated to Lithuania had we seen a frog in the lavatory, this anxiety extended not only to drains and plugholes, but to everything in their vicinity. Anything onto which germs could have leapt – handles, levers, chains, plugs, showerheads, towel rails, light switches, wall sockets – we avoided like the plague, because they *were* the plague.

In the first fifteen years of my life I never once flushed a lavatory with my bare hands. To those anxious to avoid norovirus today I recommend flushing with the ends of a scarf or a tie, also gloves, though gloves have to be thrown away once they've been used for this purpose, which makes them an expensive option unless you buy them from the market, but remember that means risking such market viruses as those attendant on receiving change or breathing in. As for trying on gloves that are sure to have been tried by someone before you, don't even consider it. Man-size Kleenex doubled and fashioned into a sort of glove itself is an alternative, provided you destroy it immediately afterwards, though you can easily get trapped in that vortex of using one to flush the lavatory and then realising you have to use another to flush the first away, and so on until you have emptied the box or lost your mind.

Best to employ your foot wherever possible. If the lever is too high you can always stand on the pedestal, so long as you don't omit to clean it as a courtesy to the person who comes after you. There are people I know who feel they need to clean their shoes after this as well, but that strikes me as neurotic. What you do if the lavatory is old-fashioned and has a chain depends on your athleticism. I had a lanky friend at school who used to invite us into the latrines to watch him do a handstand on the toilet bowl and pull the chain by making a sort of grappling hook of his feet, but I wouldn't recommend that to everybody.

It's important, once you are set on such a course – and as long as young men are spitting in the street to attract women, and young women are throwing up in it to attract men, such a course is necessary – it's important to follow it through to the letter. There's no point, for example, in being vigilant in the matter of what you touch around the cistern if you go insouciant in the matter of what you touch around the sink. Assume you have emptied a dispenser of soap onto your fingers and then scalded them for upwards of forty-five seconds in boiling water – all this goes for nothing if you then manually turn off a tap that will previously have been touched by someone who, for all you know, is not only a constitutional bare-hand chain-puller but has dropped his iPhone into the lavatory pan and fished it out without even rolling up his sleeves.

How to turn off a tap without undoing everything you turned the tap on to achieve remains one of the great hazards of using public conveniences. Unless you're lucky enough to have found taps that work electronically – and you'll encounter these only in expensive restaurants and Germany – I would propose the scarf, the tie, your elbow, or the foot option again. Turning a tap off with your foot requires considerable dexterity and balance – only ballet dancers do it well – and can be embarrassing in a crowded lavatory at the theatre, but you can always lurk in the bar – keeping your distance from other drinkers – and wait for everybody to return to their seats. So you miss the play? You'll be missing more than that when you're emptying the contents of your stomach onto your own bathroom floor.

In the end, the choice is yours. You can keep your dignity or you can keep your health.

Nani in space

I GOT CLOBBERED IN the street recently. In a hurry to make a doctor's appointment, I found myself on a narrow pavement behind two enchantingly voluble middle-aged, middle-class women, one pushing a couple of twin babies, presumably her grandchildren, whom she addressed as though they were just home from university, the other gesticulating with wild expressiveness, as though to draw the attention of pilots preparing to land at Heathrow.

What with the roar of the traffic, the screams of the babies and the women's honking conversation, my hoarse 'Excuse me' went unheard. I attempted to slip in on the twins' side but there was insufficient space between their pushchair and a road murderous with cyclists, so I had to risk the almost equally dangerous option of dodging the other woman's flailing arms. I miscalculated and she caught me with her elbow full on the jaw. 'Oh my God,' she cried, hearing the crunch, 'I'm so dreadfully sorry.' 'Madame, you have a right to animated conversation,' I told her, spitting out a tooth. 'The fault, comprising impatience and a lack of spatial awareness, is all mine. Think no more about it.' And so peace was made. But had there been a Turkish referee observing us, he would have handed her a red card.

I take it that the significance of this little parable, which also happens to be a true record of events, is not lost on readers who saw, in the flesh or on television, the gross and cruel misjudgement which did for Manchester United's chances against Real Madrid on Tuesday night. Enough has been said about the legal niceties of this incident in the sports pages of the world's press for me to pass over them with speed. Ignore those letter-of-the-law pundits who thought the sending-off had merit. It didn't. Nani, in space, innocently raised his foot in order to control a ball, just as the voluble woman innocently waved her hands to make a point, and as I walked into her fist, so Alvaro Arbeloa walked into Nani's boot, the difference being that I didn't roll on the ground clutching a part of me that hadn't been touched.

Why football hasn't introduced the hot-spot technology employed in cricket is a mystery to me. If you can tell whether a batsman has nicked a ball by X-raying the bat, you can surely tell whether a footballer has been kicked in the heart by X-raying him. It might be slow, it might necessitate an MRI scanner being rolled onto the pitch, but what's time when truth is in the balance?

There is something else I don't understand: why we didn't wake up on Wednesday morning to find that UEFA had convened an emergency session in the night, overturned the decision and handed Manchester United a passage into the last eight of the European Cup, which it would then go on to win? Or failing that, why wasn't the natural world in disorder when we woke, why weren't the sun and moon distracted from their orbits, why hadn't the sheeted dead climbed from their graves, why weren't owls killing falcons and horses eating one another?

If there were such a thing as natural justice, if the spheres moved in harmony, if God existed, then a thunderbolt would have struck and burnt to cinders the red card waved officiously by Cüneyt Çakir – a man whose name sounds too much like the insults that must get thrown at him, a man too encumbered by umlauts and cedillas to follow what is happening on the field of play.

I know – indeed no one knows better – that a game of football is just a game of football. Except that it isn't. Nothing that we do is ever just what we do. Our every action is a sort of foreshadowing of the essential Great Action whose meaning is locked away from us and might never be revealed. If there is no justice in small things, then there can be no justice in large, and life becomes a random, absurdist lottery for which we'd be fools to buy a ticket. The very reason we play games, or in my case watch them, is to affirm a metaphysical order in imitation of the ideal order we long to see but cannot.

I don't know when I stopped believing in God, or even if I ever started, but had He wanted my allegiance, all He had to do was reverse decisions too egregiously unfair to be compatible with divine intention. The wrong line call or LBW decision, the catch that wasn't caught, the low punch that wasn't noticed, the games-manship that shouldn't have been allowed, the penalty that should or shouldn't have been given, the rain that shouldn't have been permitted to fall.

How many times as a boy did I cry out against these miscarriages, not suffered by me personally, not necessarily suffered by a team or a player I supported, simply felt as wrongs that had to be righted. Truly I believed that, spurred by the force of irresistible universal outrage, a sort of Prague Spring of sport, this righting would some-how come about – Henman granted a rain-free rematch against Ivanisevic, Gatting given another chance to play Warne's ball of the century as he wasn't ready the first time, Zidane's sending-off revoked in the light of the provocation to which he'd been subjected, Manchester United reinstated as winners, referee and linesmen executed.

At the best of times, we live a hair's breadth from despair. The innocent die young, the good go unrewarded, the greedy go unpunished.

We love sport because of the brief illusion of equity it brings – so long as we can trust the judgement of those who officiate. Once they err, the entire edifice of fantasy crumbles and we are left with life as it really is, and there is too much of that already.

The Queen versus Edward Snowden

So who do you reckon won the great TV head-to-head of Christmas? Not *Downton Abbey* vs *EastEnders*, or *Doctor Who* vs *Coronation Street*, but the Queen vs Edward Snowden – Edward Snowden being the ex-CIA employee turned whistle-blower currently residing in Russia, and the Queen being the Queen, currently relaxing in Sandringham. Snowden was Channel 4's choice to give its traditional bad-taste 'up-yours' *Alternative Christmas Message* – from which we might deduce that Ratko Mladic, Miley Cyrus and Mrs Brown and Her Boys were either unavailable or too expensive. In the event, it was no contest, the referee stepping in and stopping it in favour of the Queen after fifteen seconds. Cruel, I thought, to have let it go on that long.

In fairness to Snowden, the Queen has been giving Christmas messages for a long time. She knows where to get her hair done. She knows how to sit. She knows how to modulate her voice, how confidential to appear, how to address, without being controversial, the concerns we've shared since she spoke to us last. Above all, she understands that her job is not to be wise but to administer comfort, which is to say to speak to us in platitudes. 'Who's a good boy, then?' we croon over our spaniel, tickling him behind the ears, and though he knows there's nothing remotely good about him he luxuriates in the familiar sounds, confident that, for the time being, all is right with the world. Thus the Queen, on Christmas Day, to us. 'Who's a good subject, then?'

If there is a moment when she asks herself 'Who's writing this piffle?' she conceals it well. But I don't for a moment doubt that piffle is what she recognises it to be. This, too, however, she recognises: that we wouldn't be tuning in to hear Wittgenstein after a heavy Christmas lunch.

The wisdom of knowing when wisdom is not required, and that the commonplace soothes as the recondite never will, is the wisdom that underpins our constitutional monarchy. It costs a lot to sustain but I happen to think it's worth it. If Channel 4's ruse of an alternative Christmas message has a virtue, it is to remind us how much worse off we'd be with a monarch chosen from the ranks of stand-up comedy, reality television, Holocaust denial, and that branch of snitching that comprises frightening the intelligentsia with stories that someone's reading its emails. How to stay edgy and challenging has been a ticklish problem for Channel 4 ever since its inauguration as an 'alternative' broadcaster. There's a limit to how 'other' you can be when you have to be it every night. But with the wheeling-in of that dead-eyed sanctity Edward Snowden, 4 has finally touched bottom; if this is what the transgressive looks like we might as well be watching the Disney Channel.

Don't get me wrong – I take the point that Snowden has alerted us to an inordinate predilection for snooping on the part of government agencies. But one man's inordinacy is another's sensible precaution. There is nothing new about spying. It's an impulse as old as humanity, and for good reason. People mean one another harm. Checking out our neighbours' intentions is no more than judicious unless, in the fun of doing it, we forget what we are checking for. I would recommend each party to the inordinacy versus sensible precaution debate to heed the other's fears, though there is no sign that Snowden can hear much above the sacral thrum of encouragement coming from his fellow travellers or, like them, has any interest in weighing abuse against needfulness.

He was no sooner on our screens on Christmas Day than he was invoking Orwell, a name bandied about more often by the vainglorious than the word patriotism is by scoundrels. Big Brother's electronic arsenal, Snowden reminded us, was as 'nothing compared to what we have today' – which is frightening only if we confuse the Thought Police stamping us into servility with marketing men wanting to know what we buy and sell on eBay. No, I don't want anyone to know what deodorant I use either, but that doesn't make me Winston Smith.

Cliché number two was privacy. 'A child born today,' Snowden said – though the Queen would have said it with more feeling, not to say more consciousness of its Christian echoes – 'will grow up with no conception of privacy at all. They'll never know what it means to have a private moment to themselves, an unrecorded, unanalysed thought.' Privacy is the current fetish of the educated classes, which might be explained by how little regard they show for their own, tweeting their every prejudice and perturbation, blogging whatever resemblance to cogitation passes through their minds, and distributing compromising selfies for a cruel world to snigger over.

As for the child for whose privacy Snowden expresses such heartfelt concern, he has long since abandoned all idea of an inviolable self, posting all there is to know about him on Facebook alongside a photograph of his naked girlfriend. A private moment of unrecorded thought! Reader, who wants it when you can have recorded fame instead?

With a naivety that wouldn't shame a Miss World pageant, Snowden suggests that if governments really want to know how we feel, they should just ask, 'for asking is always cheaper than spying'.

'Forgive the intrusion, but what building is it you feel like blowing up? If you'd be so good as to send us an aerial photograph, together with dates and names of personnel, the gratitude of our government would know no bounds.'

It has been said by some more beguiled by Snowden than I am that there is no evidence that all this surveillance has thwarted a single terrorist attack. I bet the Queen is thinking what I'm thinking: doesn't that mean they should be trying harder?'

Into the digital darkness

SOMETIME IN THE EARLY 1960s when my father was driving taxis in Manchester, he had that April Ashley in the back of his cab. For readers who don't remember April Ashley, let me quote from her website. 'My story begins in 1935 in a tough, working-class area of Liverpool where I was born as a boy ... In Paris, I debated with myself the decision to have a sex change ... I knew I was woman and that I could not live in a male body. I had no choice. I flew to Casablanca and the rest, as they say, is history.'

It must have been a short time after her operation in Casablanca that my father ferried her around in his taxi for a day. He liked her, found the story of her ordeal fascinating and moving – 'An education', he called it – and wouldn't tolerate any sarcasm, weird as the idea of a sex change then was. To this day he stands guard in my imagination over any inclination I might have to judge ungenerously.

So in the matter of transgender politics I can be trusted to show respect. If Germaine Greer has upset people who might have looked to her for understanding, they have my sympathy. But since she hasn't called for their operations to be reversed, or for them to be physically harmed, not a single voice should be raised against her delivering a lecture on any subject she chooses at a British university.

Our country is in a censorious mood. The more educated we are, the less we are prepared to tolerate views contrary to our own. Shake any institution of higher learning and a dozen boycotters will fall out of it. If the academic community gets its way, we will soon all be speaking with a single voice.

But it isn't just the desire to silence dissenting opinion that should worry us. Let us say that Greer didn't just happen to think differently from those she has distressed but intended, for whatever reason – because she's Australian, say – to go out of her way to needle them. Why, even then, should she be denied the right to a platform?

It isn't only in the name of free speech that the views of an itchy polemicist should be tolerated – and I say itchy polemicist promoting thought, not itchy ideologue promoting violence – but because provocation is indispensable to the workings of a sound, creative culture. The loser, when silencers have their way, is not the provocateur but the provoked. To be easily offended is to be shut off from the invigoration of that argumentative give-and-take we call liberty; not to understand the poetics of provocation is to miss out on the joys of living in a literate and robust society that excels at satire and burlesque.

We hear too much of 'phobia'. Attach 'phobia' to any cause you care for and you have ring-fenced it against the words of the critic and the devious antics of the clown alike. Nothing is to be mocked; everything – except the act of critical dissent itself – is sacrosanct. Thus have we created for ourselves an impoverished world of touchy fools who understand no mode of address other than the Internet's yes/no, like/dislike, thumbs up/thumbs down discourse of the dumb.

Take some of the responses to Martin Amis's splenetic and self-consciously snobby dismantling of Jeremy Corbyn in the *Sunday Times* last week. That the straight-faced of social media were going to throw a blue fit over this would assuredly have entered Amis's calculations. It can be fun for a writer with a comic gift to drive the over-principled into an apoplexy. That's part of what a comic gift is for. 'Dance,' says Martin Amis, and true to expectation, they dance their hobbled dance, outraged by his ridicule, sickened by the position of educational privilege from which he mocks Corbyn's intellectual penury, primly unamused by the unashamedly ad hominem nature of his attack. (No matter that with Jeremy Corbyn – a man admired for nothing more substantial than 'authenticity' – ad hominem is all there is.)

It is a strange, cabalistic world out there in the celibate darkness of digital resentment forums, where people for good reason denied a platform of their own cling to the coat-tails of those published in the daylight, froth in envious rage, share one another's small and bitter diatribes and as a matter of principle find nothing funny, not even when it patently is – as for example, Amis's really rather fond description of 'weedy, nervy, thrifty' Corbynites each 'with a little folded purse full of humid coins'. It's that word 'humid' that does the trick and marks the writer his detractors will never be.

A bad habit has evolved, below stairs, of calling any writer with whom you disagree about anything a twat, and his or her books bollocks. As a tactic, this is poor. It weakens your argument if you can only admire art made in the image of your own predilections, and shows you have neither eye nor ear for art at all.

As for snobbish derision, it is of noble ancestry, going back to Hamlet twitting Polonius, Pope, Swift, Wilde, Waugh: a line of scurrilous mirth whose slithering ambiguities make a charlie of whoever can't keep up. Equivocation is at the heart of literary insult, harnessing seriousness to comedy, earnestness to lightness, teasing the single-minded into taking offence. Sadistic? Yes, but then again no.

The impulse to irresponsible play is lost on the easily provoked who think a writer must mean what he appears to mean, say what he seems to say, or indeed say anything, because saying, reader, is the least of what a writer does.

Half the time, if it's any good, writing is a wind-up, a trap for the unwary. To be wound up in the playground was always a humiliation; to be wound up on the page is no different. We must get off our high horses. We look stupid up there.

Nights in white satin; nuns in red nighties

You can't blame richard Dawkins for getting in early with his tweet. See it from his point of view: if you are of the conviction that organised religion encourages a dangerous delusion and that Pope Benedict XVI's 'first instinct when his priests are caught with their pants down is to cover up the scandal', then the announcement of his retirement is an opportunity too good to miss. 'I feel sorry for the Pope and all old Catholic priests,' he tweeted. 'Imagine having a wasted life to look back on and no sex.'

It's a cunningly laid trap. 'A wasted life!' I hear a chorus of old priests crying. 'We've had more sex, young man, than you've had hot dinners,' before it dawns on them that Dawkins has caught them with their pants down again. But this is not a column about Dawkins or the Catholic Church. It's about sex. Or rather no sex. Imagine it, Dawkins says. So I'm trying.

Perhaps I am of an age to try. Any earlier would have been impossible. For the first forty or fifty years of your life there is only sex – the wanting, the waiting, the wondering, and then the greed for more. Other things distract for a day or so, but they are no more than an intermission. You take up chess or cycling, you try yoga, you bake your own bread and learn the names of foreign cheeses, you garden and croon over hollyhocks, but you aren't fooling anybody, least of all yourself. The fires die down briefly only in order that they can roar back into life with ever more ferocity. We are on an errand, emissaries of the future, and we deliver or we die.

Up until the age of ten, I lived opposite a convent school. From my bedroom window, I could see the convent girls running around the playground and sharing one another's lunch. Ten was too young for that to be an arousing spectacle. But it wasn't too young to wonder about the nuns who taught them. My heart broke for those nuns. Something about the way they dressed and moved told me they were denying themselves that without which life was not worth living. And what was that? I had no idea, but I could read the abnegation, or the terrible consequences of that abnegation, on their faces. You can be a sentimentalist of sex, even at ten.

Years later, I supervised a thesis on D. H. Lawrence written by a nun whose quick intelligence, demure bearing and keen but forever downturned eyes beguiled everyone who taught her.

Her work was brilliant but we believed her religion dulled her natural vitality. Once she got her first, we hoped, she would renounce her vows. And she did. We threw her a renunciation party where she got comprehensively pissed, told lewd stories, flaunted herself disgracefully, and left us all wishing she'd never read Lawrence. Celibacy may have few pleasures but in this instance it beat incontinence hands down.

My sentimentality about nuns survives. My wife once told me that in the course of directing a television documentary she miked up a nun – it was not thought appropriate that the soundman should go rummaging through her habit – and discovered she was wearing scarlet underwear. The story touched my heart. Did she have a love outside the walls that could never be consummated, or a love inside them that dared not speak its name? Or was the lingerie her trousseau as a bride of Christ? In which case, I'm with Dawkins – what a waste!

To the worldly, this sense of waste is non-negotiable. It strikes us as against nature, an act of ingratitude, a crime against the body for which the body's guardians – the ids, the egos and the rest – will exact a terrible price. We feel the sadness of it in those who blundered into self-denial without measuring its consequences, or were pushed by families hoping to find favour in the eyes of God through the sacrifice of someone else, but we are less tolerant when celibacy turns up its nose and brags of its virtue.

And so we laugh in advance of the action in *Love's Labour's Lost* when Ferdinand, King of Navarre, reminds his followers of their oath to stand for three years against their own affections 'and the huge army of the world's desires'. Fat chance of that, we think, even without Berowne's heartfelt cry that 'these are barren tasks, too hard to keep: / Not to see ladies, study, fast, not sleep'.

But celibacy's self-righteousness is no laughing matter in *Measure for Measure*, where Angelo, who 'scarce confesses that his blood flows', boils over when he sees the conventual Isabella, a woman who sets higher store by her chastity than her brother's life.

I wrote an essay on *Measure for Measure* at school, wondering that people should make such a fuss about getting their leg over. My teacher put a red pen through the lot and told me my imagination wasn't up to the moral rigours of the text. He was right. Whoever denies his blood flows might be making a great mistake, but it's not for someone who is drowning in his own semen to pass judgement. Freedom from the pesterings of nature ought not to be a contemptible ambition. And, yes, I can, now that I'm not a boy, imagine its consolations. A clear mind. Crystalline concentration. An even body temperature.

Kant railed against sexual intercourse because it made us 'things', and masturbation because it turned us into 'loathsome objects'. Be honest – in our age of unremitting porn: the soft stuff of popular culture even more trivialising than the hard stuff the Internet pumps into the brains of already deranged boys – in such drossy, sex-satiated times, don't we owe Kant a nod of recognition? No sex! Shouldn't we at least try to imagine that occasionally?

Killing is a serious business

NOT A SUBJECT IDEALLY suited to a weekend consecrated to lovers, but it has been raised and I must address it. Murder, I'm talking about. The amount of it there is about. The sheer volume of bodies. Not in actuality – though God knows there are enough bodies there ('I had not thought death had undone so many') – but in books and on the stage, particularly in film and on television, and more particularly still in that genre known as 'the thriller', though I speak as one who has never felt the thrill of thrillers. But live and let live is my motto. If murder is your bag, bag it. Me – I go to art only to wonder whether Elizabeth Bennet will eventually get to lie with Mr Darcy, and when Gregor Samsa will come down from the ceiling.

Blame the dramatist David Hare for raising this. Speaking a few days ago about a thriller series he has just completed, he warned against our coming to it with the wrong expectations. There'll be no guns, he promised, adding that 'I personally can't stand the body count in contemporary drama. I think it's ridiculous.' Amen to that. I don't agree with David Hare about everything. I am less interested in exposing the wrongs of MI5 than he is, for example. But that's a temperamental thing. I can live with more secrecy than he can. The thought of government agents working in the shadows makes me feel safe – as long, of course, as it's our government they're working for. About the body count, though, we are as one.

I haven't done much killing myself. By about my third novel I was wondering whether I was even going to allow anyone to die by natural causes. Characters make their own fates, but you can always subtly intervene. If not by miracle cure then by silence, for silence, too, is an intervention and the novelist can decide to look the other way when his characters fall ill.

The first time one of mine gave up the ghost I sank into a depression that lasted half a year. 'Cheer up,' people told me. 'It may never happen.' But it already had. I'd assisted at a deathbed scene. I'd been a party – no matter how unwilling – to the gravest of all human events. There's no cheering up after that. It's hard enough just to rejoin the living.

I did once ask a distinguished crime writer how she – funny how often it's a she – coped with all the bodies. She laughed. 'Oh, you just knock 'em off,' she said.

How you do that without feeling you're in some way an accessory is what I can't fathom. Nor do I understand how you can litter the page or the stage with corpses if you're not yourself familiar a) with the sight of them, b) with the psychology of those that turned them into corpses, and c) with murder's aftermath of remorse and sorrow. I don't say a writer needs to have fired a gun herself, but to kill in art is a crime in itself if the deed and its repercussions are not felt to outrage and perplex our humanity.

If that sounds as though I'm asking every writer who assists at a murder to be possessed of a little of the Shakespeare who wrote *Macbeth*, then yes, that is exactly what I'm asking. It's not that difficult to hear *Macbeth* if you write in English. Our language is permeated with Shakespeare and with *Macbeth* especially. Dr Johnson cited it more often in his dictionary than any other Shakespeare play, and alongside the Old and New Testaments it remains central to the way we imagine the act of taking life and the price we pay for doing so.

'If the assassination could trammel up the consequence,' Macbeth ponders – the strangled expression mimicking the strangled hope – 'we'd jump the life to come.' If. If only. 'But' – the fatal but – 'in these cases we still have judgement here.'

What makes Macbeth the most interesting murderer in literature is the ground he imaginatively covers, the dimension of pity and damnation he enters, even before he lifts a hand. If tears don't drown the wind for an assassin, you have to wonder why. Is this one too lacking in ethical and spiritual foresight to feel the enormity of the act? Is that one too motivated by hate? It's a drama of the profoundest significance either way.

After the initial fun of watching bodies pile up in a Tarantino movie, or being fed into wood chippers in *Fargo*, the being blasé starts to pall. Grand Guignol degenerates into pantomime. I enjoy the spectacle of Mr Punch laying into everyone around him, but he inhabits a universe in which assassination trammels up consequence only because it's comic.

It's not the number of bodies that makes the contemporary thriller ridiculous. It's the corresponding lack of poetic seriousness. And that's more than a passing failure of expression. To kill in art and not give a damn is a failure of mind and senses. For an antidote, go to a literary festival and hear Alice Oswald reciting *Memorial*, her version of Homer's *Iliad*, in which the victims of the Trojan War – a body count to stop the heart – are commemorated in all their disgrace and majesty.

The first to die was PROTESILAUS.
... He died in mid-air jumping to be first ashore
There was his house half-built
His wife rushed out clawing her face.

And HECTOR died like everyone else ...
a spear found out the little patch of white
Between his collarbone and his throat
Just exactly where a man's soul sits
Waiting for the mouth to open.

Did I say go and hear her? Let me put that another way. Kill to hear her.

In praise of insincerity

THE ASSUMPTION OF JEREMY Corbyn oughtn't to surprise. Not because the man himself has long been a flower in the Stop the War, Whoever Is Our Enemy Is Our Friend, And Never Mind Who That Means We Rub Shoulders With, daisy-chain-plaiting wing of the Labour Party, but because we couldn't go on forever pretending that the coexistence of the soup kitchen and the banker's bonus was just another of life's unavoidable little cruelties. Once in a while we need the hard left to pipe up.

You don't have to believe the electorate secretly hankers for a dose of Marxist–Leninism to accept that there are deep levels of justified bitterness out there waiting to be tapped. How Ed Miliband and his team of hopefuls managed not to tap them is a question still engrossing the Labour Party, but the idea that its socialism was to blame never was convincing, if only because it didn't look or sound socialist. Maybe we'd forgotten what socialists are meant to look and sound like. Well, now we've been reminded. They're meant to look and sound like Jeremy Corbyn. I can't pretend to know what draws anyone to a politician, never having been drawn to one myself, but it would seem that nostalgia has a lot to do with it in this instance. A rough beast we thought extinct has come slouching back out of the undergrowth.

As for those who are too young to remember him the first time round, they are astounded by the novelty of a politician who resembles a British Rail booking clerk moonlighting as a polytechnic sociologist, except that they won't remember what British Rail or a polytechnic was. Such an alliance, between those with faded memories of CND and funded trips to the Soviet Union, and those with no memories of anything, is proving formidable. It offers to efface, at a stroke, the occasionally shoddy pragmatism we've grown accustomed to. The campfires burn; our souls are clean; we clap along and anything feels possible.

I'm not against it. I like a singalong. And I'm a bit of a sentimentalist for the past myself. Just before the trains were handed over to Richard Branson they were almost running on time and selling sandwiches designed by Clement Freud and wines selected by Fay Weldon. Now they won't tell you what platform any train is leaving from until it's left and the food might have been prepared by Primark. So I'm with Corbyn on taking back the railways, no matter that he hasn't yet named the novelist he'd like to see selecting the wine. And I'm with him on energy companies as well. Why shouldn't the state make a profit out of heating my Jacuzzi? On protecting public libraries, too, I agree. Ditto not making the poor pay higher taxes than the rich. Ditto not burning the unemployed at stakes. If this makes me a socialist, then I'm a socialist. But here's a question: why can't we oppose the inequities of a society weighted in favour of wealth, and all the trash that wealth accumulates, without at the same time having to snuggle up to Putin, pal out with Hamas, and make apologies for extremists?

The sad collapse of Kids Company highlights the plight of neglected children; it's a national disgrace that without such charities there is no one to pick up the pieces. We should be able to admit that *and* keep Trident. *And* bomb ISIS in Syria. *And* look back on the IRA's terror campaign with something less than misty-eyed affection.

Truth isn't a carpet not a single thread of which dare be removed without the entire tapestry unravelling. In fact, the more individually brilliant the threads, the more exquisite the carpet. But the Corbyn catechism is predicated on the presence of a divine unsmiling artificer at the loom, weaving his single truth over and over again. The oppressor's wrong, weave weave, the wickedness of the West, weave weave, imperialism, weave weave, and our own responsibility, weave weave, for every act of violence directed against us. The Great Banality Carpet woven on the Great Loom of the Single Thought.

Socialism has learned from religion to keep all promises of salvation simple – no one ever yet lit a candle for nuance – and not to underestimate the allure of masochism. The faithful feel holiest when blaming themselves, except the young, who feel holiest when blaming the old. For all the wicked, colonialist things our parents did, O Lord – including the Balfour Declaration, whatever that was – we say sorry.

Corbyn's distinction is to have held on to these articles of faith while all about him have been losing theirs. In an age of facing both ways, he doggedly faces in one direction only. That this makes him authentic I have no desire to question. But our weariness with the vacillations of insincere politicians is no reason to put our trust in the rigidities of a sincere one. History teaches that the road to horror is paved with sincere schemes for mankind's amelioration.

We are fools for sincerity. 'The poetry of a teenager in love,' writes the Shakespearean scholar Jonathan Bate, 'is sincere: that is what makes it bad. The key to dramatic art is Insincerity.' The dramatist, he goes on, should only pretend to feel what he expresses; that way he can pretend to feel the opposite just as well. Politicians aren't writers. But we should value in a politician no less than in a writer the ability to feel variously, admit ambiguity, understand the equal attraction of opposing truths, and to know when to mistrust 'truth' altogether. The case against Tony Blair is sometimes that he believed nothing, and sometimes that he believed too much. Whatever the rights and wrongs of the Iraq war, it was God, he said, who whispered to him to go in. What if he was sincere in this? Do you, who abhor that war, applaud his sincerity? Or would you rather he'd been more calculating?

One thing that war does teach: the rightness of a course of action cannot be decided by the authenticity of its advocates. We should think twice before we let sincerity be our lodestone.

The ghost speech

FOUR YEARS AGO, IN these pages, I described the experience of winning the Man Booker Prize. But since a man must take the rough with the smooth, it now behoves me to describe the experience of not winning it. So here's my description. Not as good.

To be frank, I'd been expecting nothing else. It makes existential sense to me to assume failure. Count on misfortune and what's the worst that can happen? Once in a blue moon you'll be pleasantly surprised, that's all. It was in such spirits, anticipating disappointment, that I made my way to the Guildhall for this week's prize and so wasn't disappointed when disappointment struck.

Reader, I had read the runes. Checked the alignment of the planets. Noted the sorrowing way strangers had begun to look at me in the street. You never know for certain when you are going to win a prize, but you know for certain when you aren't. One sure sign, for me, is the appearance, the night before any awards ceremony, of a well-known literary figure who comes up behind me on whatever corner of the blasted heath of writerly hope I happen to be wandering – outside the London Library or at the bar of the Groucho Club – enfolds me violently in what I have to come to think of as the Hug of Death, and walks off.

Not a word is spoken. Not a murmur of sympathy or condolence. Just an anonymous philanthropic embrace calculated to squeeze out any last remnant of delusive expectation. How he knows what decision the judges will reach before they've reached it I have no idea. But he has never been wrong yet. If he doesn't appear, I win. If it's the Hug of Death, I lose. And this year he hugged me harder than he'd ever hugged me before.

I had no choice, for all that, but to write what's known in the business as the Ghost Speech. The Ghost Speech is the speech you don't expect to deliver but keep buried deep in your dinner-jacket pocket just in case. No matter how certain you are of losing, you daren't risk being wrong this one time and having to go to the microphone unprepared.

As acts of self-torture go, writing an acceptance speech for a prize you know you're not going to win is only marginally less masochistic than writing it before you're even on the longlist. But novelists are dreamers and fantasists, imagining the unimaginable and looking forward to what can never be. 'The mind dances,' Dr Johnson says of those who delight too much in silent speculation, 'from scene to scene, unites all pleasures in all combinations, and riots in delights which Nature and fortune, with all their bounty, cannot bestow.' Condemned to which pitiable folly, writers carry around innumerable acceptance speeches in their heads for prizes that do not yet exist, and for which their work would be unlikely to be considered even if they did.

I made a modest essay at a Ghost Speech this time round, a precautionary few words, no more. In it I told the true story of an encounter with a shirt salesman the day before. I had taken my dinner shirt from the hanger on which it had returned from the dry-cleaner only to discover bloodstains down the front. Had someone at the dry-cleaner's killed himself while pressing my shirt? Had he – a friend of one of the other shortlisted novelists, perhaps – known to whom the shirt belonged and imagined he was stabbing me in the heart? Or had the shirt, in a macabre act of Poe-like ominousness, bled of its own accord in my wardrobe? Whatever the explanation, I had to run quickly to Bond Street to buy a new one. Without once raising his eyes to me while wrapping it, the shop assistant said, 'Is this for tomorrow night's Man Booker Prize dinner?'

I concealed all astonishment at his conversance with the prize – Bond Street's Bond Street after all – and told him yes. Still without raising his eyes, he wished me well, saying that from what he'd read he gathered I had a good chance. (Was this Satan, the Great Enticer, speaking in a shirt salesman's guise?) I told him I had already won once and that there needed to be an overwhelming argument for a writer to receive so great an honour twice. Finally, he looked up. 'Surely the only overwhelming argument, sir,' he said, 'is a good read.'

A phrase I abominate. We don't call Mozart's *Requiem* 'a good listen', or a Rembrandt self-portrait 'a good watch'. 'In my view,' I told the salesman, 'read's best used as a verb. It sits ill as a noun. It detracts from the active, dialectical nature of the reading experience. Literature, like the life it interprets and illuminates, is a knot intrinsicate, sitting on a high hill of truth, and he that would unpick it about must and about must go . . .'

Whereupon he left me to serve another customer.

At this point in my Ghost Speech I would fix the distinguished guests with a Moses-like stare and say, 'But you all – lovers of the rich, the subtle and the complex – you know what I mean.'

An unnecessary admonition. Judges of the Man Booker Prize no longer speak of preferring novels that 'skip along'. But the phrase 'a good read', along with its bastard brother 'an easy read', still crops up in even the most serious newspapers and journals, and cannot be outed as an idiocy too often.

In the event, the winner Richard Flanagan put it better and with more magnanimity. This too tempered my disappointment. Reader, I like him. An Australian novelist who calls me 'mate' and doesn't talk about 'good reads' – how can I not like him? The others, too. Ali, Karen, Neel, Josh – my new family. How six shortlisted novelists could grow fond of one another under the pressure of such intense competition I cannot explain. But we did. Was it the last huddle of literary love before cultural extinction? Or just happy circumstance? Either way I had a good time. Only by winning could I have had a better.

Yes but no but

I'VE A PROPOSAL TO make: what if, instead of employing the Chomsky 'but' whenever something terrible is visited on us, we tried saying 'and' instead? Not just for the fun of it but to make the world a better, bigger, more inclusive space. 'But' shrinks and grudges; 'and' amplifies and allows.

Let me remind you how the Chomsky 'but' operates. 'The attack on the Twin Towers was an atrocity,' you concede, '"but"...' And here you insert whichever qualifier takes your fancy. 'The attack on the Twin Towers was an atrocity, "but" Americans are committing atrocities all the time.' 'The attack on the Twin Towers was an atrocity, "but" George Bush is a shit.' Or, how about, 'Gunning down the staff of *Charlie Hebdo* was an atrocity, "but" Israel kills journalists in Gaza.' Would anyone say that? Unless I dreamed it, Noam Chomsky just has.

So now change his 'but' to 'and' and see what happens. Take your time.

Salman Rushdie, meanwhile, has been doing sterling work on American television and in the American press fingering the 'butters'. The 'But Brigade', he felicitously calls them. As someone who has been a victim of ideologically organised 'butting' himself, he knows whereof he speaks. 'No, we cannot tolerate fatwas on writers, "but" he did insult the Prophet, and you wouldn't like it if he'd insulted Jesus or Moses.' Which is disingenuous, since most of us wouldn't mind at all.

Chomsky himself has 'butted' vociferously over the years about the fatwa imposed on Rushdie, noting that Western intellectuals were up in arms in favour of Rushdie 'but' had nothing to say when it came to the imprisoning of Holocaust deniers. A selective truth, since many Western intellectuals have opposed the imprisoning of Holocaust deniers, believing it to be a more effective punishment to leave them wandering round what's left of Auschwitz and Buchenwald with their rulers and log tables for all eternity. Besides which, the fate of a Holocaust denier touches us less deeply than that of a novelist threatened with assassination, if for no other reason than that a novelist adds to the world's stock of knowledge, while a Holocaust denier detracts from it. All life is precious, but we mourn less when a skunk dies than when a tiger does.

The equivalising of what's not equivalent is dear to the hearts of the 'But Brigadiers', who claim a purity of principle themselves, unlike the rest of us, who hypocritically defend one man's rights and not another's. There are two answers to such puritanism. The first is Leonard Cohen's: there's a crack, a crack in everything – that's how the light gets in. Avenging angels might be consistent but humans aren't. 'Everything unconditional belongs in pathology,' Nietzsche wrote, agreeing with Leonard Cohen. Only the pathological believe themselves free from those venial irregularities that make us favour novelists over deniers, tigers over skunks, even though as abstract causes they can be made to appear the same.

The second answer is that the pathological are themselves no better in practice. What principle of pure truth guides Chomsky when he equivalises a journalist killed in crossfire in Gaza with the cartoonists mowed down with malice aforethought in Paris? And while he wants us to see a parity in these deaths, the fervency of his reasoning declares him to be more outraged by those in Gaza.

So how are you getting on substituting 'and' for 'but'? Jihadists shouldn't kill journalists in Paris. And Israelis shouldn't kill journalists in Gaza. Doesn't cut the mustard, does it? The reason being – leaving aside the preposterousness of analogising massacre and mishap – that it removes the idea of consequence. The 'but' that was deemed so necessary after 9/11 – that great 'but' from which all the lesser 'buts' have sprung – was the 'but' of extenuation. It was the first, grammatical step in shifting blame from perpetrator to victim. Not only, on the back of that 'but', was America reminded that others had suffered, that America was instrumental in that suffering, and that America could therefore be said to bear a share of responsibility for what happened, the 'butters' finally came within a whisker of condoning the act of terrorism itself.

And so it has been these past few shameful weeks with the *Charlie Hebdo* massacre. Little by little, day by day, the 'But Brigade' has turned its monosyllabic screw until the cartoonists become complicit in their own demise and their murder appals us a little less. Yes the requisite noises are made – free speech non-negotiable blah blah – but the 'butters' are quick to invoke instances where we do negotiate it: anti-Semites removed from their positions, for example; anti-Semites not allowed to speak what's on their minds. Funny how it's always the freedom to be an anti-Semite the 'But Brigade' protects. And finally, in justification of murder, the issue of provocation is wheeled out, though the concept of 'asking for it' would not be entertained for a second if the crime were rape.

Pace the Papa, he who insults my mother might deserve a stern rebuke, but not with rocket launchers and Kalashnikovs. Nor does being rude to someone's ma equate to criticising his beliefs. I thought we had long ago decided we are all fair game when it comes to the gods we choose to revere, whereas our mothers, like the colour of our skin, we are given. If the Pope has a vested interest in protecting religion from scrutiny, so does the 'But Brigade' have a vested interest in drawing attention away from any atrocity that isn't perpetrated by Americans or Israelis. Except that there isn't any atrocity which isn't perpetrated by Americans or Israelis, for who else is ever on the end of the chain of repercussion, extenuation and blame that begins with that malignant 'but'?

And no I said no I won't No: Molly Bloom decides against casting a vote in the 2015 elections

Yes they're all big infants making promises I'd be twice the fool to believe even the one who looks like Gromit's friend Wallace but we got that wrong a Casanova no one can look into his big brown eyes without falling head over heels and asking to see his manifesto I bet all the girls say show me your manifesto costed he tells me which is more than can be said for any of the other parties but I'm not asking about any of the other parties I tell him looking away so I don't fall victim to his Casanova charms I'm asking about yours that makes him laugh mine doesn't do what most manifestos do that's what he says it doesn't offer a list of promises so what's a manifesto for I wonder well that's easy to answer he answers easily looking me up and down a woman really feels looked at when he does it unlike leaders of the other parties especially the one who's always offering me beers made of English hops and promising to untax my tampons no thank you not likely soft-lipped Casanova now is another matter persisting that his manifesto answers the questions I'm asking who said I'm asking any questions well we're answering them whether you're asking them or not is his answer take the deficit no you take the deficit that's just what we're going to do in our party he says take the deficit and stick it which is all right by me I won't be losing any sleep over any deficit well you should interposes the one with the long forehead from another planet the Mekon was it if you care about the future ha that's rich coming from you says Casanova what about the health service if you care about what country your children are going to inherit looking at me so now he wants me to have his children which isn't the worst offer I've ever had not the best either under the bedclothes discussing

243

deficits not my idea of a not with either of them certainly not the
Mekon who loves his wife so why is he there for me in that case
I wonder what she thinks of him telling every man woman and
child he's there for them who does he think he is Big Brother wasn't
he there for us Big Brother Is There For You will he be there when
I'm having Casanova's baby I bet he won't jealous is my guess wants
to be loved always sticking his face into other people's selfies being
there for them and promising the Good Life that doesn't sound
much like my idea of a good life no mention of glorious sunsets and
fig trees no kissing under Moorish walls just tax relief and selling
people homes they're already in and you'd think they'd give the earth
to get out of the big question is whether he'll be there for himself
come 8 May he'd be better off if you ask me leaving being there to
his Chief Whip which is a funny name enough to give a certain sort
of woman ideas not me no though I don't mind admitting a gentle
whipping never went but he isn't that sort of man you can see too
busy taking his glasses on and off quizzical with them on kindly
with them off which is where they've been ever since his party
became the protectors of babies and decent hard-working pension-
ers from the cradle to the grave the sooner in the grave the better
no that's not fair they don't want us dead at least not before we've
voted and paid our taxes which pop-eye Casanova says those with
the broadest shoulders have to bear it's only fair whoever said life
was fair but oh I must say I do love broad shoulders whether they're
bearing taxes or just being there who was it now with the broadest shoulders I've ever seen took me back to his mansion he called
it not what I'd have called a mansion me neither he said putting
a flower from Aldi in my hair but a mansion is what Casanova
calls it for tax purposes and you know where the tax will go and
when I said I had no idea but I hoped into buying me more expensive flowers he told me it was to give unemployed gay immigrants
free kidney transplants so I knew which party leader he'd be voting
for not the boyish-looking one with the tousled hair who cosies
up to whoever will give him leg room the one who doesn't think
prison is the proper place to keep prisoners presumably wants to
put them in mansions tax tax tax big crackdown even Mr Whippy's

promising crackdown on tax evasion avoidance dodging shirking shuffling equivocation fugivity or is that Casanova's non-dom thing which puts me in mind of whipping or rather not whipping because that sort of corporal is presumably not what a non-dom does but maybe won't mind being on receiving end of unless a non-sub as well O Lord the cost of having a dirty mind which some party probably the Greens is going to want to tax because where else will money come from to abolish zoos except for hen nights that's Riga finished let alone feed two hundred thousand million children starving in nuclear submarines which we'll give them the right to buy no that's the Mekon's idea having reached conclusion that a little bribery never went so long as it's costed unlike every other party which isn't costed and if you want to know how we've costed it snuggle up in bed with someone with broad shoulders and read our manifesto and ours and ours what we find us too is that voters expect require demand believe swallow that our specifics add up or subtract and as for austerity light or dark it is both necessary, and redundant as will be evident if you do the electoral sums and look at how people have acted in the past if you want to know how they will act in the future we're the only party that cuts costs and costs cuts and learns from our mistakes although there were no mistakes amen to that says Casanova or Mr All Heart No Brain or is it All Brain No Heart if you ask me not much of either but that goes for the lot of them coming on all hot air and cheap perfume no I say no I would not like to no and my heart and my brain are hurting and no I say no I won't No.

Culpability Brown

TIME WE TALKED ABOUT our culpability in the matter of terror? I put that interrogatively for fear readers might rather we talked about something else. I share the reluctance, but, as the blamers tell us, we cannot understand the motives of those we call terrorist unless we acknowledge our contribution to their state of mind, and the last thing we ever want to turn our backs on in this column is understanding.

Let me say, then, from the outset, that I get it. I understand. Many of those acts we call terror are committed because the perpetrators believe it's their duty to take vengeance on the West for its invasion of Muslim lands, the 'war on terror', the Israeli occupation, the mass incarceration and destruction of innocent Muslims, the murderous sanctions against Iraq and now Iran, the routine killing of Afghan civilians by British troops, the lax morals of Western women, the publication of *The Satanic Verses*, and other military incursions and cultural abuses too numerous to name. That they believe this we know because they tell us. And when an assassin speaks, it's provident to listen.

I say to listen, not necessarily to trust. In any circumstances it's unwise to believe what people say about their motives. If Sophocles, Shakespeare and Freud didn't teach us that, they didn't teach us anything. And even to talk of 'motives' is crude when it comes to the unseen and often unguessed-at impulses that drive us. But the reasons people give for why they act as they do at least paint a picture of what they think is inside their heads, if nowhere else, and that tells us something. It tells us who they've been listening to, for example, and what they've been reading. It sheds light on the culture of those we call terrorists – see how careful I'm being – if not their psychology. That it cannot be taken to reflect an impersonal or verifiable truth – any more than it is verifiably true that our rivals are monsters and our lovers paragons – needs no protesting.

So there you are. I get it. This is how it feels, this is what it looks like, this is the cultural terrain, inside the head of someone who plants a bomb or tries to bring down an aircraft, or walks the streets with a machete. I understand. Can I go now?

To be clear: the grievances listed above contain buried quotations, not from terrorists themselves but from Western commentators who feel some kinship with their views if not their deeds. Let's give them a single name, say Culpability Brown, since they all think we're to blame, borrow ideas freely from the same branch of Handmedown Bank, and are similarly careless in their condemnations – as, for example, in accusing British troops of killing Afghan civilians 'routinely', where 'routinely' is a rhetorical device, planted to derange even further those whose minds are full of scorpions.

Cometh the atrocity, cometh Culpability Brown. Does he wait like a spider suspended in the darkness, the opportunity to blame you and me again, reader, the reward for his infinitely banal persistence? Out into the light he crawls, anyway, in the immediate aftermath of every killing, to agree the crime is terrible, unspeakable, yes, but – ah, the callousness of that 'but' – we had it coming.

In what other context, these days, do we allow people to tell us we have it coming? This one goes about with her handbag open, that one with his wallet protruding like a free gift from the back pocket of his jeans, complains the poor pickpocket. 'I was provoked, Your Honour.' How the girls in their short summer dresses, flirty, drunken, free with their kisses, arouse the hapless rapist. 'Aren't they, ladies and gentlemen of the jury, in every meaning of the phrase, asking for it?'

This is not an argument against precaution. Though no provocation justifies a rape, it's still sensible, given who we know is out there, to be on our guard. A sad reflection on the times, though one that has no bearing on the heinousness of the crime of rape itself.

So what precautions should we take – accepting that they have no bearing on the crime of murder – when it comes to terror? What should we change? Our foreign policy, plainly. The things we do that upset jihadists, though the concept of jihad – much argued over as it is – pre-dates Bush, Blair, Salman Rushdie and the Israeli occupation. I'd be surprised if there are many who think the wars the West has fought since 9/11 have in all cases been well considered in conception or execution. Cruel and terrible mistakes have been made. But the mass murderer Saddam has gone. The Taliban, destroyers of other cultures, killers of women and children, haters of the light, might not have been routed but they are not – not yet, anyway – what they were.

No such offsetting gains against losses, however, when Culpability Brown describes the world. Only our undiluted villainousness. So let me ask a question: if we are to blame for those we call terrorists, if we create the culture in which it looks right to them to kill, aren't those commentators who excite that culture into an even greater ferment of boiling hate – who speak, for example, of British soldiers killing Afghan civilians 'routinely' (once a day? twice a day?), who collapse history until there are no two sides to any conflict – aren't they, the butters and the blamers of the press, more culpable than anyone? Our security services film potential terrorists travelling to places where they will be inflamed, when indoctrination can be achieved as effectively over here by nothing more sinister than newsprint.

If you are looking for whose hands beyond the murderers are bloody, look here. At those who, to further their own ideological ends, agitate the already unstable with lurid untruths.

Don't ask me

M Y POSITION ON WHETHER we, or anyone else, should inter-vene in Syria couldn't be clearer. I absolutely, utterly and definitively don't know. I like to think I have been consistent in this. I didn't know what I thought when the Syrian uprising started more than two years ago; didn't know when the Syrian army stormed the city of Homs; didn't know after reports of the Houla massacre reached us in May last year; didn't know when brutal-faced Syrian generals denied all involvement in any massacre; didn't know when I saw pictures of rebels bearing marked resemblance to clerics we are always trying to deport to Jordan, and don't know now.

Gas should concentrate the mind – or at least the minds of those on whom it has not been used – should it not? Gas, for God's sake. Gas, with all its hideous associations for those of us who still remember the twentieth century. Isn't gas the line that can't be crossed, and once crossed must incur not just our wrath but our strenuous and if necessary armed insistence that it will never be crossed again? Don't know. Yes but no but.

I am not asking for anyone's pity, but chief among the pains of writing a newspaper column each week is having to know what you think. No matter that you are more the craven-scrupled Hamlet than the itchy-fingered Fortinbras, a man who can 'find quarrel in a straw', you must lash yourself into opinionated action on the morn-ing that you write, fat the region's kites with the offal of the villain of the week, understanding that if your thoughts aren't bloody, they are nothing worth.

Out there at this very moment, in lofts, basements, lean-tos and neglected gardens, a thousand otherwise genial-tempered hacks are rubbing the lamp of intemperate opinion to coax out a view – immoderately enthusiastic or grossly derogatory, it hardly matters which, and the distinction probably won't be noticed anyway – on celebrity chefs, wayward footballers, twerking pop stars, tattooed nobodies and any one of a thousand comedians whose routine is indistinguishable from the others – a judgement I no sooner make than I withdraw lest you think I have a view on the matter.

But what are such artificially manufactured convictions compared to the certainties the leader of a powerful nation has to delve into himself to find when confronted, not with Jamie Oliver and potato crisps, but Bashar al-Assad and a rocket-load of sarin gas? Who'd be Obama? Damned for every action he takes and damned for every action he doesn't. It's hard not to suspect, from the pitch of their voices, that those who rail against our going in today are the very people who railed against our staying out yesterday. Or is it just that dead certainty sounds the same, no matter who you are and what it is you're being dead certain about?

So what is it we think we know? Or at least – to shrink the field to more manageable proportions of ignorance – what is it we think we know about this region of the world? Let's start with dictators. We think we are against them. His being a dictator was one reason among many for getting rid of Saddam Hussein. But then we discovered that a dictator sometimes holds together, by virtue of the violence at his disposal, factions that would otherwise do even greater damage to their country than he does. 'Iraq was better under Saddam Hussein,' say those who once blamed the West for putting him there in the first place. A dictator, it would appear, like your reflection in a mirror, depends where you're looking from. And whether Tony Blair is looking over your shoulder.

Some Egyptians, having democratically elected a man who was quick to take on the lineaments of absolutism, now look longingly back to the dictator they already had. Better the despot you know is the thinking of the Russians in relation to Syria. And Russians have some previous when it comes to alternating despots. Maybe we should listen to them from time to time. Since we are all wrong about everything, the more variously wrong voices we attend to the more comprehensively informed about our ignorance we are likely to be.

Having done dictators, let's deal with democracy. We think we are for it. Let the people choose. That was what Egyptians recently believed. But they forgot that 'the people' often choose badly. So when does a free vote that turns out to be a bad vote turn out to be undemocratic? When the side that you are on says it is. Enter the army. We, who know what we think, call any army interference in civil politics 'a coup'. Egyptians in favour of 'the coup', and who don't therefore see it as 'a coup', call it democracy in action.

If I knew what I thought I'd say that was a fair description. Using the army to remove, in the name of democracy, a democratically elected leader who thought he'd been elected to be a dictator, thereby rendering illegal the legality of his election, makes a sort of sense if only in that it makes nonsense of the idea that there can be sense.

What's happening in Egypt isn't funny, but no absurdist playwright could have left the language of ideology – the weasel words in which we wrap our beliefs and offer to know what we think – in more disarray.

> Yesterday, upon the stair,
> I met a man who wasn't there.
> He wasn't there again today
> I wish, I wish he'd go away.

But now he's gone – Mr Certainty – now Parliament has decided against intervention, I can't help thinking it's made the wrong choice. Gas for God's sake! No but yes but.

Dumb also degrades

SOMEWHERE OUT THERE, WHEREVER things went before there was an Internet, a mere mote in the eye of scandal, smaller even than the baby moon that's just been discovered running rings around Saturn, perhaps at the back of someone's drawer or pasted into an ancient journal of the heart, creased, faded, but I fear still identifiable, is a photograph of me without a shirt. I am wearing a pair of those prickly bathing trunks that men and boys were forced into in the early 1950s, made of elasticated Brillo pad, and I have my fists up like Joey Maxim, light heavyweight champion of the world. After his retirement Joey Maxim became a stand-up comedian, as I might become after mine. But I knew nothing of that at the time I posed bare-chested, trying to look menacing. I just wanted to be light heavyweight champion of the world.

Believe that and you'll believe anything. In fact, I wanted to be a novelist and literary critic, as would be obvious from the photograph, were you to see it, which I hope to God you never do. I was ten when it was taken, at a holiday camp near Morecambe, and had been forced to adopt the pose by my father who I reckoned could have been light heavyweight champion of the world had his heart been stronger. Why he couldn't see that I had no such ambition, that I felt humiliated to be photographed without a shirt, I have never understood. He was not without his own prudishness in such matters as swearing, but he couldn't sympathise with mine in the matter of exposing my chest. But I still believe today what I believed then: clothes maketh the man.

This reminiscence of delicate feeling is prompted by a story concerning Zac Efron, someone of whom I don't expect my readers to have heard. Me neither, but research tell me he stars in films made for schoolgirls, goes to the gym, and has just had his shirt ripped off at the MTV Movie Awards.

Given that Efron was at the awards to receive a prize for Best Shirtless Performance, you would expect him to have come prepared to lose his shirt again. A little powdering and plucking, or whatever you do to look like that, must surely have gone on. He did, though, tweet a thank-you afterwards to the person who unbuttoned him, a young woman called Rita Ora, of whom we also haven't heard, saying he didn't know whether he could have done it on his own, by which – since we must assume he has no difficulty unbuttoning his own shirt – he could only have meant brazenly baring what was underneath it. A confession that suggests he is not without a consciousness of modesty at least.

If I now introduce the name of Cyril Smith it is not to encourage readers to imagine him without his shirt. But there is no escaping the issue of sexual abuse at the moment, whether it's some public figure being charged, or some other public figure exonerated, and innocent or guilty, accused or accuser, it would seem that we are all being called to account in the matter of sexism and the abuse of power, what we mean by such terms, how much responsibility we bear for the seedy atmosphere of contemporary life.

Called in by *Newsnight* last week to address the hair-raising claim made by a UN investigator that sexism in the UK is worse than in other places, three highly intelligent women calmly discussed the sexualisation of women, from exploitation, to denigration, to harassment, to bullying, to rape, agreeing that while some of the UN investigator's findings were more pertinent than others, it was right nonetheless to talk about a continuum that linked small infractions of common decency to significant manifestations of contempt, denials of opportunity and acts of violence. It is easy to deride the continuum argument. Matters of apparent insignificance at the one end – things we think we should laugh off if we are good sports – and murderousness at the other. A woman playfully ripping off a man's shirt here, and Cyril Smith brutalising children there. Come on!

Something, however, is seriously amiss, and we don't get far discussing what it is, how it has come about, or how to intervene, if we refuse to accept that causes accrete, that the tone of society determines our actions within it, that the lives we allow to be held cheap in the name of a bit of fun one day are lives we might be prepared to hold cheap in far more serious circumstances the next. Maybe monsters like Jimmy Savile and Cyril Smith create themselves. But are we certain we know why they thrive when they do? And what subtle signals of allowance and even encouragement we might be sending them?

To be clear: I am not using the sexualisation of Zac Efron's body to discredit those who complain about the sexualisation of women's. On the contrary, I consider the one to be the mirror image of the other. The Page 3 girl pinned on a workshop door degrades all parties to its being there: the inanely objectified girl and those who inanely ogle her. And we should not discount the coarsening effects of inanity itself. To trivialise is also to dishonour. Dumb also degrades. Similarly degraded and inane, anyway, are the girls who shout 'phwoar' the minute a boy, a man, a Chippendale, a birthday stripper, undoes a button. I know the argument. It's irony: women enjoying being the ones who do the gawping for a change. 'How do you like it when you're at the receiving end, boys?' But we've had years of that now. If the reversal of roles was intended to liberate and empower women, then where's the evidence it has?

Someone might have a better idea – and that won't include any of the forms of purdah favoured by male societies still frozen in Neolithic terror of women – but until I hear it here's my recommendation. Let's all keep our shirts on for a bit.

The dying bug

W E ARE NOT HEALTH religionists in this column. We don't warn against excessive consumption of all the good things in life – such as Giuseppe Rinaldi 2010 Brunate Nebbiolo, or Ribena – because we know that life itself, to be pleasurable, must be excessively consumed.

And we don't celebrate austere athletic prowess, as when another pared-down British cyclist in a Lycra onesie pedals to a victory that will lead only to more aggressive, foul-mouthed bikers running red lights and mounting pavements. (I don't, notice, say that all cyclists fit that description; only that those who do – and they are recognisable by how much higher in their saddles they ride – are more to be feared whenever a Wiggins or a Froome notches up a win.)

Notwithstanding our principled bodily scepticism, however, we have just employed the part-time services of a personal trainer, David. I say 'we' because there are others in my house he is employed to service. And I say 'trainer', though when he gets to me he is not so much a personal trainer as a personal stretcher. You don't have to be in pursuit of a body beautiful to wish yourself to be the flexuously willowy creature you once were or, failing that, just to be able to pick up something you have dropped.

Seeing me stoop to retrieve a pound coin on a bus the other day, three people got up to offer me their seats. Two of them were women. The third was a good decade older than me and had a wooden leg. And please don't tell me he didn't. I know he didn't. But now that I have a personal stretcher I might as well let absurdity have its way with me entirely.

I once belonged to a health club, where it cost me £2,000 a year to amble on a treadmill for half an hour a week and sit and read

Grazia in the cooling-off area. So this is not the first time I have been struck by the irony of paying good money to do something I don't want to do, and moved heaven and earth to be saved from doing when I was a schoolboy.

For the whole time I was at grammar school I carried around in my back pocket an assortment of notes from my mother requesting that I be excused from PE, cross-country running, football, cricket and swimming on the grounds that I was bilious, hyper-sensitive, agoraphobic, vertiginous, allergic to the natural hemp from which gym ropes were manufactured, easily nauseated and afraid of water. 'All these are just excuses for being a pansy,' the PE teacher told me. 'They're not excuses, sir. They're a description,' I corrected him – for which he made me hang upside down from the wall bars for an hour. Thereafter, my mother added constitutionally pusillanimous to the list. 'That means being a pansy, sir,' I explained to the PE teacher, who hung me from the wall bars again, despite the biblical injunction against the brain ever being positioned lower than the feet.

Looking back, I realise it wasn't only gym I dreaded at school. Every class was a torment. It wasn't knowledge I objected to but instruction. Why couldn't they just tell us what books to read and leave us to get on and read them? I wasn't a rebel. I just found it impossible to listen when I was trying to think, and craved sovereignty over my imagination. You would have thought, in that case, that PE was just the ticket; I could hang upside down from the wall bars and think my own thoughts till the hour was up. The trouble was, the only thoughts I had were about killing the PE teacher.

On top of which, the gym was a locus of the unambiguous. It was regimented and militaristic. It aspired, necessarily, to the unequivocal. You cannot exercise and be amused about it. You cannot integrate the dying bug into your core workout and hold to the position that you are a spiritual being. In this way the body and the mind are each other's opposite unto death, which is why you have to choose which of them you are going to follow. The great Japanese novelist Yukio Mishima had a passion for bodybuilding as well as literature and even posed for publicity photographs in a ceremonial fundoshi. But in the end, unable to reconcile the irreconcilable, he put a sword through the bodily part of himself.

Confined to a racetrack or velodrome, the single-minded athlete is a curse only to himself. In these cathedrals of mirthlessness, he can conjoin with his co-religionists in celebration of the body ugly with no detriment to the rest of us. It's on our roads and pavements that he spreads confusion and violence, and to our parks that he brings disharmony.

A city park is a wonderful place to practise the ironic life. At once metropolis and country, neither wholly natural nor wholly artificial, home to the sedate swan and the preposterous pelican, a place of new growth that speaks urgently of death, a city park enables us to rejoice in those contrarieties that prevent us turning fanatical or tedious. But none is safe from such events as the Prudential Bike Ride, which this weekend will make a hell of central London with its 'bike-based entertainment and festival zones', for which read roads you can't cross, officious men in yellow bibs, slavishly applauding groupies, unironic *X Factor* ballads piped through giant speakers, and parks you can't enjoy. (Yes, yes, and incidental charitable intentions, but I don't deny that good can sometimes come from evil.)

Otherwise it's runners, numbered and logo'd, pounding the paths, fracturing the ambiguous quiet of city nature and frightening the already existentially bemused ducks with the ticking of their Fitbits and the zombie zedding of their headphones. Fortunately, David, my personal stretcher, is not closed to comedy. I might not be laughing when I do the dying bug, but he is. So while he will never make an athlete of me, there is a chance I will make a philosopher of him.

Weeping in the new year

I CAN'T SPEAK FOR you, reader, but for me no new year can be said to have begun until I've shed a tear. The only question is whether I shed it on the last day of the old or the first day of the new, and what in particular precipitates it. This time, I made it through the champagne, fireworks and kisses of the last night of 2013 only to be set off the following morning by the New Year's Day concert televised live from Vienna.

Daniel Barenboim, looking as though he were sucking a lemon, leading the Vienna Philharmonic through the stirring slush of Strauss. Other considerations apart, the Vienna Philharmonic is enough to make a grown man cry. Such a zest for life in their playing. Then there's the nostalgic ritual of the concert itself, dating from 1939, a year already drenched in tears, somehow brave in its continuance, given all that's gone before, and braver still in the fleeting assertion, shown in the faces of the orchestra and the audience alike, that there isn't, and never was, a finer place in the whole wide world to be on New Year's Day than Vienna. As if.

I mistrust togetherness tears, precisely because I'm susceptible to them. The band plays, emotions surge, the oceanic sensation of limitlessness beguiles you into the arms of humanity, and the next minute you're giving a Nazi salute. That's something else that gets the tear ducts working – Vienna, with its beautiful and treacherous associations; Vienna, with its power to inspire longing and loathing. 'Wonderful city where I belong' – I used to love listening to Richard Tauber sing about Vienna, but he'd had to flee it at about the time *Das Neujahrskonzert* was inaugurated, wonderful or not. Behind the tears, the questions. Ought I to be feeling what I'm feeling? Ought I to be watching at all?

In a sense, every new year is a reminder of the ones before. Small wonder they're upsetting. They mark the passage of time even more fatefully than birthdays do. The bells toll and the world is grown a little older. And without doubt, part of what's upsetting me as I watch the Vienna Philharmonic playing in 2014 is the memory of a New Year's Eve I spent in Vienna twenty years ago, waltzing with my wife of that time on Graben Street, hearing Tauber in my head, loving the snow, the glamour, the swirl of years and dresses, the fantasy of being transported back to the great days of the Austro-Hungarian Empire which would not, in truth, have been that great for me.

But then it's all fantasy, every bit of it. Yes, we'd waltzed in the snow – or at least I'd made as though to waltz – but we'd been brawling all day, with friends, with each other, with a waiter who'd brought us what we hadn't ordered at a coffee house that wasn't as good as the coffee houses we'd read about, even arguing with our friends' dog who froze fast to the icy ground the minute he set a paw outside the hotel and so expected us to take turns carrying him. A magical New Year's Eve? Only if I scissor out the dog, our arguments, the truth of the Austro-Hungarian Empire, and picture us waltzing forever in an empty landscape like figures on a music box.

New year tears work either way: remembering what was or what wasn't. And I now realise I'd been preparing them, in anticipation either of sorrow or a too-transient happiness, from the very first New Year's Eve of which I could be said to be conscious, when I sat in the kitchen watching Jimmy Shand on television, wondering why everyone I knew was at a party and I wasn't – everyone, that is, except my grandfather, who sat on a chair next to me, coughing up bile and clipping his yellow toenails with the scissors I employed to cut balsa wood.

It has to be better than this, I thought; I don't have to be the saddest boy on the planet; it doesn't just have to be me and Jimmy Shand and an old man with rotting toenails. But it was many years before it did get any better than that, and even then the exquisitely romantic New Year's Eve I longed for – waltzing in the streets of Vienna, for example, or dancing cheek to cheek with Ava Gardner in a bar in Manhattan while Yanks who looked like Fred Astaire went mad in Times Square – refused to materialise.

From the age of twelve to sixteen, I played brag on New Year's Eve with school friends, cursing the celibacy of the occasion, cursing the cards I was dealt, cursing the fact that I'd been born poor, though I couldn't have said how riches would have helped, and yet knowing that on some future New Year's Eve I would look back on these evenings with an aching fondness, missing our once-carefree celibacy, the jokes we shared, the excitement of cards, our vanished youth.

Enter girls at last, and all that happened to my New Year's Eves was that they became sadder still. You have to have reached a mature age before the girl you take to a New Year's Eve party is the girl you want to leave it with. If they were always wrong for me, I was certainly always wrong for them. My dissatisfaction with the year that had been, matched only by my dissatisfaction already with the year to come, made me a horrible companion.

For men like me, the future is simply too close to the past on New Year's Eve. We should try separating them, first by banning the countdown to midnight, then by outlawing 'Auld Lang Syne', and finally by interposing a dead or fallow year between New Year's Eve and New Year's Day. Worth it for a dry eye once in a while.

Is that a bomb you're carrying or are you just pleased to see me?

SWIFT WROTE *GULLIVER'S TRAVELS* to 'vex the world'. Pope's target was 'babbling blockheads'. Those were the days. Though constitutionally more modest, less certain of our genius and more sceptical as to our effect – for the times we live in bruise easily – we share those great satirists' ambitions. If a writer can't vex the world a little every day, why would he bother to get up in the morning?

But satire when it descends to populist jeering – that's to say when it flatters the babbling blockheads rather than lambasts them – becomes a boorish, toothless and, on occasions, even a dangerous thing. There was a signal example of this last week in the wake of seventeen police cars swooping on a suspect bus travelling along the M6 in Staffordshire.

Let me remind you of what this was all about. A passenger on the bus saw smoke coming from another traveller's bag. He didn't scream. He didn't try to jump out of the bus. He didn't tweet a fond farewell to his loved ones. He dialled 999 on his mobile phone. Highly commendable. Isn't this what mobile phones are for? That the police responded promptly to the call was highly commendable, too. We hear of 999 calls going unheeded. The operator could have said, 'Oh, yeah, pull the other one. This is Staffordshire, mate. Nothing happens in Staffordshire.'

So far, then, so good. A highly suspicious bag – I don't have to remind readers of this column that most bags don't smoke – was spotted by an alert member of the public who did the sensible thing, and the police responded sensibly in their turn. Or did they? This is where the jeerers, of whom one of the most obdurate and vociferous has been Nick Ferrari, shock-jock for LBC – don't ask me how I know this – saw their opportunity. Did it take seventeen police cars? they wanted to know. Was it necessary for some of those police cars to contain armed marksmen? (Where the point of an unarmed marksman would be I don't know.) Weren't thirteen fire engines twelve too many? Was it necessary to hold and body-search forty-eight bus passengers – forty-eight 'innocent' bus passengers, according to the *Daily Mail*? Did the police have to close the motorway, in the process stranding thousands of infuriated motorists who had *Mock the Week* to get home to. Cordons, cones, tents, decontamination units, for crying out loud! – all because, as it turned out, the smoking bag contained a fake cigarette.

The more primitive one's sense of humour, the more the contrast between a small cause and a large effect will strike one as amusing. A minor mishap creating major mayhem has been the staple of feeble sitcoms ever since the genre was invented. And so Nick Ferrari roared with that bumptious, plain man's outrage that early-morning shock-jocks are obliged to manufacture to ensure their listeners don't nod off. It was a fake cigarette, for heaven's sake. A fake cigarette!!

One of his callers reasonably reminded him that the police didn't know that when they turned up at the scene. In the same spirit, I would remind the *Daily Mail* that the police didn't know that all forty-eight passengers were innocent. The justification for having police is that we sometimes need suspiciousness investigated. But Ferrari wasn't alone in finding the idea of precautionary zeal even more hilarious than the idea of mistaking a fake cigarette for a real bomb. All the police had to do was ask, the jeerers jeered.

Ask? *Ask!* It was hard to believe one's ears. Did they mean a single bobby should have tailed the bus on his bicycle, flagged it down at the lights, boarded it with apologies all round, and asked the owner of the suspicious bag – nicely – if he was a terrorist and whether that was a bomb he was carrying? Yes, that was exactly what they did mean. And if it had turned out to be a bomb? But it wasn't, for crying out loud. It was an electronic cigarette. And how were the police to know that? By asking!

How to explain this circle of moronic illogicality? I cannot. Perhaps some people lack a conditional tense or a suppositional gene. Perhaps they lack an imagination of disaster.

Myself – and I accept I speak as someone with a highly developed imagination of disaster: but then history is on my side – I don't think seventeen police cars were too many. If anything, I'd have liked a dozen more, and a helicopter, if there wasn't one there already, and a fleet of ambulances, and a marksman (ideally armed) on every roof in Staffordshire. Were terrorism only the figment of our fears, it could be argued that this was an overreaction, but where it is both a proven fact and a fervently declared ambition, there is no such thing as overreaction.

It's sometimes said that when we go in like this, with cop-car sirens blaring and the emergency services at the ready, we hand victory to the terrorists. For this contention to be plausible, we have to imagine al-Qaeda operatives in Tora Bora tuning in to LBC and rubbing their hands at the thought of the M6 in Staffordshire being closed for half a day. 'Victory, fellow mujahideen, is ours! Tomorrow, we will see how many lanes we can shut down on the A6144.' But then I suppose global jihad has to start somewhere.

Yes, there are a few jumpy weeks ahead. Just getting people to the Games is going to be taxing, let alone getting them there safely. I'm staying home. Though even that might not be the end of it. Smoke issuing from my ears, if I happen to hear any more bilge about overreaction, might alert a neighbour who might alert the authorities who might choose to drop paras on my terrace. It's the price you pay. Only a babbling blockhead would complain.

Damnation for dummies

Is it my imagination or has everyone now been released from prison? I know it's Kenneth Clarke's declared intention to stop putting everybody in, but I must have missed the announcement that he has decided to let everybody out.

It's possible I overstate the case. Maybe it just feels as though every prison gate is swinging open because there's been so much talk of previous prisoner release – the dying but not yet dead Megrahi, for one – and the as it were imaginative release of Raoul Moat, whom we've been pardoning not from a mere custodial sentence (which he is in no condition to serve) but from eternal damnation.

I'm suffering compassion fatigue, anyway, however you explain it, which is surprising given that of late I haven't been feeling much compassion. I put it down to other people showing compassion on my behalf – not me personally, but me as citizen – and I would rather they didn't. Compassion can be overweening and rapacious. Those who pride themselves on possessing it will invade and flatten your moral garden until all that flourishes there is the weed forgiveness. I do not find the fragrance of forgiveness lovely? Depends where it grows. In a society forever feuding, yes. But where exoneration is the custom of the country, no. I think it belittles the forgiven – for even a criminal has the right to drink deep the consequences of his crime – and I consider it a perversion, akin to kissing lepers, on the part of the forgiver.

I alluded to eternal damnation a paragraph ago. Shame we no longer go in for it. It was never really ours, of course, to dispense, but there was a time when the prospect of eternal damnation was a necessary adjunct to egregious crime. But then egregious crime is something else we no longer go in for – the concept of it, I mean, the idea that some actions are so terrible that God Himself cannot forgive them. So we go on getting the crimes – the brutality, the terror – we just refuse to feel them as egregious. Our minds have shrunk. Anything above a misdemeanour, an expression of unhappiness caused by social deprivation, psychological malfunction, Zionism or the Iraq war, will no longer fit. It isn't only the idea of evil our heads reject, we refuse all gradations of wickedness – rottenness of soul, malignant spite, call them what you will: any of those examples of indurated vindictiveness from which, once upon a time, we believed we had a right to be protected.

The trouble with prisons, Kenneth Clarke has been telling us, is that they make no difference; we no sooner let offenders out than they offend again. I propose a simple solution to that problem – keep them in. Where the original offence was serious, the slightest suggestion that they will repeat it should be sufficient to extend their stay. Until when? Doomsday, if necessary. Rehabilitation is a fine ideal, but it is secondary to our protection. The first justification of the prison wall is that it separates us from those who will harm us if they can. The second is that it enables society to honour the retribution we individually crave but cannot individually exact.

Retribution troubles modern sensibilities. Isn't it just a bigger word for revenge? The letters pages of our newspapers have been running hot on the subject of revenge this week, the occasion for it being the rights and wrongs of releasing Megrahi a year ago, when he was supposed to be at death's door. We didn't believe a word of that in this column a year ago, and we don't believe a word of it now. That he is alive today, Alex Salmond, Scotland's gullible (or cynical) First Minister, ascribes to a change of scene. He was at death's door in a Scottish prison because Scottish prisons are not cheering places, but now he is back home in sunny Libya he understandably feels a little better. Since a show of gratuitous compassion for a dying mass murderer was the reasoning, I don't now see the argument for not releasing any homicide looking peaky and for whom a change of scene would work similar wonders. But then I speak in anger. The croaking raven doth bellow for revenge.

Of those who would throttle the raven's croaking, the most striking was a letter-writer to this paper, a sister of one of the Lockerbie victims, who with much dignity dismissed the relevance of Megrahi's health today or yesterday and wished him well. Those were her exact words. 'I wish him well.' I have puzzled my head over this letter all week. Why would she wish Megrahi well? Assuming him to be guilty of murdering 270 people he didn't know (and the letter-writer gives credence to the findings of the court set up to try him), why would anyone wish him well? I can see some might have theological objections to wishing him in hell, but 'well'? The same 'well' one wishes a friend, a person one loves, a saver of lives, a creator of beauty? Are there to be no distinctions? Is there no evil so great that well-wishing is not the reward for it?

Behold Dante's New Inferno, where there is no underworld, no ascending circles of sinfulness, just a flattened plain of minor miscreants to whom we extend warm greetings.

In so far as such wishing well constitutes forgiveness, I wonder what right any of us – even a close relative – has to forgive on someone else's behalf. Who hurts me can be forgiven by me alone. Yes, violence is a crime against society too. Justice must be impersonal, administered by the courts, else it's one unending vendetta. But so long as the cry for retribution goes inadequately heeded, we will live in a bitter and unjust world.

Mercy droppeth as the gentle rain from heaven? A sweet sentiment. For Shakespeare at full imaginative bore we go to Macbeth, where, in consideration of the 'deep damnation' of Duncan's murder, pity is figured 'like a naked newborn babe, / Striding the blast', and 'heaven's cherubim, horsed / Upon the sightless couriers of the air' are conceived with the power to 'blow the horrid deed in every eye, / That tears shall drown the wind'.

This is pity for the done-to, not the doer, pity simultaneously vulnerable and armed, a great heavenly force of raging sorrow, acknowledging the enormity of human outrage and the holy duty we owe to fury. 'Deep damnation', reader. Sometimes you need a religious vocabulary. Deep damnation. And where you have deep damnation you don't talk lightly of prisoner release, forgiveness, and wishing the murderer of 270 Duncans a comfortable retirement.

Remembering Odin Testostenhammur

DOPING? CORRUPTION? LET ME tell you what I know. I was once a shot-putter. Or I could have been.

'You've got the brawn for it, Jacobson,' our sports teacher told me. 'You've got the shoulders. You've got the swivel. You might even have the far-sightedness.' The clear implication was that I had every attribute of a successful shot-putter bar one. 'Would that be height, sir?' I asked. He looked down at me, shook his head and walked away. Later, I learned he'd told my only serious shot-put rival that I would never be in contention for the medals because I was called Howard Jacobson.

My rival was called Odin Testostenhammur. You can see the advantage he enjoyed. Just to go out with Odin Testostenhammur written on your back was worth another metre.

I often wonder whether I'd have made it as a star of field and track had I changed my name. But had I made it as a shot-putter, who's to say I wouldn't have ended up ruining my body with the steroids they'd have slipped into my Lucozade. I meet Odin occasionally when I'm back in Manchester. He represented England in the 1960 Olympics in Rome, unless it was the 1964 Olympics in Tokyo. He's on the bottle now, lives on his own in a cold-water flat in Droylsden, and throws squash balls at his cat for a hobby. He is flabby, gaunt-eyed and cries a lot. So does his cat. Whereas I – well, I don't.

The conclusion is inescapable. If you want a good life, don't succeed at anything too early or too well. And don't choose a profession that attracts money or attention. The minute people want to see you doing what you do, you're finished.

I must have grasped this truth instinctively at an early age, because after shot-putting I went into table tennis. The sports teacher who talked me out of shot-putting thought I'd found my niche. 'You've got the right build and temperament for ping-pong, Jacobson,' he told me. 'Short arms, strong wrists, obsessive personality.' What he actually meant was that I had the right name.

He was not alone in deriding table tennis by calling it ping-pong. Table tennis, in the popular view, was a parlour game, not a sport. Some, who'd heard of my prowess, would challenge me to a match, convinced they were in with a shot because they'd scraped home against some five-year-old at Butlins. When I thrashed them to within an inch of their lives they'd laugh, not at their own ignominy, but because nothing in the world mattered less to them than being thrashed at ping-pong. A trouncing at tiddlywinks would have hurt them more. If anything, I was the real loser for being good at something no one minded being bad at.

Though I didn't properly grasp it at the time, these were the tranquil years. Never again would I be so happy. No one envied me. No one burdened me with admiration. No one came to watch. When I won, no one congratulated me. When I lost, no one consoled me. No one bribed me to throw a match. No one offered me a backhander for inside information about other players on my team. And, most importantly of all, no one suggested doping. This, reader, I can swear with my hand on my heart: the game I played at the level I played it attracted not the slightest corruption. No sport was ever cleaner. And why? Because no one gave a damn.

Where there are no spectators, there is no sponsorship. Where there is no sponsorship, there is no money. Where there is no money, there are no officials with fingers in the pot. The lesson to be learned from this is simple. If we want honest sport, we have to stop watching it. At a stroke we could clean up football, athletics, cricket and whatever else is bent. All we have to do is stay away – don't go to the grounds and don't watch it on television – and, hey presto, the money disappears; sport is returned to its innocence and we wouldn't have to look at Ronaldo in his diamond earrings and underpants.

That still leaves the problem of national glory, I grant you. But if we didn't overvalue sport to the degree we do, countries wouldn't want to associate themselves with it and might look elsewhere to bolster patriotism.

To science, maybe. Or literature. There must be substances out there that improve the performances of poets. Let the Americans and Russians fight over that – who writes the more sonnets. And at least there'd be no point in cheating.

Poets are not meant to be in competition. We don't question the value of 'Kubla Khan' because of whatever it was that Coleridge took while he was writing it. We don't say he unfairly beat Wordsworth and ask for his plaque to be removed from his cottage in Nether Stowey. Writers are pragmatic about this sort of thing: whatever it takes, take it.

Everything is susceptible to corruption of one sort or another – humanity is one big cheat – but it matters particularly with sport which ceases to be itself the minute the outcome's rigged. It is sometimes said, and I sometimes agree, that one answer is to call open season on doping and make performance-enhancing drugs available to everybody. That way no athlete enjoys an unfair advantage over another, though what we would then call what they do is a question for philosophers, as is why we would care who does it better. I see a future in not caring.

If athletics were to enjoy one-tenth the prestige table tennis enjoys – in the sense of being played for itself, for the beauty of the strokes and the silence of the arena, for what it is not for what it brings, for the freedom it enjoys from the world's curiosity – the heat would all at once go out of it.

I don't know what Lord Coe would do with himself, but I'm confident Nike would find him something

Clowns

'W HEREOF ONE CANNOT SPEAK, thereof one must be silent.' Nothing beats a biblical admonishment. 'Judge not, that ye be not judged', the Gospel according to St Matthew. 'The simple inherit folly: but the prudent are crowned with knowledge', Proverbs. 'For we are but of yesterday and know nothing', the Book of Job. 'You need to shut the fuck up', Penn and Teller.

In this age of immoderate opinion unhampered by knowledge, we could do with a few more exhortations to quiet. 'The rest is silence,' said Hamlet finally. Even the wordiest of men know there's a time to button it. Whereof one cannot speak, etc. In fact, that sentence doesn't quite mean what it seems to mean and it wasn't Jesus or Hamlet or even Penn and Teller who delivered it. It's actually the concluding sentence of Wittgenstein's *Tractatus Logico-Philosophicus*, a work whose title alone scares me off. I find understanding Eric Cantona hard enough.

I once gave a character in a novel my inability to get past the same point in any work of philosophy, that moment when seeing is suddenly occluded and you know you can go no further. Page 14, paragraph 3, it always is. I can best describe the experience as believing you are talking to a sane man only to discover, in the opposite to a flash of light – an explosion of obscurity, let's call it – that you have all along been talking to a blithering idiot, though I accept that the blithering idiot is probably me. Upset by my bemusement, a distinguished Oxford philosopher kindly began a correspondence with me in the hope of removing this recurring obstacle to my comprehension.

Lucid letter followed lucid letter. Yes, yes, I saw it. Thanks to him, the word 'epistemological' was no longer a problem. The term 'logical positivism' neither. Another fortnight of this, I thought, and I'd be reading Heidegger for light relief. But then, in what turned out to be his final letter, came page 14, paragraph 3, and I was hurled once more into the Stygian night.

All this is but a prologue to my admitting that I don't grasp what philosophical problem concerning language and reality the sentence 'Whereof one cannot speak, thereof one must be silent' addresses – but I am going to employ it, anyway, against those who don't know their arses from their elbows and ought to shut the fuck up.

Am I thinking of anyone in particular? Well, yes, although it is invidious to choose a fool from among so many, yes, actually, I am. And it is not a single fool but a whole troupe of them. Fools by profession, whose folly takes the form of political intervention. You will have guessed that the fools in question are the Spanish clowns who stripped off in front of the separation wall in Bethlehem the other day, to demonstrate solidarity with the Palestinian cause, only to discover that they had thereby enraged the very people they had thought to help. 'Disrespectful', 'stupid' and 'disgusting' was how Palestinians described their actions. And of no value whatsoever in their struggle against Israel. Every struggle has its dignity.

To be clear, I abhor the separation wall. It is an eyesore in itself and makes tangible the failed diplomacy and cruel short-sightedness that causes such misery in the region. No Palestinian can see that wall and not wonder if the Israelis mean it to stay there forever, a constant reminder of what they never intend to change. I have been to Bethlehem and breathed the poisoned air. Build that wall and you might as well expunge all hope.

That the wall has done the job for which, in no small part, it was intended, cannot be denied. Fewer bombs now go off in the cafés of Jerusalem and Tel Aviv. This is not a negligible consideration. Viewed utilitarianly, it justifies its construction. But when hatred festers in human hearts, no edifice of brick or steel will subdue it. What the wall prevents other means will be found to enable. So the infernal logic continues. Hate, bomb, wall, hate, and anyone's guess what happens next.

What makes the Israeli–Palestinian conflict tragic, Amos Oz has long argued, is that it pits right against right. More recently he has spoken darkly of wrong against wrong. Either way, as he describes it, Israelis and Palestinians are partnered in intransigence and despondency. It is, in the end, irrelevant and meddlesome – and so far has been of little assistance to anyone – to apportion sympathy or blame. Whoever would effect change must act in full possession of what makes this tragic situation tragic. And to be in full possession of a tragedy is to understand what has before happened and been decreed, what immemorial fears and bloody histories motivate the actors, on what wheels of fire they are bound, how all participants explain justice and injustice to themselves. And should heed Othello's plea to Lodovico: 'Nothing extenuate, nor set down aught in malice.'

Naked of knowledge and imagination, and mouthing banalities – 'When you stand before this shameful fence all humanity is naked' – the Spanish clowns rushed in, buoyed by their own conceit. Were ever fools more ludicrous in their folly, or solipsists more the victim of their own unenquiring solipsism? That they knew so little of Palestinian culture as to be unaware what might constitute gross indecency to a religious people only shows how little they knew – and how little they thought they were obliged to know – of the place in which they'd made their intervention. We can guess how much they knew, or cared to know, of Israeli culture.

They are not alone. When emotion rules, every fool thinks that he is holy. And knowledge? Why, knowledge is a sort of sacrilege. Who needs it, anyway, when you can pick up what to feel from any foul rag-and-bone shop of hand-me-down convictions, put on a clown's nose and drop your pants. Though we are but of yesterday and know nothing, we will not let ignorance stop our mouths.

Whereof one cannot speak, yet one will.

It isn't a day of rest we need, it's a day unlike the day before

GOOD SHABBES. UNLESS IT'S gone 6.44 p.m. on the day this column is published, in which case it's Shabbes no longer and I shouldn't be wishing you a good one. Sorry to be punctilious, but that's how it is with religious observance. You can't be approximate.

Which goes some of the way – all right, 86.55 per cent of the way – to explaining why I've never been a good Jew in the observing sense. What time exactly does a festival start and what time exactly does it finish; when, to the second, can I turn on the oven; what constitutes work precisely and what constitutes relaxation, and can it still be called relaxation even though it doesn't relax me; if I can read a book congenial only to the spirit of Shabbes on Shabbes does that let Kafka in or Kafka out; and why shouldn't I read *The 120 Days of Sodom* in bed on a Friday night so long as I pass adverse criticism on its obscenity – all this quibbling and cavilling presupposes a pedantic God, and since I don't like pedantry why should I make an exception just because it's divine pedantry, particularly on Shabbes when I'm supposed to be relaxing?

Today is a bigger Shabbes than usual in the Jewish world because it has been chosen to launch the Shabbos Project, or ShabbatUK – and if you wonder why there are so many different ways of spelling Shabbes you put your finger on another problem I have with it. I knew where I was with Shabbes. I didn't keep it. That made me a naughty boy, but my excuse was that my father was a market man and couldn't have made a living had he not worked on Saturday and not had me to help him. In the robustly secular Manchester of the 1950s this was understood and forgiven by even the strictest rabbis. A man had to feed his family. But once Shabbes metamorphosed into Shabbat – for which blame creeping orthodoxy and Israeli pronunciation – what had been a venial omission, akin to letting down a friend, became a profanation of the sacred.

However it's pronounced, Shabbes exerts a pull on all Jews. Probably the only Jews who think about Shabbes more than those who keep it are those who don't. I don't say that when I climbed into my father's swag-filled van on Saturdays to drive to Oswestry or Worksop my thoughts were filled with the wonder of God's creation – for that's what Shabbes goes on commemorating: the day work on the world was finished – but I did sometimes fear there would be a price to pay for my impiety, and often regarded boys accompanying their fathers to the synagogue not with envy exactly but a sort of reverential curiosity. Were their hearts filled with a peace, a holiness even, that mine would never know? Were they made more serious by their religious devoirs than working as a market grafter, knocking out shepherd and shepherdess wall plaques and nests of tartan cardboard suitcases imported from Romania, made me? I didn't want to be those boys, indeed I scoffed at them, but I was still glad they were, so to speak, keeping Shabbes for me.

And there are good arguments, whatever one's faith, for a day unlike every other. In one part of myself I am pleased to have seen the back of those monotonous Sundays of the sort Dickens evoked in *Little Dorrit* – 'Melancholy streets, in a penitential garb of soot, steeped the souls of the people who were condemned to look at them out of windows in dire despondency. Everything was bolted and barred that could furnish relief to an overworked people . . . nothing to change the brooding mind, or raise it up.'

But in another I regret we have turned Sunday into one more day for driving out to shopping complexes and buying wider-screen televisions. How does that raise up the brooding mind?

We call it the day of rest, but I'm not convinced it's rest we most need. Just as I'm not convinced it was rest that God most needed on the seventh day. What had He done that was all that tiring? All right, He'd created the cosmos, set stars in the firmament, imagined great whales and winged fowls and cattle, and wished them a fruitful future, but He'd done this simply by expressing His desire that it should be so. *Fiat lux.* Let there be light. And then sitting back and admiring it. Reader, if only my job were as cushy. Let there be a column. *Fiat columna.* And lo, there was a column. And the evening and the morning were the sixth day. And for that I need to rest?

Let's agree that this is not the meaning of the seventh day. The meaning of the seventh day is the necessity to separate and distinguish, the Hebrew word for which is 'havdalah'. Having created, God now chooses to be uncreative. Between making and not making, as between the waters and the firmament, as between light and dark, and as between the holy and the profane, there must be separation. One thing is not another thing.

The moment in the Shabbes service that touches me most – philosophically – is the Havdalah benediction. Not because it brings Shabbes to an end but because it recalls to mind God the Great Discriminator, who discriminated between down here and up there, between the mundane and the special, between *Mamma Mia!* and *Mother Courage*, thus enshrining discrimination as the act that makes us Godlike.

A second soul, with each of us for the duration of Shabbes, is said to leave after the Havdalah service. Hence the sadness those who believe in such things experience as Shabbes ends. They feel diminished, single, unexceptional again. It's a wonderful idea – that for twenty-four hours (twenty-five to be exact) we accrue extra being. Let me be clear. I liked escaping the endless prescriptions of Shabbes to work the markets. We had fun. But it was just me and my dad irreligiously and ungrammatically flogging tat from the back of a van. No second souls came looking to take up abode in us in Worksop.

These things of darkness

THE PLACE COULD BE any crowded city where the one-sided war between cyclists and pedestrians rages. You – the innocent party – are walking along the pavement minding your own business when you see the enemy coming towards you. Is he riding his bicycle at full pelt, or just doing semi-wheelies while in conversation with a friend? Not sure it matters. He and his bike just shouldn't be here. You have already nearly been knocked down fifteen times this morning by cyclists jumping red lights, weaving through traffic, haring in the wrong direction down one-way streets, showing you the finger, mounting the kerb rather than slowing down or stopping – for cyclists are on the devil's errand and have no time to stop – and so you are not well disposed to them.

'You shouldn't be doing that,' you say. Perhaps you say it with more forthrightness than the cyclist – than any cyclist, puffed up with territorial aggression and an inflated sense of rectitude – can tolerate. But you are an Asperger's sufferer and don't always get your tone right. Not that that should matter. I am not an Asperger's sufferer and never get my tone right with cyclists. 'Get off the fucking pavement,' I might well have said. Which you could argue is asking for trouble, though it's no more asking for trouble than cycling on the fucking pavement. You get punched in the face, anyway, whoever you are and whatever you suffer from, not by the cyclist himself but by his friend. Call that loyalty.

The punch fells you; your head hits the pavement and you die. So what do you call that?

The judge called it 'wanting to cause some injury'. That's as opposed to 'wanting to cause grievous bodily harm'. Had the assailant intended the latter, Judge Cutler explained, the charge would have been murder. So it was lucky that he hadn't. Intended grievous bodily harm, that is. 'Lucky' is the judge's word. Lucky he'd only wanted to cause injury. 'Some' injury – unspecified. Gentle injury, maybe. Non-injurious injury. As though to emphasise how lucky he is, the sentence handed down to him is four years, before the usual deductions. So let's call that two. From which the only possible lesson we can draw is that things go worse for you if you tell off a cyclist than if you punch someone in the face and kill him.

Look, as Australians say. Look, I know it's no picnic being a judge. Adjudicating between someone else's spur-of-the-moment intentions can't be easy at the best of times, but when you've got to make such fine distinctions – between degrees of intended injury: a little bit of injury, a medium amount of injury, a heap of injury – you need moral, psychological, intuitive and mind-reading skills beyond the common. You need to be Moses, Jesus, Freud, Dostoevsky, George Eliot and Derren Brown rolled into one, and even they might have trembled before such a task.

So here's a suggestion. Why don't we just agree that punching someone in the face, whatever you intend by it and regardless of the fate of the person you've punched, is an act of barbarity for which you will be punished in a manner commensurate with the vileness of the offence and our utter abhorrence of it? Let's say ten years minimum. I won't complain if someone else says twenty.

I don't know about you, reader, but I have never been able to punch a person in the face. Maybe it's cowardice that's stopped me: a fear of being punched in the face back. But it's also squeamishness. And what's squeamishness but the outward form of an imaginative, not to say educated, reluctance? I'm talking about something more specific than wanting to cause pain. As a boy I wrestled in the school playground often enough and wasn't above administering Chinese burns or baby headlocks. 'Submit?' I used to love asking. 'Submit yet?' Though the answer was invariably a shake of the head. But a punch in the face is another thing again. Cracking bone against bone, breaking flesh, causing blood to flow, smashing into eyes and mouth – not to feel the horror and the sadness of it in advance, not to anticipate another's pain and foretell your own revulsion, is itself a mark of inhumanity, and that's before you go ahead and do it. The face, reader! That subtle and most delicate tracery of expression, the mirror of our feelings, the register of our fears and sorrows, the place from which we look out and make connection, even with our assailant. You don't touch it, that's what the law should say. Go near it with your fists and it matters not a jot whether you intend to cause 'grievous bodily harm'. It is itself an act of grievous bodily harm – and grievous spiritual harm to boot – regardless of consequences.

Judge Cutler is reputed to be a religious man who openly rejoices in his power to show leniency, as though leniency were a virtue in itself. But leniency is creditable only where it is appropriate. To be Christian is to know what's sacred. At the heart of Judaeo-Christian ethics is the inviolability of the human person, made in the image of its creator, and we don't have to believe in that creator to understand the holiness of the concept. Lose that and we lose the wherewithal to feel outraged by brutality. If we live in an age inured to daily acts of ferocity, that is in no so small measure the fault of those who think it's liberal, religious, humane or somehow cute not to cry out against them.

We make monsters out of our cruelty, but we make them out of our indulgence just as well. These things of darkness, Judge Cutler, we must acknowledge ours. And that's not a plea for leniency.

Offence is sacred

ANYBODY KNOW WHAT'S HAPPENED to the petition to boycott the film *Zoolander 2* prior to its release on account of Benedict Cumberbatch's role in it as 'the biggest androgynous supermodel in the world'? I went away, a few weeks ago, just as the petition was gathering traction, and now I'm back the tumult seems to have subsided.

That's not a complaint. I wish neither Cumberbatch nor the film ill. I just don't like not being up to speed in these matters. If something or someone is being banned, I want to be among the first to know about it.

The newspapers could be of more assistance in keeping us abreast of the progress of those witch-hunts which have become the defining characteristic of our age. Do you remember *The Times* when it was the organ of the establishment and so big you could read it naked in your club and not upset whoever was breakfasting at the next table? Somewhere very prominent – I might be wrong in imagining it was the front page – it used to carry a Court Circular which informed you not just of the comings and goings of royal personages and their footmen, but the visits of unsuitable foreign dignitaries and the wild doings of debutantes. Now it's tucked away where you can't find it. So much for the age we live in.

Well, what I propose is a version of the Court Circular, prominently positioned as in the good old days, listing the latest bans and boycotts: who is snubbing whom and why, the day's petitions to expel a politician from office, remove a boxer from contention as sports personality of the year, whatever a sports personality is, keep an American presidential hopeful out, stop the showing of a film because Benedict Cumberbatch disrespects a transgender super-model in it and therefore, by illegitimate implication, disrespects all transgender supermodels.

A sort of rolling trolling diary is what I envisage, detailing every person currently suffering harassment and abuse for entertaining views contrary to whatever they shouldn't be contrary to. That way we would know at a glance who the nation's villains are without having to go hunting for their names. And then, maybe a list of the people doing the harrying so we would know at a glance who the nation's fools are.

Cumberbatch must be pondering the fickle nature of reputation. Only a few weeks ago, just moments after flights of angels had sung his Hamlet to his final sleep, he was haranguing audiences about Syrian refugees. 'Fuck the politicians,' he had declared, to rapturous applause.

Theatre audiences love it when you throw them a fuck out of character. Throw a good cause after it and they are yours forever. And in the spring he had been a petitioner himself, calling to over-turn verdicts of gross indecency passed on homosexual men in those dark days when all human sexuality but the boring sort was illegal. Another unimpeachably good cause. And yet within a year, let me not think on't. Hero to zero within a little year.

If I say I hope the petition against *Zoolander 2* has run out of steam, it isn't because I am unsympathetic to the concerns of the androgyne/trans/non-binary individuals who were originally offended by it, albeit on the strength of a trailer and a publicity handout. But there's a principle at stake: offence, however deep the cut, does not sanction silencing.

That should be the first sentence anyone enrolling at a univer-sity hears. Good morning, students. Welcome to a liberal education where you will encounter, if we are doing our job right, much that will distress and infuriate you. The indignation you have been expressing on your first morning here, voting for the banning of all jokes and the removal from office of every lecturer with whose views you suspect you will soon be disagreeing, does you credit, but adds nothing to the sum of human reason. So you are offended by

Zoolander 2. Who isn't? Of course a satire which is directed against you hurts; that is precisely its point. Would you live in a world that has none? No ridicule because you are its object? No mockery, though mockery is the breath of life? Punch the following into your phones – *giving offence is sacred*. Oh, and try to remember how much you liked Benedict the day before yesterday.

But two days are a long time in the politics of pain. And those who should be counselling against the fashion for fraught nerves are shamefully surrendering to it. Not long ago, an eccentric Nobel Prize winner with profuse nostril hair – I mention this only to highlight his carelessness as to effect – was relieved of his duties for making a joke which, inter alia, had women as its object. An element of the joke was that women cry easily, whereupon a number of them did precisely that and there was his career sunk. The world waited for the academic institution that employed him to come to its senses, but it didn't. For universities go in fear now of the massed neuroses of their students or junior staff and, rather than risk a confrontation, capitulate to them.

The latest sacrifice on the altar of the thin-skinned is David Starkey, also once the nation's darling, but now banned from appearing in a Cambridge University promo because of his racist, classist and no doubt anti-androgyne/trans/non-binary views. Since Starkey chose to play the jester on television it has become more and more difficult to be certain what his views are. Only a blockhead would assume he believes what he says, since part of his comic shtick is to offend the faint of heart and bemuse the literal of mind. That doesn't make him the nicest of company, but Cambridge University isn't a kindergarten. We entertain a diversity of opinions, and ways of expressing them here – somebody should be saying – not all of them sympathetic. This is a place of learning, not a sanatorium. If you can't handle contrariety, you shouldn't be here.

And it's goodnight from him

IT WAS SIMON KELNER who offered me a column on this paper. I told him I wasn't sure I was up to the job of writing a thousand words every week. I'd done a stint reviewing television for the *Correspondent*, but reviewing is different – it's not just you and the inside of your head. Simon suggested I try for a few months and see how I felt. That was eighteen years ago. When I saw him recently, he asked if I'd made my mind up. I told him I hadn't.

I wrote my early columns in a camper van travelling from Perth to Broome. I recall composing one while sitting on a collapsible stool by a billabong that had been a smudge of dry dirt the day before but was now home to pelicans, wading birds and a single black swan. Another, I phoned in from a rowing boat on the heartbreak-blue waters of Shark Bay, a thousand miles from anywhere. Bottlenosed dolphins tried to nudge the phone out of my hand. In Broome itself, I wrote about watching an Aboriginal musical under a broiling night sky from which a succession of shooting stars fled like sparks from the fires of hell. In the heat, the moon rolled red like a drunkard.

Six months later I was back in London, still writing the column, but without the Australian wildlife. It changed days, changed length, changed format, and little by little I changed with it. The anecdotal mode gave way to the discursive, the ironical to the ireful, until I decided I was going in the wrong direction and changed back again.

I hadn't signed on to write opinion pieces about war and famine – I am a novelist and novelists aren't meant to have opinions – but nor did I want to dance inconsequentially upon a pinhead every week.

Making something out of nothing is a challenge to a writer; do it too often, though, and nothing comes of nothing.

What's worse, ponderousness or levity? My first responsibility, I believed, was to entertain in a spirit of high seriousness. Glide seamlessly between Rabelais and George Eliot.

But no one entertains all of the people all of the time. Kelner stopped being entertained when I began savaging other writers on the paper. And those other writers weren't much entertained either. But readers who didn't share the indurated anti-Zionism I was attacking declared themselves grateful.

In other circumstances, I might have written fewer articles on the subject. I didn't come on to the paper a polemical Zionist. If I have sometimes sounded like one, that's the paper's fault. I'm not saying I cared nothing for Israel beforehand. But there was a new ortho-doxy of anti-Zionism in the air and this paper inhaled its poisons freely. One doesn't go to war in the abstract. Had quite so many anti-Zionists not been writing for the *Independent*, and had their hostility to Israel been less a thing of myth and rhetoric, I might not have felt the call to buckle up as often as I did. But when I did buckle up, it was as a critic of their psychology, not their politics. The deep, self-deluding irrationality of hatred will always give itself away in language first.

We all learn on the job, and writing is no exception. It is said of novels that if you know what you're going to say before you say it, you won't produce a good novel. The same, to my mind, is true of writing a column. You need to snake your way to meaning, find out what's true, or at least more true than false, in the course of saying it, allow the words to discover the passion, not the passion dictate the words. The reason ideology leads us astray is that it is the expression of made-up minds. The best novels surprise their authors and the best columns end up somewhere the columnist never expected to go.

Online, the made-up mind characterises much that passes for comment. Wise columnists don't read the threads that follow their words, but once in a while it is instructive to do so. It is a jungle in which the combatants are so befuddled they forget it was you they set out to attack and end up tearing at one another. Once upon a time, the ignorant, the froward and the vain vented their spleen in letters written in green ink and sealed with a little sticker showing a dove of peace. Now there's no need for the pretence. You can revile and say so at the press of a button. This too has come to be a subject I've returned to reluctantly but often: the Gadarene-swine effect of the social media.

What's wrong with the social media can be simply stated. In the heat of violent exchange, everything but opinion gets lost. A generation has grown up that – online, at least – is deaf to tone, impervious to irony, incapable of grasping that thought can be tentative and argument exploratory. Theirs is a battleground of stated positions. One view lowers its head and charges its antlers at another. All we can hope is that in time they will all have butted themselves into unconsciousness.

I am asked whether writing columns has interfered with writing fiction. My answer is no, because I have approached both in a similar spirit. It might sound fanciful to claim that my columns have been little novels, but that was how I saw them. Essays *into* rather than *about*, dramatic pieces in which I didn't have to say what I believed, because I didn't know, or didn't want to know, or hoped that in the interactive play of images and ideas a way of looking at the world would emerge that wasn't trite, that might surprise and energise, and would give pleasure.

Pleasure to me too. For eighteen years of which, now I have finally made my mind up, I owe Simon Kelner thanks. And so I leave you.

A NOTE ON THE TYPE

The text of this book is set in Adobe Caslon, named after the English punch-cutter and type-founder William Caslon I (1692–1766). Caslon's rather old-fashioned types were modelled on seventeenth-century Dutch designs, but found wide acceptance throughout the English-speaking world for much of the eighteenth century until replaced by newer types towards the end of the century. Used in 1776 to print the Declaration of Independence, they were revived in the nineteenth century and have been popular ever since, particularly amongst fine printers. There are several digital versions, of which Carol Twombly's Adobe Caslon is one.

ALSO AVAILABLE BY HOWARD JACOBSON

ZOO TIME

Novelist Guy Ableman is in thrall to his vivacious wife Vanessa, a strikingly beautiful red-head. The trouble is, he is no less in thrall to her alluring mother, Poppy. More like sisters than mother and daughter, they come as a pair, a blistering presence that destroys Guy's peace of mind, suggesting the wildest stories but making it impossible for him to concentrate long enough to write any of them.

In flight from personal disappointment and universal despair, Guy wonders if it's time to take his love for Poppy to another level. Fiction might be dead, but desire isn't. And out of that desire he imagines squeezing one more great book.

'Carries all the intimations of angst, melancholia and comedy that make Jacobson unique'
DAILY TELEGRAPH

'Comedy is never as clever as when Howard Jacobson is on a roll and this book finds him barrelling'
INDEPENDENT ON SUNDAY

'Brilliantly composed ... crackling with Jacobson's wit, superb wordplay and boundless exuberance'
TIMES LITERARY SUPPLEMENT

ORDER YOUR COPY:

BY PHONE: +44 (0) 1256 302 699; BY EMAIL: DIRECT@MACMILLAN.CO.UK
DELIVERY IS USUALLY 3–5 WORKING DAYS. FREE POSTAGE AND PACKAGING FOR ORDERS OVER £20.
ONLINE: WWW.BLOOMSBURY.COM/BOOKSHOP
PRICES AND AVAILABILITY SUBJECT TO CHANGE WITHOUT NOTICE.

WWW.BLOOMSBURY.COM/AUTHOR/HOWARD-JACOBSON

BLOOMSBURY

WHATEVER IT IS, I DON'T LIKE IT

Howard Jacobson, the winner of the 2010 Man Booker Prize, brims with life in this collection of his most acclaimed journalism. From the unusual disposal of his father-in-law's ashes and the cultural wasteland of *Chitty Chitty Bang Bang* to the melancholy sensuality of Leonard Cohen and desolation of Wagner's tragedies, Jacobson writes with all the thunder and joy of a man possessed. Absurdity piles upon absurdity, and glorious sentences weave together to create a hilarious, heartbreaking and uniquely human collection. This book is not just a series of parts, but an irresistible, unputdownable sum which triumphantly out-Thurbers Thurber.

'[An] acutely observed collection of occasional pieces that pick at absurdist life and reveal him to be a quiz, a cultural critic gifted with precise comic timing'
THE TIMES

'Nobody does it better than Jacobson'
OBSERVER

'Yes, Jacobson is an entertainer ... And he does indeed entertain, but in a way that stimulates rather than simply amuses'
SUNDAY TELEGRAPH

ORDER YOUR COPY:

BY PHONE: +44 (0) 1256 302 699; **BY EMAIL:** DIRECT@MACMILLAN.CO.UK
DELIVERY IS USUALLY 3–5 WORKING DAYS. FREE POSTAGE AND PACKAGING FOR ORDERS OVER £20.
ONLINE: WWW.BLOOMSBURY.COM/BOOKSHOP
PRICES AND AVAILABILITY SUBJECT TO CHANGE WITHOUT NOTICE.

WWW.BLOOMSBURY.COM/AUTHOR/HOWARD-JACOBSON

BLOOMSBURY

THE FINKLER QUESTION

WINNER OF THE MAN BOOKER PRIZE 2010

Julian Treslove, a professionally unspectacular former BBC radio producer, and Sam Finkler, a popular Jewish philosopher, writer and television personality, are old school friends. Despite very different lives, they've never quite lost touch with each other – or with their former teacher, Libor Sevcik. Both Libor and Finkler are recently widowed, and together with Treslove they share a sweetly painful evening revisiting a time before they had loved and lost. It is that very evening, when Treslove hesitates a moment as he walks home, that he is attacked – and his whole sense of who and what he is slowly and ineluctably changes.

'Full of wit, warmth, intelligence, human feeling and understanding'
OBSERVER

'I don't know a funnier writer alive'
JONATHAN SAFRAN FOER

'How is it possible to read Howard Jacobson and not lose oneself in admiration for the music of his language, the power of his characterisation and the penetration of his insight?'
THE TIMES

BLOOMSBURY

IN THE LAND OF OZ

THE *SUNDAY TIMES* BESTSELLER

On what he calls 'the adventure of his life', Howard Jacobson travels around Australia, never entirely sure where he is heading next or whether he has the courage to tackle the wild life of the bush, the wild men of the outback, or the even wilder women of the seaboard cities.

In pursuit of the best of Australian good times, he joins revelers at Uluru, argues with racists in the Kimberleys, parties with wine-growers in the Barossa and falls for ballet dancers in Perth. And even as vexed questions of national identity and Aboriginal land rights present themselves, his love for Australia and Australians never falters.

'A marvellous read ... he is a comic explorer in the grandest mould'
FINANCIAL TIMES

'The most successful attempt I know to grip the great dreaming Australian enigma by the throat and make it gargle'
EVENING STANDARD

'A wildly funny account of his travels; abounding in sharp characterisation, crunching dialogue and self-parody, it actually is a book which makes you laugh out loud on almost every page'
LITERARY REVIEW

ORDER YOUR COPY:

BY PHONE: +44 (0) 1256 302 699; **BY EMAIL:** DIRECT@MACMILLAN.CO.UK
DELIVERY IS USUALLY 3–5 WORKING DAYS. FREE POSTAGE AND PACKAGING FOR ORDERS OVER £20.
ONLINE: WWW.BLOOMSBURY.COM/BOOKSHOP
PRICES AND AVAILABILITY SUBJECT TO CHANGE WITHOUT NOTICE.

WWW.BLOOMSBURY.COM/AUTHOR/HOWARD-JACOBSON

B L O O M S B U R Y